INTD 106: Conventions of College Writing

INTD 106: Conventions of College Writing

Edited by Gillian Paku and Lumen Learning

Published by SUNY OER Services
Milne Library
State University of New York at Geneseo
Geneseo, NY 14454

Distributed by State University of New York Press

Except where expressly noted otherwise, the contents of this course are based on materials originally published by Lumen Learning CC-BY Creative Commons Attribution License. The original version of this text was published as SUNY Geneseo Guide to Writing and may be accessed for free at https://courses.lumenlearning.com/suny-geneseo-guidetowriting/.

ISBN: 978-1-64176-028-7

This book was produced using Pressbooks.com, and PDF rendering was done by PrinceXML.

Contents

4: Grammar

5. Writing Process

6. Research

7. MLA Documentation

8. APA Documentation

9. Chicago/Turabian Documentation

About This Book

Your INTD 106 textbook is a compilation of articles written by instructors for universities around the country. The entire compilation is provided free of charge online through a Creative Commons license. You can access or even copy all the material here, for your own reference, even after the semester ends.

Different Versions

An electronic version is made available via your Canvas course, and also at https://courses.lumenlearning.com/suny-geneseo-guidetowriting/.

You may also purchase a physical copy at the College Bookstore. The electronic version has access to multimedia content including video, slideshows, and interactive activities. The print version will have all the same reading material, but not include the multimedia content.

About the Author

There are many different authors; look to the "Licenses and Attributions" section at the end of each chapter to identify contributors. This compilation was edited by Gillian Paku at SUNY Geneseo.

1. Usage

Introduction to Usage

Usage determines which words or forms of words you should use in a specific context – for the purposes of INTD 106 and INTD 105, that context is the conventions of standard academic English. For example, if you're trying to decide if you should use the numeral 17 or spell out the word *seventeen* in an art history essay, and whether it will take the same form in a biochemistry lab report, those decisions fall under usage. This section will also deal with capitalization, abbreviations and acronyms, and commonly confused words. Many common errors of the *there/their/they're* variety happen individually and will be pointed out to you by instructors or peer-reviewers, so we will also provide you here with resources to help check your individual tendencies and guide your decisions as you write.

Attributions

CC licensed content, Original

- Introduction to Usage. **Provided by**: Lumen Learning. **License**: *CC BY: Attribution*
- Revision and Adaptation. **Authored by**: Gillian Paku. **Provided by**: SUNY Geneseo. **License**: *CC BY: Attribution*

Writing with Numbers

The General Principle

The basic guidelines for expressing numbers are relatively simple, but the details can get very complicated, and, as with many usage issues, opinions on how to express numbers will vary. If your instructor prefers a certain format, you should use their preferred format!

When you're writing in a humanities subject (such subjects require relatively few numbers), numbers one hundred and below should be written out with letters, not numerals:

- There were **sixty-three** self-portraits in the first collection.
- The archeologists found **264** bracelets in **one** tomb.

One hundred is the magic number because over one hundred, the number cannot be spelled in one or two words. That's why numbers such as *sixteen hundred* or *four million* are written out as words rather than as numerals; yes, four million is a bigger number than one hundred mathematically, but it takes fewer words to spell out than *one hundred twenty-five*, so we write "four million," but "125."

Note that you generally do not include page numbers in either written or numerical form in your sentences (or line numbers, if, for example, you are discussing a poem or play); when such numbers appear in citational parentheses, they take their numerical form.

- In *Macroanalysis: Digital Methods and Literary History*, Matthew Jockers argues, "Big data are fundamentally altering the way that much science and social science get done" (7).
- Discussions of John Milton's readers frequently include his famous description of *Paradise Lost*'s readership as "fit audience … though few" (7.31). [Here, 7 indicates Book Seven of *Paradise Lost*; 31 indicates line thirty-one of that book of that poem. It would be inelegant and unconventional to convey this source information in the main sentence, as in the following form: "Discussions of John Milton's readers frequently include his famous description in line thirty-one of Book Seven of *Paradise Lost* of *Paradise Lost*'s readership as "fit audience …

though few." Students sometimes write like this in an attempt to avoid mistakes in bibliographical formatting, or simply to take up more space as they work toward a page limit, but this habit causes more problems than it solves. If you're still following these details, you might also note that Book Seven is represented in the citation as *7*, not as *VII* (i.e., in Arabic numerals, not in Roman numerals). This is an example of a change in documentation fashion; academics used to use Roman numerals in such cases, but the current fashion, dictated by the leading bibliographical style guide in the humanities, is to use Arabic. So now you know.]

In STEM fields (science, technology, engineering, math), where numbers are a more common feature, the convention is to spell out numbers ten and below. Larger numbers should be written as numerals:

- This study is based on **three** different ideas
- In this treatment, the steel was heated **18** different times.

Other Guidelines

If a sentence begins with a number, the number should be written out:

- **Fourteen** of the participants could not tell the difference between samples A and B.
- **Eighteen hundred and eighty-eight** was a difficult year for Vincent van Gogh.
  - ◦ You may want to revise sentences like this so the number does not come first: "The year **1888** was difficult for Vincent van Gogh."

You should treat similar numbers in grammatically connected groups alike:

- **Two** dramatic changes followed: **four** samples exploded, and **thirteen** lab technicians resigned.
- **Sixteen** people got **15** points on the test, **thirty** people got **10** points, and **three** people got **5** points.
  - ◦ In this sentence, there are two different "categories" of numbers: those that modify the noun *people* and those that modify the noun *points*. You can see that one category is spelled out (*people*) and the other is in numerals (*points*). This division helps the reader immediately spot which category the numbers belong to.

When you write a percentage the number should always be written numerically (even if it's ten or under). If you're writing in a technical field, you should use the percentage symbol (%):

- This procedure has a **7%** failure rate.

If you're writing in a nontechnical field, you should spell out the word *percent*:

- The judges have to give prizes to at least **25 percent** of competitors.

All important measured quantities—particularly those involving decimal points, dimensions, degrees, distances, weights, measures, and sums of money—should be expressed in numeral form:

- The metal should then be submerged for precisely **1.3** seconds.

- On average, the procedure costs **$25,000**.

- The depth of the water at the time of testing was **16.16** feet.

In technical settings, degree measures of temperature are normally expressed with the ° symbol rather than by the written word, with a space after the number but not between the symbol and the temperature scale:

- The sample was heated to **80 °C**.

Unlike the abbreviations for Fahrenheit and Celsius, the abbreviation for Kelvin (which refers to an absolute scale of temperature) is not preceded by the degree symbol (e.g., **12 K** is correct).

Attributions

CC licensed content, Original

- Revision and Adaptation. **Provided by**: Lumen Learning. **License**: *CC BY-NC-SA: Attribution-NonCommercial-ShareAlike*
- Revision and Adaptation. **Authored by**: Gillian Paku. **Provided by**: SUNY Geneseo. **License**: *CC BY: Attribution*

CC licensed content, Shared previously

- Style For Students Online. **Authored by**: Joe Schall. **Provided by**: The Pennsylvania State University. **Located at**: https://www.e-education.psu.edu/styleforstudents/. **Project**: Penn State's College of Earth and Mineral Sciences' OER Initiative. **License**: *CC BY-NC-SA: Attribution-NonCommercial-ShareAlike*
- Background Numbers. **Authored by**: thinunes. **Located at**: https://pixabay.com/en/background-numbers-mathematics-1143869/. **License**: *CC0: No Rights Reserved*

Abbreviations and Acronyms

Abbreviations (the shortened form of a word or phrase) and acronyms (words formed from the initial letters of a phrase) are commonly used in technical writing. In some fields, including chemistry, medicine, computer science, and geographic information systems, acronyms are used so frequently that the reader can flounder in an alphabet soup. However, the proper use of these devices enhances the reading process, fostering fluid readability and efficient comprehension.

Some style manuals devote entire chapters to the subject of abbreviations and acronyms, and Milne Library contains volumes that you can consult when needed (they move around, but were last seen to the right of the staircase leading to the second floor). Here, we provide just a few principles you can apply in using abbreviations and acronyms.

Abbreviations

- Typically, you abbreviate social titles (like *Ms.* and *Mr.*) and professional titles (like *Dr., Rev.*).
- When you abbreviate the names of people to initials, a period and a space follow each initial unless the name is reduced entirely to initials
    - J. R. R. Tolkien
    - The Notorious RBG
- Titles of degrees should be abbreviated when following someone's name. However, in résumés and cover letters, you should avoid abbreviations
    - Gloria Morales-Myers, PhD
    - I received a *Bachelor of Arts* in 2016.
- Most abbreviations should be followed with a period (*Mar.* for March), except those representing units of measure (*mm* for millimeter).
- Typically, do not abbreviate geographic names and countries (i.e., write *Saint Cloud* rather than *St. Cloud*). However, these names are usually abbreviated when presented in "tight text" where space can be at a premium, as in tables and figures.
- Use the ampersand symbol (&) in company names if the companies themselves do so in their literature, but avoid using the symbol as a narrative substitute for the word *and* in your acade-

mic writing.

- Spell out addresses (Third Avenue; the Chrysler Building) but abbreviate city addresses that are part of street names (Central Street SW).

- Try to avoid opening a sentence with an abbreviation; instead, write the word out.

Acronyms

- With few exceptions, present acronyms in full capital letters (FORTRAN; NIOSH). Some acronyms, such as *scuba* and *radar*, are so commonly used that they are not capitalized.

- Unless they appear at the end of a sentence, do not follow acronyms with a period.

  ◦ NOAA is a really great organization.

  ◦ I want to work for the USGS.

- Acronyms can be pluralized with the addition of a lowercase *s*. Don't insert an apostrophe to indicate a plural.

  ◦ Please choose between these three URLs.

- Acronyms can be made possessive with an apostrophe followed by a lowercase *s:*

  ◦ The DOD's mandate will be published today.

- As subjects, acronyms should be treated as singulars, even when they stand for plurals; therefore, they require a singular verb.

  ◦ NASA is committed to . . .

- Always write out the first in-text reference to an acronym, followed by the acronym itself written in capital letters and enclosed by parentheses. Subsequent references to the acronym can be made just by the capital letters alone. For example:

  ◦ Geographic Information Systems (GIS) is a rapidly expanding field. GIS technology . . .

- The acronym *US* can be used as an adjective (US citizen), but *United States* should be used when you are using it as a noun (In the United States, …).

Spelling, Capitalization, and Punctuation

Different abbreviations and acronyms are treated differently. You can review this PDF (https://s3-us-west-2.amazonaws.com/textimgs/Developmental+Reading+and+Writing/Commonly+used+Abbreviations+and+Acronyms.pdf) to check the proper treatment of some commonly used abbreviations and acronyms. For a much more detailed listing of abbreviations and acronyms, you can check in the back pages of many dictionaries, or consult the free online version of the *United States Government Printing Office Style Manual:* https://www.gpoaccess.gov/stylemanual/index.html

Attributions

Capitalization

Capitalization Conventions

Writers often refer to geographic locations, company names, temperature scales, and processes or apparatuses named after people, all of which have capitalization conventions that go beyond the standard rules for proper nouns that you probably remember from grade school: the name of a person or place is capitalized. There are ten fundamental conventions for capitalization:

1. Capitalize the names of major portions of your paper and all references to figures and tables. Note: Some journals and publications do not follow this rule, but most do.

   - Table 1
   - Appendix A
   - see Figure 4

2. Capitalize the names of established regions, localities, and political divisions.

   - the French Republic
   - Livingston County
   - the Arctic Circle

3. Capitalize the names of highways, routes, bridges, buildings, monuments, parks, ships, automobiles, hotels, forts, dams, railroads, and major coal and mineral deposits.

   - the White House
   - Highway 63
   - Alton Railroad

4. Capitalize the proper names of persons, places and their derivatives, and geographic names (continents, countries, states, cities, oceans, rivers, mountains, lakes, harbors, and valleys).

   - British
   - Rocky Mountains

- Chicago

- Celia Easton

5. Capitalize the names of historic events and documents, government units, political parties, business and fraternal organizations, clubs and societies, companies, and institutions.

- the Civil War

- Congress

- Ministry of Energy

6. Capitalize titles of rank when they are joined to a person's name, and the names of stars and planets. Note: The names *earth*, *sun*, and *moon* are not normally capitalized, although they may be capitalized when used in connection with other bodies of the solar system.

- Venus

- Professor Covfefe

- Milky Way

7. Capitalize words named after geographic locations, the names of major historical or geological time frames, and *most* words derived from proper names.

- Middle Jurassic Period

- the Industrial Revolution

- Petri dish

- Coriolis force

- Planck's constant

Note: The only way to be sure if a word derived from a person's name should be capitalized is to look it up in the dictionary. For example, "Bunsen burner" (after Robert Bunsen) is capitalized, while "diesel engine" (after Rudolph Diesel) is not. Such inconsistencies are in the nature of conventions! Another inconsistency is that when referring to specific geologic time frames, the *Chicago Manual of Style* says not to capitalize the words "era," "period," and "epoch," but the American Association of Petroleum Geologists says that these words should be capitalized.

8. Capitalize references to temperature scales, whether written out or abbreviated.

- 10 °F

- Celsius degrees

9. Capitalize references to major sections of a country or the world.

- the Near East

- the South

10. Capitalize the names of specific courses, the names of languages, and the names of semesters.

- Political Science 211

- Fall 2018

- Russian

Common Capitalization Errors

Just as important as knowing when to capitalize is knowing when not to. Below are a few instances where capital letters are commonly used when they should not be. When in doubt, look online or consult a dictionary, but one useful note to remember is that a proper noun is called a *proper* noun because it refers to something specific or particular, from the Latin *proprius*, meaning "one's own," or "special." That's why we say, "Second Street is a street in Geneseo," not, "Second Street is a Street in Geneseo."

1. Do not capitalize the names of the seasons, unless the seasons are personified, as in poetry ("Spring's breath"):

   - spring

   - winter

2. Do not capitalize the words north, south, east, and west when they refer to directions, in that their meaning becomes generalized rather than site-specific.

   - We traveled west. [We traveled west to the West Indies.]

   - The sun rises in the east. [The sun rises in the east in East Rochester.]

3. In general, do not capitalize commonly used words, even though their origins are in words that are capitalized. Some of these words have come to have quite specific meanings in their uncapitalized forms.

   - arctic ["Geneseo's campus can be arctic in February" is not really asking you to think about the Arctic.]

   - biblical

   - india ink

   - pasteurization

4. Do not capitalize the names of elements. Note: This is a common capitalization error, and can often be found in published work. Confusion no doubt arises because the symbols for elements are capitalized.

   - oxygen

   - californium

   - nitrogen

Attributions

CC licensed content, Original

Spelling

TURN ON YOUR SPELL CHECKER, but proceed with caution when using it. They can be extremely helpful, but they are not infallible, and they do not substitute for meticulous proofreading and clear thinking – witness a complaint from an outraged professor that a student had continually misspelled *miscellaneous* as *mescaline* (a hallucinogenic drug). The student's spell checker did not pick up the error (and probably autocorrected to *mescaline* based on what the student first typed), but the professor certainly did. Always proofread a hard copy, with your own two eyes. When in doubt, look up the word for its spelling and meaning, and to make sure that you haven't become confused or substituted a similar word by accident: malapropisms are often amusing, but they don't adhere to the conventions of standard academic English. (If you don't know what a *malapropism* is, LOOK IT UP!!) Be open to the idea that you, as a first-year student, have not yet learnt all the useful vocabulary in the English language, and, more importantly, that no professor expects you to have done so. Mistakes will occur: not recognizing the word *mescaline* makes it harder to pick up that it isn't how you spell *miscellaneous*, a word the student had possibly never written out. But the student probably experienced some moment of uncertainty about how to spell *miscellaneous,* and should therefore have been suspicious enough of the spell checker's suggestion to notice that nothing in *mescaline* matches the "-eous" sound they need. People put a lot of work into creating dictionaries – make their day by using one.

A helpful hint: along with a spell checker, your word-processing program probably has a "find" function in its editing tools. Almost all "find" functions can be accessed by pressing command + f or following these steps: edit → find → find…. If you discover an error in one iteration of a word, use the "find" function to locate other erroneous iterations and then fix them. This tip is also very helpful when you routinely mistype a word, e.g. "teh" instead of "the." You can "find all" iterations of "teh" and fix them.

Six Rules for Spelling

The *Instant Spelling Dictionary*, now in its third edition but first published in 1964, includes six basic spelling rules, adapted below. Even without memorizing the rules, you can improve your spelling simply by reviewing them and scanning the examples and exceptions until the fundamental concepts begin to sink in.

Rule 1

In words ending with a silent *e*, you usually drop the *e* when you add a suffix that begins with a vowel:

- *survive + al = survival*

- *divide + ing = dividing*

- *fortune + ate = fortunate*

Here are a few common exceptions:

manageable	singeing	mileage
advantageous	dyeing	acreage
peaceable	canoeing	lineage

Rule 2

In words ending with a silent *e*, you usually retain the *e* before a suffix than begins with a consonant.

- *arrange + ment = arrangement*

- *forgive + ness = forgiveness*

- *safe + ty = safety*

Here are a few common exceptions:

- *ninth* (from *nine*)

- *argument* (from *argue*)

- *wisdom* (from *wise*)

- *wholly* (from *whole*)

Rule 3

In words of two or more syllables that are accented on the final syllable and end in a single consonant preceded by a single vowel, you double the final consonant before a suffix beginning with a vowel.

- *refer + ing = referring*

- *regret + able = regrettable*

However, if the accent is not on the last syllable, the final consonant is not doubled.

- *benefit + ed = benefited*

- *audit + ed = audited*

Rule 4

In words of one syllable ending in a single consonant that is preceded by a single vowel, you double the final consonant before a suffix that begins with a vowel. (The rule sounds more complex than it is; just look at the examples.)

- *big + est = biggest*

- *hot + er = hotter*
- *bag + age = baggage*

Rule 5

In words ending in *y* preceded by a consonant, you usually change the *y* to *i* before any suffix that does not begin with an *i*.

- *beauty + ful = beautiful*
- *accompany + ment = accompaniment*
- *accompany + ing = accompanying* (suffix begins with *i*)

If the final *y* is preceded by a vowel, however, the rule does not apply.

- journeys
- obeying
- essays
- buys
- repaying
- attorneys

Rule 6

Use *i* before *e* except when the two letters follow *c* and have an *e* sound, or when they have an *a* sound as in *neighbor* and *weigh*.

i before *e* (*e* sound)	*e* before *i* (*a* sound)
shield	vein
believe	weight
grieve	veil
mischievous	neighbor

Here are a few common exceptions:

- weird
- either
- seize
- foreign
- ancient
- forfeit
- height

Everyday Words that are Commonly Misspelled

If you find yourself over-relying on spell checkers or misspelling the same word for the seventeenth time this year, it would be to your advantage to improve your spelling. One shortcut to doing this is to consult this list of words that are frequently used and misspelled: https://s3-us-west-2.amazonaws.com/textimgs/Developmental+Reading+and+Writing/CommonMisspellings.pdf

Many smart writers even put a mark next to a word whenever they have to look it up, thereby helping themselves identify those fiendish words that give them the most trouble. To improve your spelling, you must commit the words you frequently misspell to memory, and physically looking them up until you do so is an effective path to spelling perfection.

> One final piece of spelling advice: spell people's proper names correctly. Spell your professor's name correctly.

Attributions

CC licensed content, Original

- Revision and Adaptation. **Authored by**: Gillian Paku. **Provided by**: SUNY Geneseo. **License**: *CC BY: Attribution*

CC licensed content, Shared previously

- Style For Students Online. **Authored by**: Joe Schall. **Provided by**: The Pennsylvania State University. **Located at**: https://www.e-education.psu.edu/styleforstudents/. **Project**: Penn State's College of Earth and Mineral Sciences' OER Initiative. **License**: *CC BY-NC-SA: Attribution-NonCommercial-ShareAlike*

Commonly Misused Terms and Phrases

> When I woke up this morning my girlfriend asked me, "Did you sleep good?" I said, "No, I made a few mistakes."
>
> —Steven Wright

Everyone struggles at one time or another with finding the right word to use. We've all sent out that email only to realize we typed *there* when we should have said *their*. Have you puzzled over the distinction between *affect* and *effect* or *lay* and *lie*? You can also find billboards, road signs, ads, and newspapers with usage errors such as these boldly printed for all to see:

- "Man Alright After Crocodile Attack" (*Alright* should be *All Right*)
- "This Line Ten Items or Less" (*Less* should be *Fewer*)
- "Auction at This Sight: One Week" (*Sight* should be *Site*)
- "Violent Storm Effects Thousands" (*Effects* should be *Affects*)

This PDF (https://s3-us-west-2.amazonaws.com/textimgs/Developmental+Reading+and+Writing/CommonlyMisusedTerms.pdf) contains a list of several commonly confused words, as well as how to tell which word you should use.

You can also dig up style handbooks with recommendations on using tricky terminology within your discipline. For instance, Robert Bates' *Geowriting: A Guide to Writing, Editing, and Printing in Earth Science* explains terms commonly used in the field; medical students can turn to *The Aspen Guide to Effective Health Care Correspondence* or *Writing, Speaking, and Communication Skills for Health Professionals*.

The Chicago Manual of Style answers almost every conceivable style question—it is essentially a bible for book publishers. Never hesitate to look up a term for its proper usage if you are uncertain—there is a lot to be said for being correct.

Attributions

2. Punctuation

Introduction to Punctuation

Common Punctuation Marks

In this famous short skit, comedian Victor Borge (1909-2000) illustrates just how prevalent punctuation is (or should be) in language.

- https://youtu.be/Qf_TDuhk3No

As you've just heard, punctuation is everywhere. While it can be a struggle at first to learn the rules that come along with each mark, punctuation is here to help you: these marks were invented to guide readers through passages—to let them know how and where words relate to each other. When you learn the rules of punctuation, you equip yourself with an extensive toolset so you can better craft language to communicate the exact message you want.

Different style guides have slightly different conventions for punctuation. This module of INTD

106 will cover the MLA rules for punctuation, but we'll also make note of rules from other styles when they're significantly different.

Attributions

CC licensed content, Original

- Outcome: Punctuation. **Authored by**: Lumen Learning. **License**: *CC BY: Attribution*
- Revision and Adaptation. **Authored by**: Gillian Paku. **Provided by**: SUNY Geneseo. **License**: *CC BY: Attribution*

All rights reserved content

- Victor Borge - Phonetic Punctuation. **Authored by**: Charles Bradley II. **Located at**: https://youtu.be/Qf_TDuhk3No. **License**: *All Rights Reserved*. **License Terms**: Standard YouTube License

Ending Punctuation

The three most common punctuation marks that come at the end of a sentence are the period, the question mark, and the exclamation point. In MLA, a sentence is followed by a single space, no matter what the concluding punctuation is.

Periods

Periods indicate a neutral sentence, and as such are by far the most common ending punctuation mark. They've been at the end of every sentence on this page so far.

Question Marks

A question mark comes at the end of a question (so now you know).

Direct questions obviously use question marks, but so do rhetorical questions, which writers employ to make a point, and which do not expect an answer. Often the answer is implied or obvious, e.g. "Who would have thought that invading Russia during the bitter winter of 1812 would turn out to be a disaster for Napoleon's lightly clad troops?" At other times, rhetorical questions can be used for heightened rhetorical effect, as when Percy Bysshe Shelley ends his *Ode to the West Wind* with, "O Wind, / If Winter comes, can Spring be far behind?"

You should be careful, however, about posing rhetorical questions in formal writing because if you don't use them effectively, it can seem as if you are throwing a question out to the readers that you yourself aren't capable of answering. In particular, avoid ending the introduction to an essay with a question and then providing your answer ten pages later in your conclusion. It might seem like a smart rhetorical move, but readers actually experience it as frustrating and as an abdication of the writer's responsibility to provide their argument in their introduction.

Polite requests framed as questions also have a question mark, even though they aren't really seeking an answer, e.g., "Would you hold this beaker?"

Indirect Questions

Indirect questions can be used in many of the same ways as direct ones, but they often emphasize knowledge or lack of knowledge:

- I can't guess **how Admiral Nelson managed it**.
- I wonder **whether I looked that bad**.
- The supervisor asked **where the reports were**.

Such clauses correspond to **direct questions**, which are questions actually asked. The direct questions corresponding to the examples above are *How did Admiral Nelson manage it? Did I look that bad? Where are the reports?* Notice how different word order is used in direct and indirect questions: in direct questions the verb usually comes before the subject, while indirect questions the verb appears second. Additionally, question marks *should not be used* at the end of indirect questions.

Practice
Are the following sentences direct or indirect questions? Which need a question mark at the end?   1. Jackie wondered where her textbooks were   2. Can you pass the scalpel   3. Is anyone here   4. She asked how you were doing   5. Why won't you admit I'm right

Exclamation Points

The exclamation point is a punctuation mark usually used after an interjection or exclamation to indicate strong feelings or high volume, and often marks the end of a sentence. It's an Internet favorite:

!!!!!! I'm jUST SO!!!!!!

While this kind of statement is appropriate in that Internet context, it wouldn't work in a piece of writing in standard academic English. If you want to emphasize something in an essay, you almost always need to do it through your wording, not through an exclamation mark. Here's F. Scott Fitzgerald on the topic, and feelings haven't changed much in academia in the past century:

> Cut out all these exclamation points. . . . An exclamation point is like laughing at your own joke.
> — F. Scott Fitzgerald

Key Takeaway

Use of the exclamation mark in academic writing is generally considered poor form, as it distracts the reader and devalues the mark's significance.

Attributions

CC licensed content, Original

- Text: Periods. **Authored by**: Lumen Learning. **License**: *CC BY: Attribution*
- Revision and Adaptation of Wikipedia content. **License**: *CC BY-SA: Attribution-ShareAlike*
- Original Icons. **Authored by**: Lumen Learning. **License**: *CC BY: Attribution*
- Revision and Adaptation. **Authored by**: Gillian Paku. **Provided by**: SUNY Geneseo. **License**: *CC BY: Attribution*

CC licensed content, Shared previously

- Question. **Provided by**: Wikipedia. **Located at**: https://en.wikipedia.org/wiki/Question. **License**: *CC BY-SA: Attribution-ShareAlike*
- Content clause. **Provided by**: Wikipedia. **Located at**: https://en.wikipedia.org/wiki/Content_clause#Interrogative_content_clauses. **License**: *CC BY-SA: Attribution-ShareAlike*
- Exclamation mark. **Provided by**: Wikipedia. **Located at**: https://en.wikipedia.org/wiki/Exclamation_mark. **License**: *CC BY-SA: Attribution-ShareAlike*

Commas

Commas: these little horrors haunt the nightmares of many a professor after an evening of reading student papers. It seems nearly impossible to remember and apply the seventeen or so comma rules that seem to be given out as the standard, for example, "Use commas to set off independent clauses joined by the common coordinating conjunctions" or, "Put a comma before the coordinating conjunction in a series."

You have probably also heard a lot of tips on using commas in addition to those rules: "Use one wherever you would naturally pause," or "Read your work aloud, and whenever you feel yourself pausing, put in a comma." These techniques help to a degree, but our ears tend to trick us, and we need other avenues of attack.

Quite honestly, instructors and students both make errors in comma usage, but, as Robert Browning says, "a man's reach should exceed his grasp, / Or what's a heaven for?" In other words, our almost inevitable failure at comma rules is no excuse for not trying. Perhaps the best and most instructive way for us to approach the comma is to remember its fundamental function: *it is a separator.* Once you know this, the next step is to determine what sorts of things generally require separation. This includes most transition words, descriptive words or phrases, adjacent items, and complete ideas (complete ideas contain both a subject and a verb).

Transition Words

Transition words add new viewpoints to your material; commas before and after transition words help to separate them from the sentence ideas they are describing. Transition words tend to appear at the beginning or in the middle of a sentence. By definition, a transition word creates context that links to the preceding sentence. Typical transition words that require commas before and after them include *however, thus, therefore, also,* and *nevertheless.*

- *Therefore,* the natural gas industry can only be understood fully through an analysis of these recent political changes.

- The lead prosecutor was prepared, *however,* for a situation like this.

Note: As was mentioned, these words require commas at the beginning or middle of a sentence. When they appear between two complete ideas, however, a period or semicolon is required beforehand:

- Dr. Clint had been planning the Geology field trip with his research group for three months; *however,* when NASA called him onto a project, he couldn't say no.

- General Peters was retired. *Nevertheless,* he wanted to dictate policy in the new administration.

As you can see from these examples, comma is *always* required after transition words.

Descriptive Phrases

Descriptive phrases often need to be separated from the things that they describe in order to clarify that the descriptive phrases are subordinate (i.e., they relate to the sentence context, but are less responsible for creating meaning than the sentence's subject and verb). Descriptive phrases tend to come at the very beginning of a sentence, right after the subject of a sentence, or at the very end of a sentence.

- **Near the end of the eighteenth century**, James Hutton introduced a point of view that radically changed scientists' thinking about geologic processes.

- James Lovelock, **who first measured CFCs globally**, said in 1973 that CFCs constituted no conceivable hazard.

- All of the major industrialized nations approved, **making the possibility a reality**.

In each example, the phrase separated by the comma could be deleted from the sentence without destroying the sentence's basic meaning. If the information is necessary to the primary sentence meaning, it should **not** be set off by commas. Let's look at a quick example of this:

- Jefferson's son, Miles, just started college.

- Jefferson's son Miles just started college

You would write the first sentence if Jefferson only has one son and his name is Miles. If Jefferson only has one son, then *Miles* is not needed information and should be set off with commas.

You would write the second sentence if Jefferson has multiple sons, and it is his son Miles who just got into college. In the second sentence, *Miles* is necessary information, because until his name is stated, you can't be sure which of Jefferson's sons the sentence is talking about.

This test can be very helpful when you're deciding whether or not to include commas in your writing, especially around the titles of books or articles you mention in your essay, where students tend to spray commas at the page.

Adjacent Items

Adjacent items are words or phrases that have some sort of parallel relationship, yet are different from each other in meaning. Adjacent items are separated so that the reader can consider each item individually.

> The river caught fire on July 4, 1968, in Cleveland, Ohio.

The dates (July 4, 1968) and places (Cleveland, Ohio) are juxtaposed, and commas are needed because the juxtaposed items are clearly different from each other. This applies to countries as well as states: "Asilah, Morocco, is beautiful this time of year."

Practice

The commas have been removed from some of the following sentences. Rewrite the ones that need correction, adding the commas back in.

1. Sergi Sousa the top-ranked shoe designer in Rhode Island is going to be at the party tonight.
2. Sergi only wears shoes that he created himself.
3. Nevertheless he is incredibly courteous and polite to everyone he meets.
4. He was born in Barcelona Spain on April 19 1987.

Coordinating Conjunctions: FANBOYS

We also discuss coordinating conjunctions in the Grammar Module of INTD 106. These are words that join two words or phrases of equal importance. The mnemonic FANBOYS helps us remember the seven most common: *for*, *and*, *nor*, *but*, *or*, *yet*, and *so*.

When these conjunctions join two words or phrases, no comma is necessary (for more than two, take a look at "Commas in Lists" just below):

- Minh turned off the lights but left the door unlocked.
  - "Minh turned off the lights" is a complete phrase; "left the door unlocked" is not. No comma is required before *but*.
- Danny studied the lifespan of rhinoceroses in their native Kenya and the lifespan of rhinoceroses in captivity.
  - "Danny studied the lifespan of rhinoceroses in their native Kenya" is a complete idea; "the lifespan of rhinoceroses in captivity" is not. No comma is required before *and*.

When these conjunctions are used to join two complete ideas, however, a comma is required:

- We could write this as two separate sentences, but we've chosen to join them together here.
  - Both "We could write this as two separate sentences" and "We've chosen to join them

together here" are complete ideas. A comma is required before the *but*.

Practice

The commas have been removed from some of the following sentences. Rewrite the ones that need correction, adding the commas back in.

1. Aamir and Tyesha went on a trip to California.

2. Aamir was nervous but Tyesha was excited.

3. They had been to East Coast before but never to the West.

4. Aamir became less nervous after he looked up a few tourist guides and journals online.

5. When they came home Tyesha had not enjoyed herself but Aamir had.

Commas in Lists

The serial comma is used to separate adjacent items—different items with equal importance—when there are three or more. This is so the reader can consider each item individually. Here are a few examples:

- Weathering may extend only a few centimeters beyond the zone in **fresh granite**, **metamorphic rocks**, **sandstone**, **shale**, and **other rocks**.

- This approach **increases homogeneity**, **reduces the heating time**, and **creates a more uniform microstructure**.

In the first sentence, the commas are important because each item presented is distinctly different from its adjacent item. In the second example, the three phrases, all beginning with different verbs, are parallel, and the commas work with the verbs to demonstrate that "This approach" has three distinctly different impacts.

The Serial Comma (a.k.a the Oxford Comma)

Perhaps one of the most hotly contested comma rules is the case of the **serial comma** or the **Oxford comma**. MLA style (as well as APA and *Chicago*) requires the use of the serial comma—AP style highly recommends leaving it out. But what is the serial comma?

The serial comma is the comma before the conjunction (*and, or,* and *nor*) in a series involving a parallel list of three or more things. For example, "I am industrious, resourceful**, *and*** loyal." The serial comma can provide clarity in certain situations. For example, if the *and* is part of a series of three or more phrases (groups of words) as opposed to single words:

Medical histories taken about each subject included smoking history, frequency of exercise, current height and weight, and recent weight gain.

The serial comma can also prevent the end of a series from appearing to be a parenthetical:

I'd like to thank my sisters, Beyoncé and Rhianna.

Without the serial comma, it may appear that the speaker is thanking his or her two sisters, who are named Beyoncé and Rhianna (which could be possible, but isn't true in this case). By adding the serial comma, it becomes clear that the speaker is thanking his or her sisters, as well as the two famous singers: "I'd like to thank my sisters, Beyoncé, and Rhianna."

By always using a comma before the *and* in any series of three or more, you honor the distinctions between each of the separated items, and you avoid any potential reader confusion.

> **Note:** Some professors and many journals prefer to leave out the serial comma. For the journals, it is literally cheaper to print fewer commas. Because of this, the serial comma is not recommended in AP style. When clarity, not finances, is your concern, we recommend you employ the serial comma.

Practice

The commas have been removed from the following sentences. Rewrite them, adding the correct commas back in.

1. Ava's favorite meals are cauliflower soup steak and eggs lasagna and chicken parmigiana.
2. Victor tried to make dinner for her. Unfortunately his skills are mostly limited to eating buying or serving food.
3. Victor and Ava decided to choose a restaurant and go out to eat.

Comma Overuse

A sure way to irritate educated readers of your work is to give them an overabundance of commas. It is easy but dangerous to take the attitude that Sally once did in a *Peanuts* comic strip, asking Charlie Brown to correct her essay by showing her "where to sprinkle in the little curvy marks."

Perhaps the best way to troubleshoot your particular comma problems, especially if they are serious, is to identify and understand the patterns of your errors. We tend to make the same mistakes over and over again; in fact, many writers develop the unfortunate habit of automatically putting commas into slots such as these:

- between the subject and verb of a sentence
- after any number
- before any preposition
- before or after any conjunction

Practice

Read the following sentences. How many of them have unnecessary commas? Write your corrected sentences below.

1. The bushings, must be adjusted weekly, to ensure that the motor is not damaged.

2. Other manufactured chemicals that also contain bromine are superior for extinguishing fires in situations where people, and electronics are likely to be present.

3. The price of platinum will rise, or fall depending on several distinct factors.

Just as it is common for someone to have to look up the same tricky word dozens of times before committing its proper spelling or use to memory, you may need to reference comma rules multiple times before they feel natural to use. As with spelling, commas (or the absence of commas) must be repeatedly challenged in your writing.

As you improve your comma usage, you will learn to recognize and reevaluate your sentence patterns, and the rewards are numerous. There is no foolproof or easy way to exorcise all of your comma demons, but a great place to start is reminding yourself of the comma's basic function as a separator and justifying the separation of elements. In the end, you'll have to make a habit of reading, writing, and revising with comma correctness in mind. INTD 105 and INTD 106 are great places for breaking old habits and learning new ones before you launch into the rest of your career at Geneseo and beyond.

Attributions

CC licensed content, Original

- Revision and Adaptation. **Provided by**: Lumen Learning. **License**: *CC BY-NC-SA: Attribution-NonCommercial-ShareAlike*
- Image of comma. **Provided by**: Lumen Learning. **License**: *CC BY: Attribution*
- Revision and Adaptation. **Authored by**: Gillian Paku. **Provided by**: SUNY Geneseo. **License**: *CC BY: Attribution*

CC licensed content, Shared previously

- Style For Students Online. **Authored by**: Joe Schall. **Provided by**: The Pennsylvania State University. **Located at**: https://www.e-education.psu.edu/styleforstudents/. **Project**: Penn State's College of Earth and Mineral Sciences' OER Initiative. **License**: *CC BY-NC-SA: Attribution-NonCommercial-ShareAlike*

Semicolons

[If you don't know why the abbreviation *TL;DR* is ironic, you should read this page. Trust us that the material won't be too long, and you'll be glad you did read it.]

The semicolon is one of the most misunderstood and misused punctuation marks; in fact, it is often mistaken for the colon (which we'll discuss next). However, these two punctuation marks are not interchangeable. A semicolon connects two complete ideas (a complete idea has a subject and a verb) that are connected to each other. Look at this sentence, for example:

> Robinson's statue is presently displayed in the center of the exhibit; this location makes it a focal point and allows it to direct the flow of museum visitors.

The first idea tells us where Robinson's statue is, and the second idea tells us more about the location and its importance. Each of these ideas could be its own sentence, but by using a semicolon, the author is telling the reader that the two ideas are connected. Often, you may find yourself putting a comma in the place of the semicolon; that habit is grammatically incorrect. Using a comma that way creates a **comma splice**, which we'll also discuss later in this module.

> Remember: a comma can join a complete idea to other items while a semicolon needs a complete idea on either side.

The semicolon can also be used to separate items in a list when those items have internal commas:

- As a photographer for National Geographic, Renato had been to a lot of different places including São Paulo, Brazil; Kobe, Japan; Kyiv, Ukraine; and Barcelona, Spain.

- As an engineering assistant, I had a variety of duties: participating in pressure ventilation surveys; completing daily drafting, surveying, and data compilation; and acting as a company representative during a roof-bolt pull test.

Practice

Do the following sentences need a comma or a semicolon?

1. Kieran never throws anything away ___ he's convinced he'll need these things someday.

2. Because I left my keys at my apartment ___ I had to stay on campus and wait for my roommate.

3. Zebras are the most popular animals at my local zoo ___ however ___ elephants are my favorite animal.

4. The company had four primary locations: Boston, Massachusetts ___ San Antonio, Texas ___ Chicago, Illinois ___ and Little Rock, Arkansas.

Attributions

CC licensed content, Original

Colons

The colon: well-loved but sadly misunderstood. The colon is not used just to introduce a list; it is far more flexible. The colon can be used after the first word of a sentence or just before the final word of a sentence. The colon can also be used to introduce a grammatically independent sentence. Thus, it is one of the most powerful punctuation marks.

The colon is like a sign on the highway, announcing that something important is coming. It acts as an arrow pointing forward, telling you to read on for important information. A common analogy used to explain the colon is that it acts like a flare in the road, signaling that something meaningful lies ahead.

Use the colon when you wish to provide pithy emphasis.

> To address this problem, we must turn to one of the biologist's most fundamental tools: the Petri dish.

Use the colon to introduce material that explains, amplifies, or summarizes what has preceded it.

> The Petri dish: one of the biologist's most fundamental tools.

> In low carbon steels, banding tends to affect two properties in particular: tensile ductility and yield strength.

The colon is also commonly used to present a list or series, which comes in handy when there is a lot of similar material to join.

> A compost facility may not be located as follows: within 300 feet of an exceptional-value wetland; within 100 feet of a perennial stream; within 50 feet of a property line.

Practice

Is the colon used correctly in the following sentences?

1. Stores need strict rules for making returns: consumers abuse them.

2. A store refund may be, for example: a cash refund, a store credit, or a gift card.

3. A store may charge a restocking fee in the following circumstances: (1) If the item is removed from plastic wrapping; (2) If the box is torn; (3) If tags or labels have been removed from the item.

4. If a store's policy differs from the state-wide 7-day policy, then the store must: place a written notice about their policies, in language that consumers can understand, so that it can be easily seen and read.

5. California law is very exact about posting store policy: The policy must be displayed either at each entrance to the store, at each cash register and sales counter, on tags attached to each item, or on the company's order forms, if any.

Attributions

CC licensed content, Original

- Revision and Adaptation. **Provided by**: Lumen Learning. **License**: *CC BY-NC-SA: Attribution-NonCommercial-ShareAlike*
- Image of colon. **Provided by**: Lumen Learning. **License**: *CC BY: Attribution*
- Revision and Adaptation. **Authored by**: Gillian Paku. **Provided by**: SUNY Geneseo. **License**: *CC BY: Attribution*

CC licensed content, Shared previously

- Semicolons, Colons, and Dashes. **Authored by**: Joe Schall. **Provided by**: The Pennsylvania State University. **Located at**: https://www.e-education.psu.edu/styleforstudents/c2_p5.html. **Project**: Penn State's College of Earth and Mineral Sciences' OER Initiative. **License**: *CC BY-NC-SA: Attribution-NonCommercial-ShareAlike*
- Colons. **Authored by**: Julie Sevastopoulos. **Provided by**: Grammar-Quizzes. **Located at**: http://www.grammar-quizzes.com/punc-colons.html. **License**: *CC BY-NC-SA: Attribution-NonCommercial-ShareAlike*

Practice Activities: Commas, Semicolons, and Colons

Commas and Semicolon

Read the following sentences. Determine if the empty spaces need a semicolon, a comma, or no punctuation:

Pyura spinifera __ commonly called the sea tulip __ is a species of ascidian that lives in coastal waters at depths of up to 260 feet. As with almost all other ascidians __ sea tulips are filter feeders. Its name comes from the organism's appearance __ it looks like a knobby "bulb" or flower attached to a long stalk. Sea tulips come in a variety of colors, including white, pink, yellow, orange, and purple __ note that __ the coloration of sea tulips depends upon their association with a symbiotic sponge that covers their surface.

Sea Tulips

You may spot this plant in ocean waters near Sydney __ Australia __ Central Coast __ Australia __ and Newcastle__ Australia.

Semicolons and Colons

Are the semicolons and colons used correctly in the following sentences? The sentences have been numbered to aid in your comments.

(1) The Antikythera mechanism is an ancient analogue computer likely used for several purposes including: predicting astronomical positions and eclipses and calculating Olympiads: the cycles of the ancient Olympic Games. (2) The device is a complex clockwork mechanism composed of at least 30 meshing bronze gears. (3) Its remains were found as one lump; it was recovered from a shipwreck, and the device was originally housed in a wooden box. (4) This lump was later separated into 82 separate fragments after extensive conservation work.

(5) The artifact was recovered probably in July 1901 from the Antikythera shipwreck off the Greek island of Antikythera. (6) Believed to have been designed and constructed by Greek scientists; the instrument has recently been dated to 205 BC. (7) After the knowledge of this technology was lost at some point in antiquity, technological artifacts approaching its complexity and workmanship did not appear again until the development of mechanical astronomical clocks in Europe in the fourteenth century.

(8) All known fragments of the Antikythera mechanism are kept at the National Archaeological Museum, Athens.

Colons

Is the colon used correctly in the following sentences? Write the corrected sentence.

1. There are three methods of attracting earthworms from the ground: worm charming, worm grunting, and worm fiddling.

2. The activity can be performed: to collect bait for fishing or as a competitive sport.

3. As a skill and profession, worm charming is now very rare: with the art being passed through generations to ensure that it survives.

4. In most competitions, the collector of the most worms in a set time is declared as the winner: they usually have a zone in which to perform their charming, measuring three yards square.

5. The activity is known by several different names and the apparatus and techniques vary significantly: (1) Most worm charming methods involve vibrating the soil, which encourages the worms to the surface; (2) Worm grunting generally refers to the use of a "stob," a wooden stake that is driven into the ground, and a rooping iron, which is used to rub the stob; (3) Worm fiddling also uses a wooden stake but utilizes a dulled saw which is dragged along its top.

See the online version for answers: https://courses.lumenlearning.com/suny-geneseo-guidetowriting/chapter/practice-activities-semicolons-and-colons/

Attributions

Hyphens and Dashes

Hyphens

In an earlier edition, *The Oxford Manual of Style* states, "If you take hyphens seriously you will surely go mad." People disagree about their use in certain situations, but we're confident about your sanity if you learn generally to use hyphens properly; indeed, they help you to write efficiently and concretely.

The Hyphen's Function

Fundamentally, the hyphen is a joiner. It can join several different types of things:

- two nouns to make one complete word (house-plant)

- an adjective and a noun to make a compound word (accident-prone)

- two words that, when linked, describe a noun (agreed-upon sum, two-dimensional object)

- a prefix with a noun (un-American)

- double numbers (twenty-four)

- numbers and units describing a noun (1000-foot face; a 10-meter difference)

- "self" words (self-employed, self-esteem)

- new word blends (cancer-causing, cost-effective)

- prefixes and suffixes to words, in particular when the writer wants to avoid doubling a vowel or tripling a consonant (anti-inflammatory; shell-like)

- multiple adjectives with the same noun (blue- and yellow-green beads; four- and five-year-olds)

A rule of thumb for the hyphen is that the resulting word must act as one unit; therefore, the hyphen creates a new word that has a single meaning. Usually, you can tell whether a hyphen is necessary by applying common sense and mentally excluding one of the words in question, testing how the words would work together without the hyphen. For example, the phrases "high-pressure system," "water-repellent surface," and "fuel-efficient car" would not make sense without hyphens, because you would not refer to a "high system," a "water surface," or a "fuel car." As your ears and eyes become attuned to proper hyphenation practices, you will recognize that both meaning and convention dictate where hyphens fit best.

Examples of Properly Used Hyphens

Some examples of properly used hyphens follow. Note how the hyphenated word acts as a single unit carrying a meaning that the words being joined would not have individually.

small-scale study	two-prong plug	strength-to-weight ratio	high-velocity flow	frost-free lawn
self-employed worker	one-third majority	coarse-grained wood	decision-making process	blue-green algae
air-ice interface	silver-stained cells	protein-calorie malnutrition	membrane-bound vesicles	phase-contrast microscope
long-term-payment loan	cost-effective program	time-dependent variable	radiation-sensitive sample	long-chain fatty acid

When Hyphens Are Not Needed

By convention, hyphens are not used after words ending in –*ly*, nor when the words are so commonly used in combination that no ambiguity results. In these examples, no hyphens are needed:

finely tuned engine	blood pressure	sea level
real estate	census taker	atomic energy
civil rights law	public utility plant	carbon dioxide

Note: Phrases containing the word *well* like *well known* are contested. *Well* is an adverb, and thus many fall into the school of thought that a hyphen is unnecessary. However, others say that leaving out the hyphen may cause confusion and therefore include it (*well-known*). The standard in MLA is as follows: When it appears before the noun, *well known* should be hyphenated. When it follows the noun, no hyphenation is needed.

- Sarah Palin is a **well-known** person.
- Sarah Palin is **well known.**

Prefixes and Suffixes

Most prefixes do not need to be hyphenated; they are simply added in front of a noun, with no spaces and no joining punctuation necessary. The following is a list of common prefixes that do not require hyphenation when added to a noun:

after	anti	bi	bio	co
cyber	di	down	hetero	homo
infra	inter	macro	micro	mini
nano	photo	poly	stereo	thermo

Note: The prefix *re* generally doesn't require a hyphen. However, when leaving out a hyphen will cause confusion, one should be added. Look at the following word pairs, for example:

- *resign* (leave a position) v. *re-sign* (sign the paper again)
- *recreation* (an activity of leisure) v. *re-creation* (create something again)

Common suffixes also do not require hyphenation, assuming no ambiguities of spelling or pronunciation arise. Typically, you do not need to hyphenate words ending in the following suffixes:

able	less	fold	like	wise

Commonly Used Word Blends

Also, especially in technical fields, some words commonly used in succession become joined into one. The resulting word's meaning is readily understood by technical readers, and no hyphen is necessary. Here are some examples of such word blends, typically written as single words:

blackbody	groundwater	airship
downdraft	longwall	upload
setup	runoff	blowout

Practice

1. Students can participate in (self paced/self-paced) learning.
2. Rather than sit in a (six hour-long/six-hour long/six-hour-long) class, students can study at their convenience.
3. Would you like the (three or four-course/three- or four-course) meal tonight?
4. He's behaving in a very (childlike/child-like) manner.

Dashes

The dash functions almost as a colon does in that it adds to the preceding material—but with extra emphasis. Like a caesura (a timely pause) in music, a dash indicates a strong pause, then gives emphasis to material following the pause. In effect, a dash allows you to *redefine* what was just written, making it more explicit. You can also use a dash as it is used in the first sentence of this paragraph: to frame an interruptive or parenthetical-type comment that you do not want to de-emphasize.

- Jill Emery confirms that Muslim populations have typically been ruled by non-Muslims—specifically Americans, Russians, Israelis, and the French.

- The dissolution took 20 minutes—much longer than anticipated—but measurements were begun as soon as the process was completed.

There is no "dash" button on a computer keyboard. Instead, use the "symbol" option in your word processor; or use the Mac shortcut option + shift + —. A dash is longer than a hyphen and means something different, so don't type a hyphen if a dash is what you need.

Practice

Is the dash used correctly in the following sentences?

1. A good leader should be—passionate, patient, productive and positive.

2. Politicians want to serve and improve the lives of people—really!

3. Life is ninety per cent perspiration—my kindergarten teacher told me—and ten per cent inspiration.

The dash we typically use is technically called the "em dash," and it is significantly longer than the hyphen. There is also an "en dash"—whose length is between that of the hyphen and the em dash, and its best usage is to indicate inclusive dates and numbers:

- July 6–September 17

    ◦ The date range began on July 6 and ended on September 17.

- Barack Obama (1961–)

    ◦ This indicates the year a person was born, as well as the fact that he or she is still alive.

- pp. 148–56

    ◦ This indicates pages 148 through 156. With number ranges, you can remove the first digit of the second number if it's the same as the first number's.

The en dash can also be used for flight or train routes.

- The London–Paris train will be running thirty minutes late today.

Like the em dash, the en dash is not on the standard computer keyboard. Select it from word processor's symbol map (or if you have a Mac, you can type **option** + –), or it may even be inserted automatically by your word processor when you type inclusive numbers or dates with a hyphen between them. In most contexts, a hyphen can serve as an en dash, but in professional publications—especially in the humanities—an en dash is correct.

When you type the hyphen, en dash, and em dash, it is a convention that no spaces should appear on either side of the punctuation mark.

Practice

Read the following passage. Identify any errors with hyphens or dashes. Write the corrected version of the passage below:

John Milton Cage Jr. (1912-1992) was an American composer, music theorist, writer, and artist. A pioneer of indeterminacy in music and the non-standard use of musical instruments, Cage was one of the leading figures of the post—war avant-garde. Critics have lauded him as one of the most influential American composers of the twentieth-century.

Cage is perhaps best known for his 1952 composition 4′33″ a performance of the absence of deliberate sound. Musicians who present this piece do nothing aside from being present for the duration specified by the title. The content of the composition is not "four minutes and 33 seconds of silence"—as is often assumed, but rather the sounds of the environment heard by the audience during performance.

For answers, visit https://courses.lumenlearning.com/suny-geneseo-guidetowriting/chapter/hyphens-and-dashes/.

Attributions

CC licensed content, Original

- Revision and Adaptation. **Provided by**: Lumen Learning. **License**: *CC BY-NC-SA: Attribution-NonCommercial-ShareAlike*
- Revision and Adaptation. **Authored by**: Gillian Paku. **Provided by**: SUNY Geneseo. **License**: *CC BY: Attribution*

CC licensed content, Shared previously

- Style For Students Online. **Authored by**: Joe Schall. **Provided by**: The Pennsylvania State University. **Located at**: https://www.e-education.psu.edu/styleforstudents/. **Project**: Penn State's College of Earth and Mineral Sciences' OER Initiative. **License**: *CC BY-NC-SA: Attribution-NonCommercial-ShareAlike*
- Hyphens & Capitalization in Headings. **Authored by**: Julie Sevastopoulos. **Provided by**: Grammar-Quizzes. **Located at**: http://www.grammar-quizzes.com/punc-hyphen.html. **License**: *CC BY-NC-SA: Attribution-NonCommercial-ShareAlike*
- Dashes (em dash). **Authored by**: Julie Sevastopoulos. **Provided by**: Grammar-Quizzes. **Located at**: http://www.grammar-quizzes.com/punc-dashes.html. **License**: *CC BY-NC-SA: Attribution-NonCommercial-ShareAlike*
- Modification of John Cage (errors added). **Provided by**: Wikipedia. **Located at**: https://en.wikipedia.org/wiki/John_Cage. **License**: *CC BY-SA: Attribution-ShareAlike*

Apostrophes

Possession

With possessives, the apostrophe is used in combination with an *s* to represent that a word literally or conceptually possesses what follows it.

- a student's paper

- the county's borders

- a nation's decision

- one hour's passing

Apostrophes with Words Ending in s and with Plurals

Singular words, whether or not they end in *s*, are made possessive by adding an apostrophe + *s*. For plural words, we typically indicate possession simply by adding the apostrophe without an additional *s*. However, for a plural that does not end in an *s* (e.g., *bacteria*), we would add an apostrophe + *s*.

- Illinois's law

- Mars's atmosphere

- interviewees' answers

- the bacteria's life cycle

- her professors' office (an office shared by two of her professors; if it were just one professor we would write *her professor's office*)

> **Note:** Practices for handling apostrophes with words ending in *s* vary from style to style, sometimes using syllable count as the determining factor, for example, so be sure to check the rules in your course's discipline.

Contractions

A contraction is a shortened phrase. *He will* becomes *he'll*, *are not* becomes *aren't*, *would have* becomes *would've*, and *it is* becomes *it's*. In all of these cases, the apostrophe stands in for the missing letters.

You may find yourself being steered away from using contractions in your standard, academic papers. Write to your teacher's preference. Leaving out contractions can possibly make your writing sound too formal and stilted, but using contractions can make your writing sound too informal and casual. And don't eliminate contractions in your papers just to up your word count!

> **Note:** Double contractions, like *wouldn't've* or *I'd've* are considered non-standard and should be avoided in formal written language.

Some Common Errors

Now that we've learned about both contraction and possession, let's take a look at some of the most common (or at least most called out) errors people make.

Its versus It's

- https://youtu.be/Yhaa214UKvA

This rule also applies to *your* vs. *you're* and *their* vs. *they're*. The best way to use these correctly is to remember that possessive pronouns never have an apostrophe: if there's an apostrophe with a pronoun, it's a contraction, not a possessive.

Should've versus Should of

- *Should of, would of, could of*
- *Should've, would've, could've*

This mistake is due to the pronunciation. Out loud both of these phrases sound exactly the same. However, remember that the original phrase is *should have*, as in "I should have done that." The phrase *should of* should never occur. Unfortunately, the only way to remember this is rote memorization (or perhaps a closer examination of the word *of*).

Acronyms and Numbers

In technical writing, acronyms and numbers are sometimes pluralized with the addition of an apostrophe + *s*, but this convention is falling out of favor, and there is typically no need to put an apostrophe in front of the *s*. Therefore, *SSTs* (sea surface temperatures) is more acceptable than *SST's* when your intention is simply to pluralize.

> Ideally, use the apostrophe before the *s* with an acronym or a number only to show possession (e.g., "an 1860's law"; "DEP's testing") or when confusion would otherwise result ("mind your *p*'s and *q*'s").

When talking about a specific decade *the 1920s* should be shortened to *the '20s*. Notice that the apostrophe curls away from the numbers, indicating that the missing characters originally appeared prior to the apostrophe.

Practice

Select the response from the list that best completes the sentence.

1. Betty Crocker actually came from an (employees/employee's/employees') imagination.

2. Back in the (1930s/1930's/1930s'), Betty Crocker was a name everyone knew.

3. A television commercial asked, "(Who's/Whose) the person (who's/whose) cookies we love?"

4. As (woman's/women's/womens') fashions changed, the company updated (Betty Crocker's/Betty Crockers') image.

5. A commercial told us, "Buy Betty Crocker. (It's/Its) quality you can trust!"

For answers, visit https://courses.lumenlearning.com/suny-geneseo-guidetowriting/chapter/apostrophes/.

Attributions

Quotation Marks

There are three typical ways quotation marks are used. The first is pretty self-explanatory: you use quotation marks when you're directly quoting.

- He said, "I'll never forget you." It was the best moment of my life.

- Yogi Berra famously said, "A nickel ain't worth a dime anymore."

If you're just writing an approximation of something a person said, you would *not* use quotation marks:

- She told me about Pizza the three-toed sloth yesterday.

- He said that he would be late today.

The second is when you're calling attention to a word. For example:

- I can never say "Worcestershire" correctly.

- How do you spell "definitely"?

> **Note:** It is this course's preference to use italics in these instances:
>
> - I can never say *Worcestershire* correctly.
> - How do you spell *definitely*?
>
> However, using quotation marks is also an accepted practice. Check with your instructor.

The last use is **scare quotes**. This is the most misused type of quotation mark. People often think that quotation marks mean emphasis.

- Buy some "fresh" chicken today!

- We'll give it our "best" effort.

- Employees "must" wash their hands before returning to work.

However, when used this way, the quotation marks insert a silent "so-called" into the sentence, which is often the opposite of the intended meaning.

Where Do Quotation Marks Go?

Despite what you may see practiced—especially in advertising, on television, and even in business letters—the fact is that the period and comma go inside the quotation marks almost all of the time. Confusion arises because the British system is different.

- Correct: The people of the pine barrens are often called "pineys."

- Incorrect: The people of the pine barrens are often called "pineys".

However, the semicolon, colon, dash, question mark, and exclamation point fall outside of the quotation marks (unless the quoted material has internal punctuation of its own).

- This measurement is commonly known as "dip angle"; dip angle is the angle formed between a normal plane and a vertical.

- Built only 50 years ago, Shakhtinsk—"minetown"—is already seedy.

- When she was asked the question "Are rainbows possible in winter?" she answered by examining whether raindrops freeze at temperatures below 0 °C. (Quoted material has its own punctuation.)

- Did he really say "Dogs are the devil's henchmen"? (The quotation is a statement, but the full sentence is a question.)

Practice

Has the following passage been punctuated correctly? Write any corrections below:

Gabrielly and Marcelo both knew a lot of "fun facts" that they liked to share with each other. Yesterday Gabrielly said to Marcelo, "Did you know that wild turkeys can run up to twenty-five miles per hour?"

"Well, an emu can run twice that speed," Marcelo responded.

"Did you know that there's a dinosaur-themed park in Poland called JuraPark Bałtów"? Gabrielly asked.

Marcelo then told her about "Rusik, the first Russian police sniffer cat, who helped search for illegal cargoes of fish and caviar".

For answers, visit https://courses.lumenlearning.com/suny-geneseo-guidetowriting/chapter/quotation-marks/.

Attributions

Editorial Brackets

The main use of editorial brackets is in quotations, where they can be used to clarify information that you lose when you take the quotation out of its original context. Here's a brief passage:

> In June, 1992, the California Attorney General's office accused the Sears Company of overcharging on automobile repairs. By way of excuse for their errors, Sears ran newspaper advertisements that stressed the huge number of repairs performed annually.

However, in your essay, you only want to quote the second sentence, where "their errors" has no clear definition. In order to do this, you could write the following: "By way of excuse for their [overcharging], Sears ran newspaper advertisements that stressed the huge number of repairs performed annually."

The brackets let the reader know that while the word *overcharging* wasn't specifically in the wording in the original quotation, you are confident that it was implied there.

> When using editorial brackets, therefore, you need to be careful not to change the original meaning of the quotation.

Another use of brackets is when there is a spelling or informational error in the original quotation, as in, "To disengage gears, fist [sic] lock the mechanism." The term *sic* means that the typo was in the original source of this quotation. More technically, *sic* indicates that the reader should trust the accuracy of the quotation even though it looks like it contains an error; one obvious side effect is that if you insert *sic*, it shows that the error was the original writer's doing, not yours.

Practice

Read the following passages. Imagine you want to quote the numbered sentences. Each sentence would appear separately. Use editorial brackets if you think they are necessary to indicate the clearest way to present each sentence to a reader who isn't able to see the whole passage.

(1) Mount Vesuivus is a stratovolcano in the Gulf of Naples, Italy, about 5.6 mi east of Naples and a short distance from the shore.

(2) It consists of a large cone partially encircled by the steep rim of a summit caldera caused by the collapse of an earlier and originally much higher structure.

(3) Mount Vesuvius is best known for its eruption in CE 79 that led to the burying and destruction of the Roman cities of Pompeii, Herculaneum, and several other settlements.

For answers, visit https://courses.lumenlearning.com/suny-geneseo-guidetowriting/chapter/brackets/.

Attributions

CC licensed content, Original

- Text: Brackets. **Provided by**: Lumen Learning. **License**: *CC BY: Attribution*
- Revision and Adaptation. **Authored by**: Gillian Paku. **Provided by**: SUNY Geneseo. **License**: *CC BY: Attribution*

CC licensed content, Shared previously

- Modification of Mount Vesuvius (errors added). **Provided by**: Wikipedia. **Located at**: https://en.wikipedia.org/wiki/Mount_Vesuvius. **License**: *CC BY-SA: Attribution-ShareAlike*

Ellipses

An ellipsis (plural *ellipses*) is a series of three periods.

As with other punctuation marks, there is some contention about its usage, namely, whether or not there should be a space between the periods (. . .) or not (...). MLA, APA, and *Chicago*, the most common style guides for students, support having spaces between the periods. Other documentation styles you may encounter, such as in journalism, may not.

Quotations

Like the editorial brackets we just learned about, you will primarily see ellipses used in quotations, where they indicate a missing portion. According to most conventions, ellipses don't require editorial brackets because they are understood already to include an editorial decision to elide material, but be aware that instructors might have their own preferences. Look at the following passage:

> Sauropod dinosaurs are the biggest animals to have ever walked on land. They are instantly recognized by their long, sweeping necks and whiplashed tails, and nearly always portrayed moving in herds, being stalked by hungry predators.
>
> In recent years, a huge amount of taxonomic effort from scientists has vastly increased the number of known species of sauropod. What we now know is that in many areas we had two or more species co-existing.

The passage contains more information than you need to include in your essay. Here's how to cut it down:

> Sauropod dinosaurs are the biggest animals to have ever walked on land. They are instantly recognized by their long, sweeping necks and whiplashed tails. . . . In recent years . . . [research has shown] that in many areas we had two or more species co-existing.

In the block quotation above, you can see that the first ellipsis appears to have four dots. ("They are instantly recognized by their long, sweeping necks and whiplashed tails. . . .") However, this is just a period followed by an ellipsis. This is because ellipses **do not** remove punctuation marks when the original punctuation still is in use; they are instead used in conjunction with original punctuation. This is true for all punctuation marks, including periods, commas, semicolons, question marks, and exclamation points.

> By looking at two sympatric species (those that lived together) from the fossil graveyards of the Late Jurassic of North America . . . , [David Button] tried to work out what the major dietary differences were between sauropod dinosaurs, based on their anatomy.

One of the best ways to check yourself is to take out the ellipsis. If the sentence or paragraph is still correctly punctuated, you've used the ellipsis correctly. (Just remember to put it back in!)

Practice

Read the paragraphs below:

Camarasaurus, with its more mechanically efficient skull, was capable of generating much stronger bite forces than *Diplodocus*. This suggests that *Camarasaurus* was capable of chomping through tougher plant material than *Diplodocus*, and was perhaps even capable of a greater degree of oral processing before digestion. This actually ties in nicely with previous hypotheses of different diets for each, which were based on apparent feeding heights and inferences made from wear marks on their fossilized teeth.

Diplodocus seems to have been well-adapted, despite its weaker skull, to a form of feeding known as branch stripping, where leaves are plucked from branches as the teeth are dragged along them. The increased flexibility of the neck of *Diplodocus* compared to other sauropods seems to support this too.

Do the following quotations use ellipses – and surrounding punctuation – correctly?

1. This suggests that *Camarasaurus* was capable of chomping through tougher plant material than *Diplodocus*. . . This actually ties in nicely with previous hypotheses of different diets for each.

2. Diplodocus seems to have been well-adapted, . . . to a form of feeding known as branch stripping.

For answers, visit https://courses.lumenlearning.com/suny-geneseo-guidetowriting/chapter/ellipses/.

Pauses

> The ellipsis can also indicate . . . a pause. This use is typically informal, and not typically a convention of standard academic English.

Attributions

Parentheses

Parentheses are most often used to identify material that acts as an aside (such as this brief comment) or to add incidental information. **Use them sparingly in academic prose**: generally, your essay should be tightly enough written that material either belongs because it is central, or does not belong in there at all.

Key Takeaway

It is almost never appropriate to put evidence in brackets since brackets signal incidental material: the evidence that supports your argument is the basis of the whole essay, not incidental to it.

Other punctuation marks used alongside parentheses need to take into account their context. If the parentheses enclose a full sentence beginning with a capital letter, then the end punctuation for the sentence falls *inside* the parentheses. For example:

> Typically, suppliers specify air to cloth ratios of 6:1 or higher. (However, ratios of 4:1 should be used for applications involving silica or feldspathic minerals.)

If the parentheses indicate a citation at the end of a sentence, then the sentence's end punctuation comes *after* the parentheses are closed:

> In a study comparing three different building types, respirable dust concentrations were significantly lower in the open-structure building (Hugh et al., 2005).

Finally, if the parentheses appear in the midst of a sentence (as in this example), then any necessary punctuation (such as the comma that appeared just a few words ago) is delayed until the parentheses are closed.

You can also use parentheses to provide acronyms or full names for acronyms. For example, "We use the MLA (Modern Language Association) style guide here," or "The Modern Language Association (MLA) style guide is my favorite to use."

Remember, parentheses always appear in pairs. If you open a parenthesis, you need another to close it!

> **Note:** In technical writing, there are additional rules for using parentheses, which can be more nuanced. While we won't discuss those rules here, it's important to bear their existence in mind, especially if you're considering going into a more technical field.

Practice

Have the parentheses been used correctly in the following sentences? Correct any errors you find.

1. (Escobar et al., 2014) wrote about this phenomenon in their most recent paper.
2. NASA (National Aeronautics and Space Administration) just announced three new initiatives.
3. Michael lost the lab rat. (He also lost his temper).
4. Helena took the viola compositions (her favorites) and gave Davi the violin pieces.

For answers, visit https://courses.lumenlearning.com/suny-geneseo-guidetowriting/chapter/parentheses/.

Attributions

Punctuation Clusters

Occasionally, you'll come across an instance that seems to require multiple punctuation marks right next to each other. Sometimes you need to keep all the marks, but other times, you should leave some out.

- You should never use more than one ending punctuation mark in a row (period, question mark, or exclamation point). When quoting a question, you would end with a question mark, not a question mark and a period:
    - Carlos leaned forward and asked, "Did you get the answer to number six?"
- If an abbreviation, like *etc.*, ends a sentence, you should only use one period.
    - I think we'll have enough food. Mary bought the whole store: chips, soda, candy, cereal, etc.
- However, you can place a comma immediately after a period, as you can see above with *etc.*:

- "If an abbreviation, like *etc.*, ends a sentence"

- Periods and parentheses can also appear right next to each other. Sometimes the period comes after the closing parenthesis (as you can see in the first bullet), but sometimes it appears inside the parentheses. (This is an example of a sentence where the period falls within the parentheses.)

Practice
Identify punctuation errors in the following sentences. Write the corrected sentences below: 1. Dana had a lot of skills: reading, writing, note-taking, listening, etc.. 2. My partner looked over and asked, "Why do you have so much ignimbrite in the sample?." 3. Lucinda was the reigning Kahoot Queen (i.e. she had been fastest in last week's class).

Practice Activities: Punctuation

Ending Punctuation

Are ending punctuation marks used appropriately in these sentences? Explain why or why not. The sentences have been numbered to aid in your comments:

(1) One famous eighteenth-century thoroughbred racehorse was named Potooooooooo, or Pot-8-Os! (2) He was a chestnut colt bred by Willoughby Bertie, 4th Earl of Abingdon, in 1773, and he was known for his defeat of some of the greatest racehorses of the time. (3) With a well-to-do background like this, where do you suppose his strange name came from. (4) The horse once had a stable lad, who facetiously misspelled *potatoes*. (5) Apparently, the owner thought the misspelling was funny enough to adopt it as the horse's real name!

Hyphens

Identify the compounds in the following sentences. All compounds have been treated as open compounds (compound words that are neither made into one word nor joined by hyphens). Correct any compounds that this is incorrect for:

1. This is all publicly available information.
2. Ana bred a new yellow orange squash last week.

Apostrophes

Read the following passage. Identify any errors with apostrophes. Write the corrected words below:

Thanks to NASAs' team of sniffers, led by George Aldrich, astronauts can breathe a little bit easier. Aldrich is the "chief sniffer" at the White Sands Test Facility in New Mexico. His job is to smell items before they can be flown in the space shuttle.

Aldrich explained that smells change in space and that once astronauts are up there, their stuck with whatever smells are on board with them. In space, astronauts aren't able to open the window for extra ventilation. He also said that its important not to introduce substances that will change the delicate balance of the climate of the International Space Station and the space shuttle.

Attributions

CC licensed content, Original

- Practice Activities: Punctuation. **Provided by**: Lumen Learning. **License**: *CC BY: Attribution*
- Revision and Adaptation. **Authored by**: Gillian Paku. **Provided by**: SUNY Geneseo. **License**: *CC BY: Attribution*

CC licensed content, Shared previously

- Modification of Potooooooooo (errors added). **Provided by**: Wikipedia. **Located at**: https://en.wikipedia.org/wiki/Potooooooooo. **License**: *CC BY-SA: Attribution-ShareAlike*

Public domain content

- George Aldrich (errors added). **Provided by**: NASA. **Located at**: http://spaceflight.nasa.gov/shuttle/support/people/galdrich.html. **Project**: Behind the Scenes: Meet the People. **License**: *Public Domain: No Known Copyright*

3. Sentence Structure

Introduction to Sentence Structure

One of the advantages of INTD 188 and INTD 105 is that we can take the opportunity to think about the linguistic building blocks that form the larger structures of essays, and take the further opportunity to practice using them. Not all linguistic structures scale up: the guidelines for effective sentences can bend in the service of paragraphs. However, if you're going to write in a way that doesn't meet regular expectations, you need to know the conventions from which you're deviating. Knowing the conventions before you riff on them is the difference between enjoying an innovative drum solo and suffering the noise of a drum kit falling down a flight of stairs. In this module, we will isolate the unit of the sentence, learn its conventional uses, and see how sentences help us to organize our ideas to identify which items belong together and which should be separated.

Each conventionally complete standard English sentence has a grammatical subject, a predicate (which can take the minimal form of a verb), and punctuation. That's good to know, but you will write like a second-grader if you don't have variety in your sentence length and structure. Gary Provost illustrates why:

> This sentence has five words. Here are five more words. Five-word sentences are fine. But several together become monotonous. Listen to what is happening. The writing is getting boring. The sound of it drones. It's like a stuck record. The ear demands some variety. Now listen. I vary the sentence length, and I create music. Music. The writing sings. It has a pleasant rhythm, a lilt, a harmony. I use short sentences. And I use sentences of medium length. And sometimes when I am certain the reader is rested, I will engage him with a sentence of considerable length, a sentence that burns with energy and builds with all the impetus of a crescendo, the roll of the drums, the crash of the cymbals–sounds that say, "Listen to this, it is important."

College-level writing involves a combination of short, medium, and long sentences. This need to create a sound that pleases the reader's ear is not simply a requirement of creative writing; you need to bear it in mind for lab reports and abstracts, too, since the readers of those genres of writing will no more enjoy monotony than you do. Provost's quotation invites you to listen, so we've illustrated the phenomenon of monotony in the following video, too. [1]

- https://youtu.be/k7ccnFw84cQ

In order to create this variety, you need to know how sentences work and how to create them. In this section we will identify the parts of sentences and learn how they fit together to create music in writing.

Attributions

CC licensed content, Original

- Introduction to Sentence Structure. **Provided by**: Lumen Learning. **License**: *CC BY: Attribution*
- Revision and Adaptation. **Authored by**: Gillian Paku. **Provided by**: SUNY Geneseo. **License**: *CC BY: Attribution*

CC licensed content, Shared previously

- Modification of Notepad. **Authored by**: Simon Mettler. **Located at**: https://thenounproject.com/term/notepad/154767/. **License**: *CC BY: Attribution*

All rights reserved content

- This Sentence Has Five Words. **Authored by**: Nick Schneider. **Located at**: https://youtu.be/k7ccnFw84cQ. **License**: *All Rights Reserved*. **License Terms**: Standard YouTube License

---

1. Provost, Gary. *100 Ways to Improve Your Writing*, Signet:1985, pp. 60–61.

Basic Parts of a Sentence

> I like the construction of sentences and the juxtaposition of words—not just how they sound or what they mean, but even what they look like.
>
> —Don DeLillo

Subject and Predicate

Every complete, standard sentence has a subject and a predicate. You were probably taught some time in elementary school that the **subject** of a sentence is often the noun, pronoun, or phrase or clause the sentence is about, and certainly there is a large overlap between the *grammatical* concept of a subject and this sense of it as a *topic*. In most clear sentences, the subject of your sentence will also answer the "who" of the basic narrative question we ask of sentences, "Who does what?" However, it's more accurate to define the subject of a sentence not as its topic but as the more strictly grammatical issue of *what the verb in the sentence agrees with in number*. Let's look at one typically sophisticated college-level sentence to illustrate these ideas:

- Einstein's general theory of relativity has been subjected to many tests of validity over the years.

A careless answer to "who does what?" in this sentence might pick up *Einstein*, a particularly famous "who," as the subject. But the grammatical unit that agrees with the verb form "has been subjected" is not "Einstein," but rather "Einstein's general theory of relativity." That's the grammatical subject of this sentence, but the sentence is not really "about" Einstein's general theory of relativity. Rather, the sentence is about subjecting that theory to many tests of validity. Here, then—and in many sentences complex enough to appear in college-level writing—the grammatical **subject** of the sentence is only tangentially what the sentence is about. To put that another way, the conceptual subject of this sentence is not the grammatical subject of this sentence. Many writers will find it easier to think about the conceptual subject than the grammatical subject, but if you want to get good at negotiating and forming college-level sentences, you'll appreciate being able to focus on the grammatical subject as *what the verb in the sentence agrees with in number*.

Just as the "has been subjected" verbal element helps us to identify the grammatical subject of this sentence, it would also lead us to a more pertinent answer to "who does what?" here; i.e., who *has subjected*

Einstein's theory to such testing? The answer to the "who" question is something like "scholars" or "skeptics" or "scientists at CERN." The reason those characters don't appear in this sentence, leaving us unsure exactly who is performing the action signaled by the verb, is because this sentence is in the passive voice—we'll cover that idea later in this module.

A further point about the grammatical subject in this sentence is that you can distinguish a *simple subject* from a *whole subject* (there's a reason we don't define subjects this way when you first encounter them in elementary school!). "Einstein's general theory of relativity" is the *whole subject* of this sentence: the element that is most fully predicated by the verb. The *simple subject* is the part of the whole subject that determines whether the verb will be singular or plural. In our example, the simple subject is "theory." You could change "Einstein" to a different singular or even a plural noun without affecting the verb and / or you could change the nature of the theory without affecting the verb (although of course you would thereby alter the meaning of the sentence; we're making a grammatical point here, not a conceptual one):

- *Newton's* theory of *gravity* **has been subjected** to many tests of validity over the years.
- *Copernican thinkers'* theory of *heliocentrism* **has been subjected** to many tests of validity over the years.

You cannot, however, change "theory" to "theories" without affecting the form of the verb, so "theory" is the simple subject here:

- Einstein's general **theories** of relativity **have** been subjected to many tests of validity over the years.

Here are a couple more examples of subjects in action:

- Although a majority of caffeine drinkers think of it as a stimulant, heavy users of caffeine say the substance relaxes them.
  - whole subject that agrees with the verb "say" = "heavy users of caffeine"
  - simple subject that determines the plural verb form = "users"
  - Notice that the introductory phrase, "Although a majority of caffeine drinkers think of it as a stimulant," is not a part of the subject or the predicate of the complete sentence.
- In a secure landfill, the soil on top and the cover block storm water intrusion into the landfill.
  - There are two subjects in this sentence: *soil* and *cover*. This is a *compound subject,* making up the whole subject of "the soil on top and the cover."
  - Notice that the characters in this sentence (the answer to "who does what?") are not human agents, but rather the inanimate objects "soil" and "cover." Although humans are social creatures who gravitate toward what other humans are doing as interesting narratives (think about how many of your private conversations revolve around "who does / did what?"), we easily understand non-human agents when we can clearly see them performing some action; i.e., What do soil and a cover do here? They block storm water intrusion.
- Surrounding the secure landfill on all sides are impermeable barrier **walls**.
  - In an *inverted sentence,* the predicate comes before the subject. You won't run into

this sentence structure very often as it is pretty rare in standard, academic English.

The **predicate** is the rest of the sentence after the subject. Given how we have defined *subject* above, you won't be surprised to see that the predicate begins with the form of the verb that agrees with the whole subject. A common definition of a grammatically complete sentence in standard English is that it has a subject and a verb, e.g. "Water evaporates." In this case, the predicate is synonymous with the verb. However, **predicate** also includes the material attached to a verb, known as the *complement*. In those very common cases, *verb + complement = predicate*. In other terms you might be familiar with, a predicate can include the verb, a direct object, and an indirect object.

- The pressure in a pressured water reactor **varies from system to system.**

- In contrast, a boiling water reactor **operates at constant pressure.**

- The pressure **is maintained at about 2250 pounds per square inch** then **lowered to form steam at about 600 pounds per square inch.** *(compound predicate)*

    ◦ There are two predicates in this sentence: "is maintained at about 2250 pounds per square inch" and "lowered to form steam at about 600 pounds per square inch"

Practice

Identify the subject and predicate of each sentence (paraphrased from Stacy Clifford Simplican's *The Capacity Contract*, pp. 86-87). Identify the whole and simple subjects where relevant. Identify the verb in each predicate:

1. Charles Mills's treatment of race and social contract theory offers fruitful inroads for a project on disability.

2. Mills specifically targets Rawls's depoliticized construction of rational capacity.

3. For Mills, Rawls's reliance on a depoliticized theory sustains the systematic omission of racial oppression from discussions of disability and neglects inequalities in cognitive capacities.

Direct Object

A direct object—a noun, pronoun, phrase, or clause acting as a noun—follows and receives the action of the main verb. To put that another way, the direct object is "acted on" by the verb, so a direct object can be identified by putting *what?, which?,* or *whom?* in its place.

- Copernicus refutes Ptolemy.

    ◦ Whom does Copernicus (the subject) *refute* (the verb)? Answer: Ptolemy (the direct object). Ptolemy is acted on by, or receives, the refutation Copernicus offers.

- Lavoisier used curved glass **discs** fastened together at their rims, with wine filling the space between, to focus the sun's rays to attain temperatures of 3000° F.

  - The action (*used*) is directly happening to the object (*discs*); i.e., What did Lavoisier use? He used discs.

- The housing assembly of a mechanical pencil contains its **workings**.

  - The action (*contains*) is directly happening to what? Answer: to the mechanical pencil's *workings*, so *workings* is the direct object.

- A 20 percent fluctuation in average global temperature could reduce biological **activity**, shift weather **patterns**, and ruin **agriculture**. *(compound direct object)*

  - The actions (what the fluctuation *could do*) are directly happening to what? To multiple objects: the fluctuation *could reduce activity*, *could shift patterns*, and *could ruin agriculture*.

- On Mariners 6 and 7, the two-axis scan platforms provided much more **capability** and **flexibility** for the scientific payload than those of Mariner 4. *(compound direct object)*

  - The action (*provided*) is directly happening to multiple objects (*capability* and *flexibility*); i.e. What did the two-axis platforms provide? They provided much more capability and flexibility.

Not all verbs take a direct object. Remember that a direct object is some form of a noun. You can't create a direct object for the verb "to sleep," for example ("I sleep bed" or "I sleep Thomas"). Such verbs that don't take a direct object are called *intransitive verbs*. Verbs that do take a direct object are called *transitive verbs*.

Indirect Object

An indirect object—a noun, pronoun, phrase, or clause acting as a noun—receives the action expressed in the sentence. It can be identified by inserting *to* or *for*.

- The company is designing **senior citizens** a new walkway to the park area.

  - The company is not designing new models of senior citizens; they are designing a new walkway *for* senior citizens. Thus, *senior citizens* is the indirect object of this sentence.

  - *Walkway* is the direct object of this sentence, since it is the thing being designed.

- Please send **the personnel office** a résumé so we can further review your candidacy.

  - You are not being asked to send the office somewhere; you're being asked to send a résumé *to* the office. Thus, *the personnel office* is the indirect object of this sentence.

  - *Résumé* is the direct object of this sentence, since it is the thing you should send.

Note: Objects can belong to any verb in a sentence, even if the verbs aren't in the main clause. For example, let's look at the sentence "When you give your instructor your assignment, be sure to include your name and your class number."

- *Your instructor* is the indirect object of the verb *give*.

- *Your assignment* is the direct object of the verb *give*.

- *Your name* and *your class number* are the direct objects of the verb *include*.

Practice

Identify the grammatical objects in the following sentences. Are they direct or indirect objects?

1. The cooler temperatures brought about by nuclear war might end all life on earth.

2. On Mariners 6 and 7, the two-axis scan platforms provided the scientific payload much more capability and flexibility than those of Mariner 4.

3. In your application letter, tell the potential employer that a résumé accompanies the letter.

Attributions

CC licensed content, Original

- Revision, Adaptation, and Original Content. **Provided by**: Lumen Learning. **License**: *CC BY: Attribution*

- Revision and Adaptation. **Authored by**: Gillian Paku. **Provided by**: SUNY Geneseo. **License**: *CC BY: Attribution*

CC licensed content, Shared previously

- Basic Patterns and Elements of the Sentence. **Authored by**: David McMurrey. **Located at**: https://www.prismnet.com/~hcexres/textbook/twsent.html. **License**: *CC BY: Attribution*

Common Sentence Structures

Basic Sentence Patterns

Subject + verb

The simplest of sentence patterns is composed of a **subject** and *verb* without a direct object or complement. It uses an **intransitive verb**, that is, a verb requiring no direct object:

- Control **rods** *remain* inside the fuel assembly of the reactor.
- The **development** of wind power practically *ceased* until the early 1970s.
- The **cross-member** exposed to abnormal stress eventually *broke*.
- Only two **types** of charge *exist* in nature.

Subject + verb + direct object

Another common sentence pattern uses the <u>direct object</u>:

- **Silicon** *conducts* <u>electricity</u> in an unusual way.
- The anti-reflective **coating** on the the silicon cell *reduces* <u>reflection</u> from 32 to 22 percent.

Subject + verb + indirect object + direct object

The sentence pattern with the INDIRECT OBJECT and <u>direct object</u> is similar to the preceding pattern:

- **I** *am writing* HER about a number of <u>problems</u> that I have had with my computer.
- **Austin, Texas**, *has* recently *built* its CITIZENS a <u>system</u> of bike lanes.

Practice
Identify the basic sentence pattern of the sentences below:

1. All amplitude-modulation (AM) receivers work in the same way.

2. The supervisor mailed the applicant a description of the job.

3. We have mailed the balance of the payment in this letter.

Attributions

CC licensed content, Original

- Revision, Adaptation, and Original Content. **Provided by**: Lumen Learning. **License**: *CC BY: Attribution*

- Revision and Adaptation. **Authored by**: Gillian Paku. **Provided by**: SUNY Geneseo. **License**: *CC BY: Attribution*

CC licensed content, Shared previously

- Basic Patterns and Elements of the Sentence. **Authored by**: David McMurrey. **Located at**: https://www.prismnet.com/~hcexres/textbook/twsent.html. **License**: *CC BY: Attribution*

Sentence Punctuation Patterns

In the following passage about Queen Elizabeth I, you don't need to pay much attention to the words: concentrate on the punctuation.

Elizabeth I's reign from 1558 to 1603 is known as the Elizabethan era. The period is famous for the flourishing of English drama, led by playwrights such as William Shakespeare and Christopher Marlowe (who may have been one of Elizabeth's double agents), and for the seafaring prowess of English adventurers such as Sir Francis Drake (who was a pirate as well as a global circumnavigator). Towards the end of Elizabeth's reign, a series of economic and military problems weakened her popularity. Elizabeth is acknowledged as a charismatic performer and a dogged survivor in an era when government was ramshackle and limited, and when monarchs in neighboring countries faced internal problems that jeopardized their thrones. After the short reigns of Elizabeth's half-siblings, her forty-four years on the throne provided welcome stability for the kingdom and helped forge a sense of national identity.

The "Darnley Portrait" of Elizabeth I of England

Here is the punctuation of the passage with the words removed:

_____.   _____,
_____   (_____),
_____   (_____).   _____,
_____.
_____
,   _____.
_____,   _____.

As you can see, the fairly basic information in this passage has a fairly basic punctuation structure. It simply uses periods, commas, and parentheses. It's correct, but it's not very sophisticated; it provides information rather than analysis or argument, and the closest it comes to complexity is when it tucks some intriguing details away in parentheses, suggesting that the author is unwilling to coordinate that information with their fairly bland central claims. At college, therefore, you should also master the following punctuation patterns because they occur very frequently both in reading and writing argumentative prose, which is typically more complex than either verbal speech or the writing you might have done at high school:

- _____; _____.

  ◦ Elizabeth was baptized on 10 September, 1533; Archbishop Thomas Cranmer stood as one of her godparents (*the semi-colon joining two related but complete sentences*).

- _____; however, _____.

  ◦ The English took the defeat of the Spanish armada as a symbol of God's favor; however, this victory was not a turning point in the war (*the semi-colon before a conjunctive adverb, e.g. however, moreover, therefore, thus, consequently, furthermore, unfortunately. Notice also the comma after the conjunctive adverb.*).

- _____: ____, ____, and ____.

  ◦ The period is famous for the flourishing of English drama, led by several well-known playwrights: William Shakespeare, Christopher Marlowe, and Francis Beaumont (*a colon introducing a list*).

As you write, it's best to use a variety of these patterns. If you use the same pattern repeatedly, your writing can seem boring. More importantly, if what you're writing never calls for the complications signaled by the punctuation of a conjunctive adverb, the urgency of a semi-colon holding together two complete thoughts, or the elaboration of a list introduced by a colon, you might in fact be writing something that *is* boring.

Practice

The sentences in this passage follow a single punctuation pattern: _____. Revise the passage to create variety. Try out some of the more complex patterns appropriate to college-level writing while you have the models right here in front of you.

Johann Sebastian Bach wrote six Cello Suites. The Cello Suites are suites for unaccompanied cello. They are some of the most frequently performed and recognizable solo compositions ever written for cello. Each movement is based around a baroque dance type. This basis is standard for a Baroque musical suite. The cello suites are structured in six movements each. Each includes a prelude; an allemande; a courante; a sarabande; two minuets, two bourrées, or two gavottes; and a final gigue. The Bach cello suites are considered to be among the most profound of all classical music works.

Attributions

Run-On Sentences

A *run-on* sentence consists of two or more grammatical sentences not separated by either a coordinating conjunction (*for, and, nor, but, or, yet, so—a.k.a. FANBOYS*) or any mark of punctuation this sentence is itself a run-on sentence. To put that definition another way, run-on sentences occur when two or more independent clauses are improperly joined. The most infamous form of the run-on sentence is the *comma splice*, in which two independent clauses are joined by a comma without a coordinating conjunction.

Let's look at two examples of run-on sentences. The second one is a comma splice:

- Often, choosing a topic for a paper is the hardest part it's a lot easier after that.

- Books do not always have the most complete information, it is a good idea then to look for articles in specialized periodicals.

Both of these sentences have two independent clauses. Each clause should be separated from another with a period, a semicolon, a colon, or a comma *and* a coordinating conjunction:

- Often, choosing a topic for a paper is the hardest part. It's a lot easier after that.

- OR: Often, choosing a topic for a paper is the hardest part; it's a lot easier after that.

- Books do not always have the most complete information; it is a good idea then to look for articles in specialized periodicals.

- OR: Books do not always have the most complete information. It is a good idea then to look for articles in specialized periodicals.

- OR: Books do not always have the most complete information, so it is a good idea then to look for articles in specialized periodicals. [This is the "comma *and* a coordinating conjunction" solution: *so* is one of the FANBOYS.]

Notice that a run-on sentence can usually be resolved by more than one method.

> **Note:** Don't define a run-on sentence as a sentence that goes on and on. A run-on sentence might be lengthy, but its defining feature is incorrect punctuation, not length. For example, look at this quotation from *The Great Gatsby*:

> Its vanished trees, the trees that had made way for Gatsby's house, had once pandered in whispers to the last and greatest of all human dreams; for a transitory enchanted moment man must have held his breath in the presence of this continent, compelled into an aesthetic contemplation he neither understood nor desired, face to face for the last time in history with something commensurate to his capacity for wonder.

> If you look at the punctuation, you'll see that this quotation is a single sentence, but F. Scott Fitzgerald manages commas and semicolons in such a way that, despite its considerable length, the sentence is grammatically sound. Length is no guarantee of a run-on sentence.

Common Causes of Run-Ons

As the Fitzgerald example above demonstrates, length is no guarantee of a run-on sentence. The confusion between lengthy and run-on sentences arises perhaps because English speakers know an independent clause when they read it, even if they don't know its technical name. We pause at the end of independent clauses, recognizing that the grammatical unit of the sentence has come to its end. When another independent clause then follows, without the pause marked by punctuation, it feels as if we have to kick our minds back into gear too quickly, or as if we are being dragged forward unwillingly. That experience makes even a relatively short run-on sentence feel long to us, as in this example: "Jonathan Swift's last years were unhappy he suffered from Ménière's disease."

We often write run-on sentences because we sense that the sentences involved are closely related and dividing them with a period just doesn't seem right. We may also write them because the parts seem too short to need any division, like in "Swift loved Esther Johnson but he probably did not marry her." However, "Swift loved Esther Johnson" and "he probably did not marry her" are both independent clauses, so they need to be divided by a comma *and* a coordinating conjunction—not just a coordinating conjunction by itself.

Another common cause of run-on sentences is mistaking adverbial conjunctions (some common examples are *however, moreover, therefore, thus, consequently, furthermore, unfortunately*) for coordinating conjunctions (the FANBOYS words). For example if we were to write, "Swift loved Esther Johnson, however he probably did not marry her," we would have produced a comma splice. The correct sentence would read, "Swift loved Esther Johnson; however, he probably did not marry her." If you manage to write a five-page college-level essay without using an adverbial conjunction, you should check the sophistication of your thoughts. This pattern, where an adverbial conjunction is preceded by a semi-colon and followed by a comma, is fundamental to complicating a thought, so it should appear in your writing, and you should punctuate it correctly. (Fun fact: adverbial conjunctions are also known as *conjunctive adverbs*. Regardless of the terminology, punctuate them correctly when you write them.)

Fixing Run-On Sentences

Before you can fix a run-on sentence, you'll need to identify the problem. You can often trust your own sense that a sentence is dragging; that sense frequently arises when a sentence is run-on rather than lengthy (think back to the Gary Provost quotation that opens this module; long sentences can be highly effective, but you have to be in control of them). Be alert to adverbial conjunctions and to coordinating conjunctions; you can use your word-processing program's "find" feature to locate common ones like "however" or "therefore" or "so," and then check the punctuation. That proofreading might sound onerous, but you won't have to do it often before you learn to think about those parts of speech while you're drafting; soon after that, you'll become competent automatically. And, of course, you don't need to wait until you've written fifteen pages before you start to check; take a look at your first couple of pages slowly and carefully to kickstart the editing process. If trusting your own feel for English and trouble-shooting obvious words still leave you with some dubious sentences, you can isolate them and ask whether the parts are independent clauses. Remember, only independent clauses can stand on their own. This also means they *must* stand on their own; they can't run together without correct punctuation. (Yes, this paragraph makes deliberately heavy use of semi-colons to prevent run-ons—we're glad you noticed!)

Let's take a look at a few more run-on sentences and their revisions:

1. Some of the hours I've earned toward my associate's degree do not transfer, however, I do have many general education credits the University will accept.

2. Some respondents were highly educated professionals, others were from small villages in underdeveloped countries.

3. The opposite is true of stronger types of stainless steel they tend to be more susceptible to rust.

The first sentence is a comma-splice sentence. The adverbial conjunction *however* is being treated like a coordinating conjunction. There are two easy fixes to this problem. The first is to turn the comma before *however* into a period. If this feels like too hard of a stop between ideas, you can change the comma into a semicolon instead.

- Some of the hours I've earned toward my associate's degree do not transfer. However, I do have many general education credits the University will accept.

- Some of the hours I've earned toward my associate's degree do not transfer; however, I do have many general education credits the University will accept.

In the second example, we again have two independent clauses. The two clauses provide contrasting information. Adding a conjunction could help the reader move from one kind of information to another. However, you may want that sharp contrast. Here are two revision options:

- Some respondents were highly educated professionals, while others were from small villages in underdeveloped countries.

- Some respondents were highly educated professionals. Others were from small villages in underdeveloped countries.

The third sentence is a run-on as well. "The opposite is true of stronger types of stainless steel" and "they tend to be more susceptible to rust" are both independent clauses. The two clauses are very closely related because the second clarifies the information provided in the first. The best solution is to insert a colon between the two clauses:

The opposite is true of stronger types of stainless steel: they tend to be more susceptible to rust.

When you are punctuating independent clauses, the difference between a semi-colon and a colon can be subtle, and is not necessarily subject to hard-and-fast rules. Both colons and semi-colons connect independent clauses when the clauses contain closely related material, but we prefer the colon when the second independent clause amplifies, explains, or summarizes the information in the first independent clause. In the example above, the second clause explains what "the opposite" refers to in the first clause.

Practice

Identify the run-on sentences in the following paragraph:

I had the craziest dream the other night. My cousin Jacob and I were on the run from the law. Apparently we were wizards and the law was cracking down on magic. We obviously had to go into hiding but I lost track of Jacob and then I got picked up by a cop. He was scary, he had fangs. However I was able to convince him that the government was corrupt and that he should take me to my escape boat.

Attributions

CC licensed content, Original

- Revision, Adaptation, and Original Content. **Provided by**: Lumen Learning. **License**: *CC BY: Attribution*
- Revision and Adaptation. **Authored by**: Gillian Paku. **Provided by**: SUNY Geneseo. **License**: *CC BY: Attribution*

CC licensed content, Shared previously

- Punctuation: Commas. **Authored by**: David McMurrey. **Located at**: https://www.prismnet.com/~hcexres/textbook/gram1.html. **License**: *CC BY: Attribution*

Sentence Fragments

Fragments are grammatically incomplete sentences—they are phrases and dependent clauses. These are grammatical structures that cannot stand on their own: they need to be connected to an independent clause to work in writing. So how can we tell the difference between a sentence and a sentence fragment? And how can we fix fragments when they already exist?

Common Causes of Fragments

Part of the reason we write in fragments is because we often speak that way. However, there is a difference between colloquial speech and standard academic English, and it is important to write in full sentences when you are in that formal situation. Additionally, fragments often come about in writing because a sentence may already seem too long.

Non-finite verbs (gerunds, participles, and infinitives) can often trip people up as well. Since non-finite verbs don't act like verbs, we don't count them as verbs when we're deciding if we have a phrase or a clause. Let's look at a few examples of these:

- Running away from my mother.
- To ensure your safety and security.
- Beaten down since day one.

Even though all of the above have non-finite verbs, they're phrases, not clauses. In order for these to be clauses, they would need an additional verb that acts as a verb in the sentence.

Words like *since, when,* and *because* turn an independent clause into a dependent clause. For example, "I was a toddler in 1999" is an independent clause, but, "Because I was a toddler in 1999" is a dependent clause. This class of word includes the following:

after	although	as	as far as	as if		as long as	as soon as
as though	because	before	even if	even though	every time	if
in order that	since	so	so that	than		though	unless
until	when	whenever	where	whereas		wherever	while

Relative pronouns, like *that* and *which,* do the same type of thing as those listed above.

Coordinating conjunctions (our FANBOYS) can also cause problems. If you start a sentence with a coordinating conjunction, make sure that it is followed a complete clause, not just a phrase!

As you're identifying fragments, keep in mind that command (a.k.a. *imperative*) sentences are *not* fragments, despite not having a subject. Commands are the only grammatically correct sentences that lack a subject:

- Drop and give me fifty!

- Count how many times the word *fragrant* is used during commercial breaks.

Fixing Sentence Fragments

Let's take a look at a couple of examples:

1. Nicola appeared at the committee meeting last week. And made a convincing presentation of her ideas about the new product.

2. The committee considered her ideas for a new marketing strategy quite powerful. The best ideas that they had heard in years.

3. Ana spent a full month evaluating Matthew's computer-based instructional materials. Which she eventually sent to her supervisor with the strongest of recommendations.

The phrase, "And made a convincing presentation of her ideas about the new product," in example one contains no subject, so the easiest fix is to simply delete the period and combine the two statements:

Nicola appeared at the committee meeting last week and made a convincing presentation of her ideas about the new product.

There is no verb contained in the phrase "the best ideas they had heard in years." By adding "they were" to the beginning of this phrase, we have turned the fragment into an independent clause, which can now stand on its own:

The committee considered her ideas for a new marketing strategy quite powerful; they were the best ideas that they had heard in years.

What about example three? Let's look at the clause "Which she eventually sent to her supervisor with the strongest of recommendations." This is a dependent clause; the word *which* signals this fact. If we change "which she eventually" to "eventually, she," we also turn the dependent clause into an independent clause.

Ana spent a full month evaluating Matthew's computer-based instructional materials. Eventually, she sent the evaluation to her supervisor with the strongest of recommendations.

As with run-on sentences, there are often multiple ways to solve the problem of fragments. We're modeling some options for you here, but our models aren't necessarily the only answers.

Practice

Identify the fragments in the sentences below. Why are they fragments? What are some possible solutions?

1. The corporation wants to begin a new marketing push in educational software. Although, the more conservative executives of the firm are skeptical.

2. Include several different sections in your proposal. For example, a discussion of your personnel and their qualifications, your expectations concerning the schedule of the project, and a cost breakdown.

3. The research team has completely reorganized the workload. Making sure that members work in areas of their own expertise and that no member is assigned proportionately too much work.

Parallel Structure

Parallel structures are sequences of coordinated words, phrases, or clauses that are of the same grammatical structure. Parallel structure can be applied to a single sentence, a paragraph, or even multiple paragraphs. Compare the two following sentences:

- Rural landlords wanted income from rent, to farm parts of their own estate, and being middlemen for agricultural trade.

- Rural landlords wanted income from rent, from farming parts of their own estate, and from being middlemen for agricultural trade.

Most people find the second sentence easier to comprehend than the first because the second sentence uses parallelism—the "from" launches three different forms of desired income, so that the reader easily understands that rent, farming, and being middlemen are all options. The first sentence is more confusing because the concepts don't line up grammatically: the first and third options (*rent* and *being middlemen*) have "wanted income from" as their root; the second time (*to farm parts*) has perhaps only "wanted" as its root. While the first sentence is technically correct, it's awkward and makes it easy to trip up over the mismatching items. Parallelism improves writing style and readability, and it makes sentences easier to process.

Compare the following examples:

- Lacking parallelism: "She likes cooking, jogging, and *to read*."
    - Parallel: "She likes cooking, jogging, and reading."
    - Parallel: "She likes to cook, jog, and read."
- Lacking parallelism: "He likes to swim and *running*."
    - Parallel: "He likes to swim and to run."
    - Parallel: "He likes swimming and running."

Once again, the examples above combine gerunds (a noun formed by adding *-ing* to a verb) and infinitives (the form a verb takes when preceded by *to*). To make them parallel, the sentences should be rewritten with just gerunds or just infinitives. Note that the first nonparallel example, while inelegantly worded, is grammatically correct: "cooking," "jogging," and "to read" are all grammatically valid conclusions to "She likes."

- Lacking parallelism: "The dog ran across the yard, jumped over the fence, and **down the alley sprinted**."

- Grammatical but not employing parallelism: "The dog ran across the yard and jumped over the fence, and **down the alley he sprinted**."

- Parallel: "The dog ran across the yard, jumped over the fence, and **sprinted down the alley**."

The nonparallel example above is *not* grammatically correct: "down the alley sprinted" is not a grammatically valid conclusion to "The dog." The second example, which does not attempt to employ parallelism in its conclusion, is grammatically valid; "down the alley he sprinted" is an entirely separate clause.

Parallelism can also apply to names. If you're writing a research paper that includes references to several different authors, you should be consistent in your references. For example, if you talk about Jane Goodall and Henry Harlow, you should say "Goodall and Harlow," not "Jane and Harlow" or "Goodall and Henry." This is something that would carry on through your entire paper: you should use the same mode of address for every person you mention.

You can also apply parallelism across a passage:

> Manuel painted eight paintings in the last week. Jennifer sculpted five statues in the last month. Zama wrote fifteen songs in the last two months.

Each of the sentences in the preceding paragraph has the same structure: Name + *-ed* verb + number of things + *in the* past time period. When using parallelism across multiple sentences, be sure that you're using it well. If you aren't careful, you can stray into being repetitive. Unfortunately, really the only way to test this is by re-reading the passage and seeing if it "feels right." While this test doesn't have any rules to it, it can often help.

Here's a more sophisticated example that's useful, too, because it makes a move that often occurs in academic writing: elaborating on an initial claim. This example is adapted from Keith Wrightson's *English Society 1580-1680* (p. 134):

> Those best placed to prosper were the yeomanry, whether they were freeholders owning their own land or substantial tenants. If freeholders, they were immune from the rent increases of the period. If large tenants, they were commonly profiting from their farming enough to afford rent increases with comparative ease.

Practice

Do of the following sentences correctly employ parallelism? If not, revise the sentences.

1. Kya is really good at writing poems and making pottery. Atswei is a good singer and a good dancer.

2. Don't forget to let the dog out or to feed the cats.

3. In this paper, we will reference the works of Walton and Sir John Cockcroft.

4. Whenever he drives, Reza pays attention to what he's doing and is watching the drivers around him.

Parallelism and Repetition

Parallelism can also involve repeated words or repeated phrases. Inexperienced writers often think that repetition should be avoided at all costs, probably because someone once warned them, usefully enough, about redundancy. However, in sophisticated writing, repetition is a way to highlight what is important. You should repeat keywords frequently enough throughout an essay that your reader is in no danger of losing your thread; parallelism offers a further opportunity to create cohesion and to emphasize crucial points. Here are a few rhetorically powerful examples of repetition in parallel positions:

- "**The inherent vice** of capitalism is the unequal sharing of blessings; **the inherent virtue** of socialism is the equal sharing of miseries." —Winston Churchill

- "Let every nation know, whether it wishes us well or ill, that we shall **pay any price, bear any burden, meet any hardship, support any friend, oppose any foe** to assure the survival and the success of liberty." —John F. Kennedy

- "And that government **of the people, by the people, for the people**, shall not perish from the earth." —Abraham Lincoln, *Gettysburg Address*

These repeated phrases seem to bind the work together and make it more powerful—and more inspiring. This use of parallelism can be especially useful in writing conclusions of academic papers.

Attributions

Practice Activities: Parallel Structure

Parallelism

Read the following passage. Correct any errors in parallelism that you find. Remember, non-parallel items can be grammatically correct, but making them parallel will improve your writing style. Write your correct answer:

"The Bone Wars" refers to a period of intense fossil speculation and discovery in American history (1872–1892). The wars were marked by a heated rivalry between Edward Drinker Cope and Othniel Charles Marsh. At one time, Edward and Marsh were amicable: they even named species after each other. Over time, however, their relationship soured, likely due in part to their strong personalities. Cope was known to be pugnacious and possessed a quick temper. Marsh was slower, more methodical, and introverted. Eventually, each of the two paleontologists would resort to underhanded methods to try to out-compete the other in the field, resorting to bribery, theft, and destroying bones.

By the end of the Bone Wars, both Cope and Marsh were financially and socially ruined by their attempts to disgrace each other, but their contributions to science and the field of paleontology were massive. Several of Cope's and Marsh's discoveries are the most well-known of dinosaurs: Triceratops, Allosaurus, Diplodocus, and Stegosaurus. Their cumulative discoveries defined the then-emerging field of paleontology. Before Cope's and Marsh's discoveries, there were only nine named species of dinosaur in North America. Judging by pure numbers, Marsh "won" the Bone Wars: Cope discovered a total of 56 new dinosaur species, but Marsh had found 80.

Academic Sentences

Look at the following items. Identify and address any issues with parallelism.

1. Low self-esteem can manifest itself in various behaviors. Some individuals may become paralyzed at the prospect of making a decision. Other individuals may bend their wills to others' in order to keep the peace. Yet another symptom is the retreat from society as a whole—to become isolated.

2. The influence of genetics on human behavior has been shown through studies of twins who were separated at birth. Not only do these sets of individuals share many physical characteristics, but they also tend to have the same sort of interests and biases and utilize similar mental processes.

3. *Nocturne in Black and Gold (The Falling Rocket)* by James Abbott McNeil Whistler is very emblematic of the impressionist movement: its dark colors, contrast, and lack of definite form reflect the attitudes of the day.

Attributions

CC licensed content, Original

- Practice Activities: Parallel Structure. **Provided by**: Lumen Learning. **License**: *CC BY: Attribution*
- Revision and Adaptation. **Authored by**: Gillian Paku. **Provided by**: SUNY Geneseo. **License**: *CC BY: Attribution*

CC licensed content, Shared previously

- Modification of Bone Wars (errors added). **Provided by**: Wikipedia. **Located at**: https://en.wikipedia.org/wiki/Bone_Wars. **License**: *CC BY-SA: Attribution-ShareAlike*

Active and Passive Voice

Passive can be an ambiguous term in writing because it can refer to a grammatical construction, but it can also refer to the way a sentence "feels," usually meaning something like "flat" or "abstract" or "devoid of clear narrative action." **Voice** is similarly ambiguous: it can also refer to the general "feel" or "style" of the writing (as in the advice to find your own voice), or it can be used in a more technical sense when applied to a verb to indicate whether the subject of a sentence acts or is acted upon. In this section, we will focus on the technical sense as we discuss active and passive voice.

You've probably heard of the passive voice—perhaps in a comment from a teacher or in the grammar checker of a word processor. In both of these instances, you were probably guided away from the passive voice. Why is this the case? Why is the passive voice so disliked? After all, it's been used three times on this page already (four times now). The first possible answer is that using the passive too frequently can obfuscate the central narrative of your writing. A related answer is that teachers issue a blanket warning against it because students need a relatively sophisticated grasp of the exceptions to the rule in order to use the passive effectively. What might be too much information for a schoolchild, however, constitutes useful information for a college-level writer. There are certainly instances where the passive voice is a better choice than the active.

One way to think about the difference between these two grammatical voices is that an active voice sentence is written in the form of "A does B," for example, "Carmen sings the song." A passive voice sentence is written in the form of "B is done by A," for example, "The song is sung by Carmen." Both constructions are grammatically correct; the difference is one of voice. You might notice that this definition works for transitive verbs (verbs that take a direct object); only transitive verbs can take the passive voice.

Let's look at a couple of more complicated examples of the passive voice:

- I've been hit! (*or,* I have been hit!)

- When Jasper's car was struck from behind, he was thrown from it.

In these sentences, the grammatical subject of the sentence is not the person (or thing) performing the action (represented by a verb). "I," the subject of the first example, did not perform the action of hitting. Jasper's car, the grammatical subject in the second, did not perform the action of striking from behind. Unlike the sentence about Carmen's singing, where even the passive version lets us know who is doing what through the phrase "by Carmen," these sentences don't tell us who or what causes the action. **Put another way, the passive voice can "hide" who performs an action.** Despite these sentences being completely grammatically sound, we don't know who hit "me" or what struck the car. This issue is why the passive voice can obfuscate the clear narrative of a piece of writing – imagine that you are "I' or you are "Jasper" – you probably very much want to know who or what hit you, and who or what struck your car! Not being provided with that information leaves you with an unclear (and probably deeply unsatisfying) narrative. It also puts pressure on context to make things clear for the reader – we can't tell whether the first example here means "Gunfire hit me!" or "Jimmy hit me!" but those are very different rhetorical situations.

Key Takeaway

In academic writing, you often demand a lot from your reader simply because a reader has to follow a sophisticated train of thought and its evidence across several pages; writing habits that make your central narrative harder to perceive can exhaust that reader, so we generally prefer the active to the passive voice. We'll discuss the exceptions to that preference shortly.

Grammatically, the passive is created using a double structure. Both parts must be present in order for a sentence to be in the passive voice. The passive takes a form of the verb *to be* (e.g., the song **is** sung; it **was** struck from behind) as an *auxiliary verb*, paired with the *past participle form of the main verb* (e.g., the song is **sung**; it was **struck** from behind). Remember that *to be* conjugates irregularly. Its forms include *am, are, is, was, were, will be, is being, will have been*, and *have been*.

Although the past participle is a past tense form of a verb, notice that in a passive construction, the verb's tense is not determined by that past participle, but rather by the tense of the auxiliary, *to be:* "I covered the story" is in the past tense in this active sentence because the past form of "to cover" is "covered;" however, "I am covered by health insurance" is in the present tense, despite also containing the past participle, because the tense is determined by the auxiliary verb in this passive construction; i.e., "am." Compare that tense to "I was covered," "I will be covered," or "I have been covered:" all different tenses, but all passive. **Don't confuse the passive voice with the past tense.**

Furthermore, be aware that English sometimes uses the same form for the past participle and for adjectives. Consider the sentence, "I was scared." Is this a passive construction ("I was scared by the explosion") or an adjective ("I was scared; I was anxious")? Thinking about how you want the word to function grammatically will help you present it to your reader in its most appropriate form, and will also prevent you from launching an ill-fated witch-hunt after anything (like adjectives and the past form of verbs) that so much as looks like a past participle.

Remember, *to be* also has more complex forms like *had been, is being*, and *was being*.

- Mirella **is being** pulled away from everything she loves.
- Pietro **had been** pushed; I knew it.
- Unfortunately, my car **was being** towed away by the time I got to it.

Because *to be* has other uses than just creating the passive voice, we need to be careful when we identify passive sentences. It's easy to mistake a sentence like "She had been failing" or "He is educated" for a passive sentence. However, in "She had been falling," *had been* simply indicates that the action took place in the past. In "He is educated," *is* is a linking verb. If there is no "real" action taking place, *is* is simply acting as a linking verb.

Key Takeaway

Passives are not the simplest grammatical constructions ever, but here are two key features that will help you identify the passive voice:

1. Both the auxiliary and the main verb in its past participle form need to be present. And…

2. The grammatical subject of the passive sentence will not be the entity performing the verb.

Usage

Passive constructions can produce grammatically tangled sentences such as this:

> Groundwater flow is influenced by zones of fracture concentration, as can be recognized by the two model simulations (see Figures 1 and 2), by which one can see . . .

The sentence is becoming a burden for the reader, and probably for the writer too. As often happens, the passive voice here has smothered potential verbs and kicked off a runaway train of prepositions. But the reader's task gets much easier in the revised version below:

> Two model simulations (Figures 1 and 2) illustrate how zones of fracture concentration influence groundwater flow. These simulations show . . .

To revise the above, all we did was look for the two buried things (simulations and zones) in the original version that could actually *do* something, and make them the grammatical subjects of the sentence by placing them in front of active verbs. This is the general principle to follow as you compose in the active voice: place concrete nouns that can perform work in front of active verbs. In other words, tell your reader that most interesting narrative information – who does what.

Practice

Are the following sentences in the active or passive voice?

1. The pill bugs drank more sugared water than any other insect in the dish.

2. The samples were prepared in a clean room before being sent out for further examination.

---

3. Lady Macbeth was arguing with her husband when she suddenly realized she needed to repent.

4. Brahe was a very serious scientist with unique interests.

5. When Monet returned to Giverny, his gardens had been replanted.

Attributions

CC licensed content, Original

- Revision and Adaptation. **Provided by**: Lumen Learning. **License**: *CC BY-NC-SA: Attribution-NonCommercial-ShareAlike*

- Revision and Adaptation. **Authored by**: Gillian Paku. **Provided by**: SUNY Geneseo. **License**: *CC BY: Attribution*

CC licensed content, Shared previously

- The Passive versus Active Voice Dilemma. **Authored by**: Joe Schall. **Provided by**: The Pennsylvania State University. **Located at**: https://www.e-education.psu.edu/styleforstudents/c1_p11.html. **License**: *CC BY-NC-SA: Attribution-NonCommercial-Share-Alike*

Revising Weak Passive-Voice Sentences

As we've mentioned, the passive voice can be a shifty operator. It can cover up its source—that is, who's doing the acting—as this example shows:

- **Passive:** The personal details **will be collected** according to the criteria stated in the letter.
  - *Collected by whom, though?*
- **Active: The voter fraud commission** will collect personal details according to the criteria stated in the letter.

It's this ability to hide the actor or agent of the sentence that makes the passive voice a powerful tool, but also a tool of the powerful. How do you feel about phrases like, "It has been said. . .," or "The system is rigged," or "People have been mistreated," or "Mistakes were made"? When we obscure the narrative clarity of a sentence, nameless, faceless forces seem to loom; language can victimize or exculpate, and it's not easy to know who to believe if you can't follow the narrative. At any rate, you can see how the passive voice can cause wordiness, indirectness, and comprehension problems, and it's important to know which questions to ask to shed light on the narrative.

Passive	Question	Active
Your figures **have been reanalyzed** in order to determine the coefficient of error. The results **will be announced** when the situation is judged appropriate.	Who analyzes, and who will announce?	**We** have reanalyzed your figures in order to determine the range of error. **We** will announce the results when the time is right.
With the price of housing at such inflated levels, those loans **cannot be paid** off in any shorter period of time.	Who can't pay the loans off?	With the price of housing at such inflated levels, **homeowners** cannot pay off those loans in any shorter period of time.
After the arm of the hand-held stapler **is pushed** down, the blade from the magazine **is raised by** the top-leaf spring, and the magazine and base.	Who pushes it down, and who or what raises it?	After **you** push down on the arm of the hand-held stapler, **the top-leaf spring** raises the blade from the magazine, and the magazine and base move apart.
However, market share **is being lost by** 5.25-inch diskettes as is shown in the graph in Figure 2.	Who or what is losing market share, who or what shows it?	However, **5.25-inch diskettes** are losing market share as the graph in **Figure 2** shows.

Passive	Question	Active
For many years, federal regulations concerning the use of wire-tapping **have been ignored**. Only recently **have** tighter restrictions **been imposed** on the circumstances that warrant it.	Who has ignored the regulations, and who is now imposing them?	For many years, **government officials** have ignored federal regulations concerning the use of wire-tapping. Only recently has **the federal government** imposed tighter restrictions on the circumstances that warrant it.

Practice

Convert these passive voice sentences into the active voice. Under what circumstances is the active voice a better choice for each of these sentences?

1. The process, which was essential for the experiment's success, was completed by Enzo.

2. The PowerPoint that I worked on all day long is being presented by Justin.

3. After the pattern has been applied to the fabric, work on the 3D printing can be started.

We've discussed in some detail why the passive can be problematic and why active sentences tend to aid clarity. Don't get the idea, though, that the passive voice is always wrong and should never be used. It is a good writing technique when we don't want to be bothered with an obvious or too-often-repeated subject and when we need to rearrange words in a sentence for emphasis. The next page will focus more on how and why to use the passive voice, but take another quick look now at that practice set you just completed. Can you imagine a circumstance where it doesn't matter that it was Enzo specifically who completed the process? Where you were more concerned about your own work on the PowerPoint than on who ended up presenting it? Where applying the pattern and then printing it were done by a machine whose function was so self-evident that it would feel redundant to say that, for example, "The 3D printer will print the pattern in 3D"? It's time to harness the power of a properly employed passive voice. . .

Attributions

CC licensed content, Original

- Revision and Adaptation. **Provided by**: Lumen Learning. **License**: *CC BY: Attribution*
- Revision and Adaptation. **Authored by**: Gillian Paku. **Provided by**: SUNY Geneseo. **License**: *CC BY: Attribution*

CC licensed content, Shared previously

- Power-Revision Techniques: Sentence-Level Revision. **Authored by**: David McMurrey. **Located at**: https://www.prism-net.com/~hcexres/textbook/hirev2.html#passive. **License**: *CC BY: Attribution*

Using the Passive Voice

There are several different situations where the passive voice is more useful than the active voice. The passive is not "wrong"–you just have to be mindful of when you do or do not use it. Here are some common scenarios where the passive has a use:

- When you don't know who did the action: *The paper had been moved.*

    - The active voice would be something like this: "Someone had moved the paper." If you don't know who the someone was and you want to avoid sounding like you're blaming someone, the passive allows you to communicate the information about the paper without assigning responsibility or blame to anyone. You may or may not want the vague element of mystery this formulation entails ("*Should* I care who moved the paper? Why don't we know who moved the paper??"). A mood of mystery can be especially helpful in writing fiction, but this passive construction can also signal a more straightforward lack of knowledge.

- When you know who performed the action, but you don't consider that information important: *The Petri dish had been sterilized and the new bacteria had been added.*

    - Presumably anybody would have gone through the standard procedure for sterilizing the dish in the same way, and would also have followed the protocols for adding the bacteria. These cases where the methodology is prescribed and the expectation is that experimenters or researchers or students are following rules that are not individualized (and that others in different times and places could replicate those actions to test the results) often occur in the natural and social sciences and are why those disciplines often (but not exclusively) employ the passive voice in formal writing.

- When you want to deliberately hide who did the action: *The paper had been ripped.*

    - Three guesses as to who ripped the paper when the speaker uses this passive formulation! Using the passive puts the focus on the paper's fate rather than on the person who ripped it, as the culprit is completely left out of the sentence.

- When you want to emphasize the person or thing the action was done to: *Clarissa was hurt by her family's insistence on a lucrative marriage to the odious Mr. Solmes.*

    - Because of the power of our narrative expectations, which lead us to anticipate that the grammatical subject of a sentence will also be the agent of the action (i.e., that we will be told a.s.a.p. in a sentence the answer to "who does what?"), we automatically focus on the subject of the sentence. Using passive to push someone who isn't the agent into the subject position is particularly effective if your larger unit of writing (your whole paragraph, or your whole essay) focuses on that person. Here, for example, Clarissa is the heroine of an eponymous eighteenth-century novel; we can almost guarantee that an essay containing this sentence would be more about Clarissa than about the odious but minor character of Mr. Solmes, or even about Clarissa's family's mercenary motivations. If most sentences in this essay are active and have Clarissa as both the grammatical subject and the narrative agent, this passive construction will fit more coherently into that whole.

- A subject that can't actually *do* anything: *Caroline was hurt when she fell into the trees.*
  - While the trees hurt Caroline, they didn't actually do anything. Thus, it makes more sense to have Caroline as the subject rather than saying, "The trees hurt Caroline when she fell into them." You could say, "Falling into the trees hurt Caroline" (because it's the action of falling into trees that hurts, not trees in and of themselves), but again, you can guarantee that Caroline was the primary agent (the person performing the action that caused this hurt), and we find narratives clearer when the "who" element of "who does what?" occupies the grammatical subject position in the sentence. Notice that this formulation—*Caroline was hurt*—essentially renders the past participle an adjective rather than a passive construction. Other examples would include *exhausted, astonished,* or *inebriated* – there are many past participles that function like adjectives and would seem strained if you re-worded them into active constructions. How often have you ever heard anyone say, "Alcohol inebriated us" versus "We were inebriated"?

Note: It's often against convention in scholarly writing to use the first-person singular pronoun *I*. One reason for that disapproval stems from the fact that scholars want to emphasize the science or research as opposed to the author of the paper. This emphasis often results in the passive voice being the best choice. This preference for the passive is not the case in other formal settings, such as essays in the humanities, or in résumés and cover letters. Some instructors feel strongly one way or the other—how your instructor feels about, or how your discipline conventionally handles, the relationship between first-person pronouns and the passive voice is a valid question for you to pose.

Practice

Consider the following instances. In each case, determine why the writers might want to use active or passive voice. Write an example sentence based on their circumstances.

1. Antonella made an error in her calculations that ruined an experiment. This error ended up costing both time and materials. She has to write a report to her boss. What might she say about the experiment?

2. Isabel is writing a supernatural thriller. Her main character, Liam, notices that his keys aren't where he left them. How might Isabel word this realization?

3. Tiago is writing a cover letter to apply for a new job. He is listing out tasks that he does at his current job. How would he want to word these items?

Using the Passive

Now that we know there are some instances where passive voice is the best choice, how do we use the passive voice to its fullest? The answer lies in writing direct sentences—in passive voice—that have simple subjects and verbs. This way, even if we are deviating from the usual narrative clarity of an agent in the grammatical subject position performing the action represented by the verb, we are still helping our readers to see quickly what our sentences are about. Compare the two sentences below:

- Photomicrographs were taken to facilitate easy comparison of the samples.

- Easy comparison of the samples was facilitated by the taking of photomicrographs.

Both sentences are written in the passive voice, but for most ears the first sentence is more direct and understandable, and therefore preferable. Depending on the context, it does a clearer job of telling us what was done and why it was done. Especially if this sentence appears in the "Experimental" section of a report (and thus readers already know that the authors of the report took the photomicrographs), the first sentence neatly represents what the authors actually did—took photomicrographs—and why they did it—to facilitate easy comparison. "Photomicrographs" is clearly a more useful noun to put in the subject position than "easy comparison of the samples," which is longer and lacks any specific vocabulary, or "the taking," which is so awkward that we call it "turgid."

Practice

Read the following sentences. Are they using the passive effectively? If there are any errors, rewrite the sentences accordingly.

1. The machine needs to be reset at 10:23, 11:12, and 11:56 every night.

2. The final steps, which need to be finished before the sun sets over the mountains, are going to be completed by Kajuana.

3. The difficult task of measuring minute fluctuations in weight was made easier by the use of a new digital scale.

The passive voice can also be used following relative pronouns like *that* and *which*.

- I configured the production computer environment **that was provisioned** for me.

- Adrián's lab rat loves the treats **that are given** to him.

- Brihanna has an album **that was signed** by the Beastie Boys.

In each of these sentences, it is grammatically sound to omit (or *elide*) the relative pronoun and *to be*. Elision is used with a lot of different constructions in English; we use it shorten sentences when things are understood. However, we can only use elision in certain situations, so be careful when removing words! If you aren't confident about whether you're eliding or just cutting information, err on the side of caution and leave all the words in place (elisions that cause confusion are a common fault when students need to revise essays to a slightly shorter length and try to shave individual words rather than cut a whole section). You may find these elided sentences more natural:

- I configured the production computer environment **provisioned** for me.

- Adrián's lab rat loves the treats **given** to him.

- Brihanna has an album **signed** by the Beastie Boys

Attributions

Practice Activities: Active and Passive Voice

Passive to Active

Convert these passive voice sentences into the active voice:

1. Alana's experiments were crushed by the Geology lab door.
2. The passive voice has likely been heard of by you.
3. Rebecca's favorite spot in the lecture hall had been taken by the time she got to class.
4. When the passive voice is overused, you often end up with writing that feels flat and abstracted.

Active or Passive

Read the following sentences. Are they using the passive effectively? Or should they be rewritten as active sentences?

1. Maren was hit by several branches as she slid down the hill.
2. A lot of discussion about whether technology is hurting or helping our ability to communicate has been inspired by this increase in Twitter subscriptions.
3. Listeners are encouraged by the lyrics to cast aside their fear and be themselves.

Attributions

CC licensed content, Original

- Revision and Adaptation. **Authored by**: Gillian Paku. **Provided by**: SUNY Geneseo. **License**: *CC BY: Attribution*

4: Grammar

Why Is Grammar Important?

Sometimes students are self-conscious about their speech and worry that the way they talk is incorrect, but diversity is a value to celebrate. There are many different types of English—all of which are dynamic and complex. However, each variety is appropriate in different situations. When you're talking with your friends, you can use slang and cultural references—if you speak in formal language, you can easily come off as uptight or rude. If you're sending a casual message via social media you don't need to worry too much about capitalization or strict punctuation. Texting five exclamation points standing alone might get your point across perfectly. To take a different perspective, how many times have you heard people of older generations ask what *smh* or *rn* mean? *The variety of English you use marks a particular cultural set.* You effortlessly switch codes as you converse with different people in different contexts every day, and your professors are code-switchers, too – listen to their language in Wegmans or on the sidelines of a sporting event.

You are already a competent user of many codes of English because you have been using them for years (or for approximately a week if you're talking in memes…). You may or may not yet feel as comfortable with the particular subset of English we use for the fairly formal act of writing at college. Most college writing requires you to adhere to the conventions of standard English, a phrase that often appears on the syllabus of an INTD 105 section, and of many other courses that meet Geneseo's departmental writing requirements. This particular type of English exists to facilitate communication within the academic culture to which you now belong, so college students learn its standardized conventions. Of course, standard English is not somehow a default code that is "beyond" culture: it is the marker of the culture of

well educated people, and the historical choice to dub this variety "standard" is a product of privilege and power. Many college instructors are keenly aware of this political aspect of standard English. Regrettable

– or outrageous – as it may be politically, when you speak or write unconventionally in an academic setting, others might make judgements about who you are as a person: "lazy," "careless," and "incompetent" are some common judgements; on the other hand, if you have some mastery of the conventions, you might be judged to be "diligent," "careful," and "scholarly." We need to acknowledge the dynamics of standard English while recognizing also that it facilitates the clear and accurate communication of complex, well founded ideas to other people within the context of higher education, and within many professions. When you learn how to use the language, you can craft your message to communicate more accurately what you want to convey in a way that large numbers of your peers will comprehend, which is also a powerful political privilege and responsibility.

This shared ability to communicate is where grammar comes in. Grammar is a set of conventions (and sometimes rules) that dictate how standard English works. You might be accustomed to groaning at the mere mention of grammar, and thinking that those who care about it must be in dire need of a social life, especially if your only explicit encounters with English grammar were rules ("articles must precede nouns") and jargon ("dangling participles," anyone?) at some point in middle school. You'll find at college that many professors view good grammar as a method of allowing you to join scholarly conversations and to have a voice that can be heard clearly. Professors are not generally trying to control or crush you with grammar, but rather to demonstrate – and give to you – the tools to be your own best advocate and an active participant in the educational environment. Professors want to know what you're thinking; grammar helps you to tell them.

Whether in a tweet or a term paper, representing our thoughts and opinions in writing is not always easy. Although we're pretty competent most of the time in our native language, and readers usually work with us to make sense of what they are pretty sure we must have meant, you're in a lucky minority if you have never written an email or text (let alone an academic essay) that has confused its recipient or frustrated you by being hard to put into words. Not unlike pouring liquids from one graduated cylinder to another, we all encounter some degree of error when translating what we're thinking to symbols on a page. And when we manage to put something in writing, we make further errors assuming how an audience will receive and analyze the intended meaning of those words. What we mean to communicate has a habit of getting lost in translation, if only because our mental lives are too complex (or, sometimes, too murky) for the act of writing to ever be foolproof. There are key ways to push back against these difficulties, however, and chief among them is our willingness to recognize and apply the conventions of grammar to our writing so that how we write does not distract from, but rather emphasizes, what we intend. By coming to terms with grammar as an adaptable system of communication, we foster stronger, more confident voices tailored to the dialogues we value most. Steven Pinker, a noted psycholinguist, comments on the importance of grammar in accurately relaying information to our peers:[1]

> It [grammar] should be thought of... as one of the extraordinary adaptations in the living world: our species' solution to the problem of getting complicated thoughts from one head into another. Thinking of grammar as the original sharing app makes it much more interesting. By understanding how the various features of grammar are designed to make sharing possible, we can put them to use in writing more clearly, correctly, and gracefully.

As a result of our familiarity with grammar, in other words, we grow closer to spanning the gap between our mind and the minds of those around us, but it is a process that advances one convention at a time.

1. Steven Pinker, *The Sense of Style* p. 79

As you go through this module, bear in mind that these are the principles and conventions for just one type of English, but you should also remember that they are tools your professors want you to wield well as you construct your scholarly self. This will not be an exhaustive survey of grammar, nor will it begin with the most basic concepts. It focuses on the problems that occur most frequently in Geneseo undergraduate writing as students look to join scholarly conversations. Some students will already be familiar with some of these ideas, and we hope that our introduction enables them to recognize that familiarity as their good fortune. Part of the democratic impulse that informs grammar is offering all students the chance to encounter and practice these conventions in an environment that will expect you to employ them: exercises in INTD 106 and more complex written assignments in INTD 105 give you the grounding to write in your other courses. Once you know what you're looking for, there's no substitute for practice, and we invite you furthermore to mentally frame this practice in INTD 106 and INTD 105 not as an isolated exercise to "get through" but as part of a larger picture of yourself as a college student with a valuable voice.

Attributions

CC licensed content, Original

- Why Is Grammar Important?. **Provided by**: Lumen Learning. **License**: *CC BY: Attribution*
- Revision and Adaptation. **Authored by**: Gillian Paku. **Provided by**: SUNY Geneseo. **License**: *CC BY: Attribution*

CC licensed content, Shared previously

- Conversation Balloons. **Authored by**: bartek001. **Located at**: https://pixabay.com/en/conversation-balloons-anger-545621/. **License**: *CC0: No Rights Reserved*
- Toolkit. **Authored by**: Brian Ejar. **Located at**: https://thenounproject.com/term/toolkit/154266/. **License**: *CC BY: Attribution*

Antecedent Clarity

In order to think about "antecedent clarity," you'll need to be comfortable with the relationship of pronouns to nouns. Here's a quick reminder of those concepts:

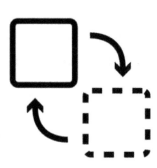

> Anna decided at the beginning of Anna's first semester at Geneseo that Anna would run for thirty minutes every day. Anna knew that Anna would be taking a literature course with a lot of reading, so along with buying print copies of all the novels Anna's professor assigned, Anna also bought the audiobooks. That way Anna could listen to the audiobooks as Anna ran.

The solution to the awkwardness of this paragraph is to employ pronouns:

> Anna decided at the beginning of **her** first semester at Geneseo that **she** would run for thirty minutes every day. **She** knew that **she** would be taking a literature course with a lot of reading, so along with buying hard copies of all the novels **her** professor assigned, Anna also bought the audiobooks. That way **she** could listen to **them** as **she** ran.

This second paragraph is more natural. Instead of repeating nouns multiple times (in this case, one example of the subset of nouns known as "proper nouns," which name a person or place: "Anna"), we were able to use pronouns in many (but not all!) places. A pronoun replaces a noun, and because a pronoun is replacing a noun, its meaning is dependent on the noun that it is replacing. This noun is called the **antecedent**. Let's look at the two sentences we just read again:

- Because a pronoun is replacing a noun, *its* meaning is dependent on the noun that *it* is replacing. This noun is called an **antecedent**.

The pronoun *it*, in two forms (*Its* and *it*), has the antecedent "a pronoun." **Whenever you use a pronoun, you must also include an antecedent noun.** Without the antecedent, your readers (or listeners) won't be able to figure out what the pronoun is referring to. Let's look at a couple of examples:

- Jason's classmates look to him for leadership.
- Trini attends her psych lab every Tuesday morning.
- Sean often has to reorganize his lab reports.

- Kimberly is a Presidential Scholar. She has presented several papers at different undergraduate Communications conferences.

So, what are the antecedents and pronouns in these sentences?

- **Jason** is the antecedent for the pronoun *him*.
- **Trini** is the antecedent for the pronoun *her*.
- **Sean** is the antecedent for the pronoun *his*.
- **Kimberly** is the antecedent for the pronoun *she*.

PRACTICE

Identify the antecedent in the following examples:

1. The bus is twenty minutes late today, like it always is.
2. I would never be caught dead wearing boot sandals. They are an affront to nature.

We've already defined an **antecedent** as the noun (or phrase) that a pronoun is replacing. The phrase *antecedent clarity* simply means that it should be clear to whom or what the pronoun is referring. In other words, readers should be able to understand the sentence the first time they read it—not the third, fourth, or tenth time, or only after they have had to go backwards to reread the previous sentence. Our opening example about Anna and her audiobooks feel belabored because we can all grasp its concepts and its vocabulary easily: we were ready to move to pronouns after the first sentence. Most college-level writing is more sophisticated than the narrative about Anna, however, so we need some additional nuance about antecedent clarity.

When writers are new to a field, they sometimes do not achieve antecedent clarity because they worry that if they repeat the key terms in full rather than moving quickly to pronouns, they will irritate an expert reader; for example, students imagine their professor as their only reader, and don't want to tell an expert what surely is old news. But the inexperienced writers also do not want to seem unfamiliar with a concept themselves. Put another way, they think that they will signal to their readers a lack of certainty about a term if they keep spelling it out in full. Imagine that you had never before encountered the term *chiaroscuro*, but now you have to write about it. Knowing that your instructor is familiar with the term, and not wanting to seem uncertain about it, you write something like,

> *Chiaroscuro* is a term that describes the contrast of dark and light paint to create three-dimensionality. We are familiar with its dramatic effects, as when Rembrandt employs it, but it is not always clear whether it is useful because it can seem too much like a spotlight. Sometimes that creates a dramatic effect but sometimes it is a distraction because it might shift the viewer's focus to the interplay of dark and light rather than keeping it on the subject of the painting.

Because the writers relies too much on abstract and unclear pronouns, writing like this feels anxious, which is probably the opposite of the writer's intended effect. And, almost inevitably, what "it" refers to in here is not just *chiaroscuro*: think about the "it" in "it is not always clear" (for a moment, the "clear" vocabulary does suggest that the writer is still referring to *chiaroscuro*, and then we realize that's not the case) or when "it" starts to refer to "the viewer's focus." Not providing antecedent clarity pushes more responsibility for making sense of the passage onto the reader, but the writer really should take – and want – the bulk of the responsibility.

An inverse issue with antecedent clarity is what cognitive scientist Steven Pinker calls "the curse of knowledge." Here is the curse of knowledge in action, described in attention-grabbing terms as a form of stupidity:

> The kind of stupidity I have in mind has nothing to do with ignorance or low IQ; in fact, it's often the brightest and best informed who suffer the most from it. I once attended a lecture on biology addressed to a large general audience at a conference on technology, entertainment, and design. The lecture was also being filmed for distribution over the Internet to millions of other laypeople. The speaker was an eminent biologist who had been invited to explain his recent breakthrough in the structure of DNA. He launched into a jargon-packed technical presentation that was geared to his fellow molecular biologists, and it was immediately apparent to everyone in the room that none of them understood a word. Apparent to everyone, that is, except the eminent biologist. When the host interrupted and asked him to explain the work more clearly, he seemed genuinely surprised and not a little annoyed. This is the kind of stupidity I'm talking about. / Call it the Curse of Knowledge: a difficulty in imagining what it is like for someone else not to know something that you know. [1]

Writers almost inevitably suffer from the curse of knowledge: if you have thought hard enough about something to have generated several pages of analytical writing on it, or to have researched the larger scholarly conversation on it, you know quite a lot about it. If you have thought about that topic in sophisticated ways and have focused precisely on an issue, you may well know more about your particular topic than your instructor, let alone your peers. In this very common situation, writers misjudge how clearly they are writing because they cannot escape their own knowledge on the topic (hence the "curse" of being trapped). They *write about* how they understand their argument, rather than *writing to* a readership who wants to learn. You might have already perceived that as well as being a problem of clarity that can be addressed through some grammatical concepts like antecedent clarity (assuming erroneously that everyone knows what you're talking about as you build your intricate tower of an argument), the curse of knowledge explains why even the most diligent proofreading of your own essay will not catch a huge problem like the curse of knowledge. You need a reader who exists outside your own brain if you really want to make that move from writing about something to writing to your readers, but it's that "writing to" that helps you join the generous and energizing give-and-take of a scholarly conversation rather than simply displaying what you know.

Key Takeaway

Bearing in mind how clear antecedents relate to Pinker's Curse of Knowledge can help you shift from *writing about* something to *writing to* your audience. Knowing yourself what you mean isn't the point of writing academically; help *others* to know what you're talking about.

1. Steven Pinker, *The Sense of Style* p. 59

Here are some examples of common mistakes that can cause confusion, as well as ways to fix each sentence.

Let's take a look at our first sentence:

> Rafael told Matt to stop changing his INTD 105 presentation.

When you first read this sentence, is it clear if the presentation is Rafael's or Matt's? Is it clear when you read the sentence again? Not really, no. Since both Rafael and Matt are singular, third person, and masculine, it's impossible to tell whose presentation is being changed (at least from this sentence).

How would you best revise this sentence? Look at the suggested revisions online at https://courses.lumenlearning.com/suny-geneseo-guidetowriting/chapter/antecedent-clarity/.

Let's take a look at another example:

> Zuly was really excited to try French cuisine on her semester abroad in Europe. They make all sorts of delicious things.

When you read this example, is it apparent who the pronoun *they* is referring to? You may guess that *they* is referring to the French—which is probably correct. However, this is not actually stated, which means that there isn't actually an antecedent. Since every pronoun needs an antecedent, the example needs to be revised to include one.

How would you best revise this sentence? Look at the suggested revisions online at https://courses.lumenlearning.com/suny-geneseo-guidetowriting/chapter/antecedent-clarity/.

Balancing your own confidence in the topic, your awareness of key terms, and the curse of knowledge, how would you manage the nouns and pronouns in the following example?:

Examples

In (Keynes's / his) seminal text, (Keynes / he) asserts that governments ought to intervene when circulation comes to a halt, but that is not to say (Keynes / he) is opposed to the economic structure of capitalism; rather, (Keynes / he) simply values checks and balances in times of crisis.

Here are a couple more situations where college-level writing often lacks antecedent clarity. The first is when the pronoun is demonstrative. Demonstrative pronouns substitute for things being pointed out. They include *this, that, these,* and *those.*

This and *these* refer to something that is "close" to the speaker, whether this closeness is physical, emotional, or temporal. *That* and *those* are the opposite: they refer to something that is "far."

- Do I actually have to read all of *this* by tomorrow?
  - By using "this," the speaker is indicating a text that is close by.

- *That* dissected fish is not coming anywhere near me.
  - The speaker is distancing herself from the object in question, which she doesn't want to come any closer. The far pronoun helps indicate that.

- You're telling me you guessed all of *these* correct answers?
  - The speaker and the audience are likely looking directly at the answers in question, so the close pronoun is appropriate.

- *Those* paintings are all really derivative of Picasso.
  - The speaker gestures towards a wider group by using the far "those."

Key Takeaway
The antecedents of demonstrative pronouns (and sometimes the pronoun *it*) can be more complex than those of personal pronouns.

- **Animal Planet's puppy cam has been taken down for maintenance.** I never wanted *this* to happen.

- I love Animal Planet's panda cam. **I watched a panda eat bamboo for half an hour.** *It* was amazing.

In the first example, the antecedent for *this* is the concept of the puppy cam being taken down. In the second example, the antecedent for *it* in this sentence is the experience of watching the panda. That antecedent isn't explicitly stated in the sentence, but comes through in the intention and meaning of the speaker.

PRACTICE
In the following sentences, determine if *this*, *that*, *these*, or *those* should be used. 1. Tyesha looked at her meal in front of her. "____ looks great!" she said. 2. Lara watched the '67 Mustang drive down the street. "What I wouldn't give for one of ____." 3. "What do you think of ____?" Ashley asked, showing me the three paint samples she had picked out.

But notice that all those examples rely on direct speech and real-life interaction. When I discuss paint samples with you, I know that you can see exactly what I'm talking about, so I don't need to say, "What do you think of *these paint samples*?" **You don't have the convenience of shared time and space when you are communicating via writing**, however, and you're probably discussing ideas more complex than selecting paint samples if you're writing a college-level analytical essay, so you typically do need to pair your demonstrative pronoun with the noun or phrase it refers to, at least frequently if not all of the time. Inexperienced academic writers worry that they will sound redundant if they repeat their nouns rather than using pronouns, or if they pair demonstrative pronouns with the concept being demonstrated. In fact, because you're demanding a lot of mental effort from your reader to follow an argument across 5-10 pages, not 5-10 spoken words, your readers will thank you for reassuring them often in your writing that your key terms haven't changed, you haven't become abstract in your argument, and you aren't expecting the readers themselves to hold all your key terms in their minds while you systematically offer up only pronouns because you know that you're still discussing the same "oxygen transport by hemoglobin in the blood" you always were.

Another place to be careful about antecedent clarity is in the **topic sentences of paragraphs**. One function of topic sentences is to transition from the previous paragraph to a related new idea. You might think that because you just wrote a paragraph on oxygen transport by hemoglobin in the blood and are ready to move now to introducing the relevant protein structures that you can safely refer to oxygen transport by hemoglobin in the blood as "it" or "this concept" in your new topic sentence. But topic sentences have to pull your readers across some serious white space on the page and in their minds: when readers finish a paragraph, they expect to be done with that paragraph's topic, so it's a very good idea to reiterate the key noun or phrase in full when you launch into how it's related to what you want to focus on next.

Key Takeaway

Reading an academic essay is cognitively demanding. Frequently reiterate key terms in full rather than over-relying on pronouns, especially in topic sentences where you need readers to recall your previous point clearly in order to move cohesively to your next point.

To make that concept of reiterating your key terms feel tangible, imagine a professor writing a two-page letter of recommendation for you. The professor is talking about only you in the letter: there are paragraphs on your stellar classroom performance, and your willingness to revise, and your appearances at undergraduate conferences, and your excellent community service projects – but the professor never writes your name again after the first sentence. Never repeating key terms in full (here, the proper noun that is your name) wastes the opportunity to really make a memorable impression on that potential employer of yours. Academic essays work the same way: *restate your key terms!*

Key Takeaways

As you write, then, keep these three things in mind:

- Make sure your pronouns always have an antecedent.

- Make sure that it is clear what their antecedents are.
- Make sure you regularly restate the antecedent in full to keep your key terms vivid.

Attributions

CC licensed content, Original

- Text: Antecedent Clarity. **Provided by**: Lumen Learning. **License**: *CC BY: Attribution*
- Revision and Adaptation of Pronouns and Antecedents (Practice). **Provided by**: Lumen Learning. **License**: *CC BY-NC-SA: Attribution-NonCommercial-ShareAlike*
- Revision and Adaptation. **Authored by**: Gillian Paku. **Provided by**: SUNY Geneseo. **License**: *CC BY: Attribution*

CC licensed content, Shared previously

- Pronouns and Antecedents. **Authored by**: Julie Sevastopoulos. **Provided by**: Grammar-Quizzes. **Located at**: http://www.grammar-quizzes.com/pronoun_placement.html. **License**: *CC BY-NC-SA: Attribution-NonCommercial-ShareAlike*
- Image of two squares. **Authored by**: Didzis Gruznovs. **Provided by**: The Noun Project. **Located at**: https://thenounproject.com/search/?q=replace&i=201238. **License**: *CC BY: Attribution*

Antecedent Agreement

A refinement of the idea of antecedent clarity involves asking whether the pronouns you use to refer back to your nouns and concepts match the person and number of the antecedent. When that matching happens, we say that the pronoun **agrees** with its antecedent. Let's look at a couple of examples:

- I hate it when Zacharias tells me what to do. **He**'s so full of **himself**.

- The Finnegans are shouting again. I swear you could hear **them** from across town!

In the first sentence, *Zacharias* is singular, third person, and masculine. The pronouns *he* and *himself* are also singular, third person, and masculine, so they agree. In the second sentence, *the Finnegans* is plural and third person. The pronoun *them* is also plural and third person.

Person and Number

Some interesting issues with agreements surround indefinite pronouns:

- Every student should do his or her best on this assignment.

- If nobody lost his or her calculator, then where did this come from?

Words like *every* and *nobody* are singular, and match, at the level of formal grammar, with singular pronouns. Here are some more words that fall into this category of indefinite pronouns:

anybody	anyone	anything	each	either	every
everybody	everyone	everything	neither	no one	nobody
nothing	one	somebody	someone	something	

Some of these may feel "more singular" than others, but they all are technically singular. Thus, using "he or she" is correct in terms of antecedent agreement insofar as both those pronouns are singular. **However, for many academics, correctness is only one value to consider.** Another value might be the level of formality they want. Being hyper-correct in your writing will sound very formal and might alienate some readers. The trade-off between being correct and losing readers is a genuine consideration; **many academic writers would rather be read by a wider audience than be credited with correctness.**

As you may have noticed, the phrase "he or she" (and its other forms) can make your sentences clunky, so concerns about stylistic elegance might also outweigh correctness. When such clunkiness threatens, undergraduate writers often write something like this:

- The way each individual speaks can tell us so much about him or her. It tells us what groups they associate themselves with, both ethnically and socially.

As you can see, in the first sentence, *him or her* agrees with the indefinite pronoun *each*. However, in the second sentence, the writer has shifted to the plural *they*, even though the writer is talking about the same group of people. Your writing seems smoother if your agreement is **consistent**, so one better solution might be to make the antecedent of "they" a plural noun, like "people" in this example:

- The way people speak can tell us so much about them. It tells us what groups they associate themselves with, both ethnically and socially.

Forming a plural antecedent appeals more to most of us than the now unpopular method of avoiding the clunky "he or she" by deciding that the default "neutral" pronoun is "he," as in this version:

- The way each individual speaks can tell us so much about him. It tells us what groups he associates himself with, both ethnically and socially.

For many people, the sexism underpinning the choice of the masculine pronoun to represent a gender-neutral "anybody" means that they will never use this solution. Others will alternate between defaulting to "he" or to "she" to refer to indefinite antecedents throughout a piece, or will default always to "she."

Another solution, an increasingly popular one, is to embrace what's known as "singular *they*." We use singular *they* in speech all the time, in formulations like "To each their own" or "Someone is singing in the corridor. If they haven't stopped in two minutes, I'm going to have to take drastic measures." But it has also been used in writing for centuries, including by Chaucer, Shakespeare, Austen, and Dickens, who all knew a thing or two about effective writing. **Singular *they* was the American Dialect Society's Word of the Year for 2015: it provides a stylistically attractive solution to English's lack of a gender-neutral pronoun, and it has been welcomed by people who identify as genderqueer and who feel that "he" and "she" don't necessarily exhaust all the gender possibilities.** If you think about your own speech, it's very likely that you use *they* as a singular pronoun for someone whose gender you don't know, and don't want to assume.

> **Note:** At Geneseo, many faculty and students would rather avoid perpetuating sexist language than be correct about the number and person of an indefinite antecedent. Many professors endorse singular *they*, but not all, so it's a reasonable topic to broach with individual instructors. In many cases, you have choices, and our best advice is to aim for consistency within your own style.

Here's a paragraph that uses "he or she" liberally:

> Every writer will experience writer's block at some point in his or her career. He or she will suddenly be unable to move on in his or her work. A lot of people have written about writer's block, presenting different strategies to "beat the block." However, different methods work for different people. Each writer must find the solutions that work best for him or her.

How would you best revise this paragraph? Look at the suggested revisions online at https://courses.lumenlearning.com/suny-geneseo-guidetowriting/chapter/antecedent-agreement/.

Were those revisions what you expected them to be?

Case

Some of the most common pronoun mistakes occur with the decision between "you and I" and "you and me." People will often say things like "You and me should collaborate on this presentation." Or—thinking back on the rule that it should be "you and I"—they will say "Dr. Brewer assigned the task to both you and I." However, both of these sentences are grammatically incorrect. Remember that every time you use a pronoun you need to make sure that you're using the correct case.

Let's take a look at the first sentence: "You and me should collaborate on this presentation." Both pronouns are the subject of the sentence, so they should be in subject case: "You and I should collaborate on this presentation."

In the second sentence ("Dr. Brewer assigned the task to both you and I"), both pronouns are the object of the sentence, so they should be in object case: "Dr. Brewer assigned the task to both you and me."

Attributions

CC licensed content, Original

- Text: Antecedent Agreement. **Provided by**: Lumen Learning. **License**: *CC BY: Attribution*
- Revision and Adaptation. **Authored by**: Gillian Paku. **Provided by**: SUNY Geneseo. **License**: *CC BY: Attribution*

CC licensed content, Shared previously

- Image of handshake. **Authored by**: Lauren Manninen. **Provided by**: The Noun Project. **Located at**: https://thenounproject.com/search/?q=agree&i=11865. **License**: *CC BY: Attribution*

Subject & Verb Agreement

The basic idea behind subject-verb agreement is pretty simple: all the parts of your sentence should match (or **agree**). Verbs need to agree with their subjects in **number** (singular or plural) and in **person** (first, second, or third). In order to check agreement, you simply need to find the verb and ask who or what is doing the action of that verb. This is another of those grammatical concepts that sound like something you could never get wrong… but we just got it wrong in that sentence. It should read, "this … sounds like," not, "this … sound like." The verb "to sound" modifies "this," not "grammatical concepts." One of our WLC tutors notes,

"To read first-year student writing with subject-verb agreement in mind is often to unearth a glittering treasure-trove of grammatical errors." Incorrect subject-verb agreement is not an error you're likely to make when you're comfortable with the subject matter you're writing about, but as written assignments across the curriculum push you out of your comfort zone (which happens to everyone), this grammatical point is one where the stress seems to show.

Person

Agreement based on grammatical person (first, second, or third person) is found mostly between verb and subject. For example, you can say "I am" or "he is," but not "I is" or "he am." This is because English grammar requires that the verb and its subject agree in person. The pronouns *I* and *he* are first and third person respectively, as are the verb forms *am* and *is*. The verb form must be selected so that it has the same person as the subject.

Number

Agreement based on grammatical number can occur between verb and subject, as in the case of grammatical person discussed above. In fact, the two categories are often conflated within verb conjugation patterns: there are specific verb forms for first person singular, second person plural and so on. Some examples:

- **I** really **am** (1st pers. singular) vs. **We** really **are** (1st pers. plural)

- The **experiment succeeds** (3rd pers. singular) vs. The **experiments succeed** (3rd pers. plural)

More Examples

Compound subjects are joined by a coordinating conjunction (and, or, neither, nor). They are plural because there are more than one of them, and, typically, their verbs should be plural, too. Look at the following sentence for an example:

- A pencil, a protractor, and a calculator **are** necessary for the assignment.

Using the principle that "in order to check agreement, find the verb and ask who or what is doing the action of that verb," you would ask here, "What *is* necessary?" The answer is, "A pencil, a protractor, and a calculator," which are three things, so the concept is plural and requires **are**, not **is**, for agreement. If we only needed a calculator, we would write, "A calculator **is** necessary for the assignment." A subject isn't compound just because it is plural: "Calculators are necessary" is a plural subject that takes a plural verb, but it isn't a compound subject because *calculators* are the only thing you need.

And, just to nuance this discussion a little more, some compound subjects actually take a singular verb because they form a singular concept. You might say, for example, "Spaghetti and meatballs is delicious" because "spaghetti and meatballs" functions as one concept (the meal). You can say, "Spaghetti and meatballs are delicious," but that means that you are considering *spaghetti* and *meatballs* as two different entities, not as a meal. Meatballs and ice cream are delicious, but meatballs and ice cream is not.

Verbs do not agree with nouns that are in prepositional phrases. To make verbs agree with their subjects, follow this example:

- The performance of the three plays **is** the topic of my talk.

The subject of "my talk" is *performance,* not *plays,* so the verb should be singular. Using the principle that "in order to check agreement, find the verb and ask who or what is doing the action of that verb," you would ask here, "What is the topic?" The answer is, "The performance." "The three plays" are nouns in a prepositional phrase because they follow the preposition "of."

In the English language, verbs usually follow subjects. But when this order is reversed, the writer must make the verb agree with the subject, not with a noun that happens to precede it. For example:

- Beside the house **stand** sheds filled with tools.

The subject is *sheds*; it is plural, so the verb must be *stand.* Using the principle that "in order to check agreement, find the verb and ask who or what is doing the action of that verb," you would ask here, "What stands?" The answer is "Sheds stand," not "The house stands."

Here's a grey area: do we use a singular or plural verb when agreeing with a noun that is singular in grammar but plural in meaning? For example, do we say, "The faculty meets" or "The faculty meet"? Other examples include *team, committee, administration, press, class, staff,* and *audience.* Generally, in American standard English (but not in British standard English), these collective nouns agree with singular verbs: "The faculty meets," "The audience applauds," "The legal team investigates," "The administration obfuscates." However, when members of the collective group are acting individually, the noun and its agreeing verb are often treated as plural: "The Geology faculty are going on various field trips with their students this week."

Agreement

All regular verbs (and nearly all irregular ones) in English agree in the third-person singular of the present indicative by adding a suffix of either -s or -es.

Look at the present tense of *to love*, for example:

Person	Number	
	Singular	Plural
First	*I love*	*we love*
Second	*you love*	*you love*
Third	*he/she/it loves*	*they love*

The highly irregular verb *to be* is the only verb with more agreement than this in the present tense:

Person	Number	
	Singular	Plural
First	*I am*	*we are*
Second	*you are*	*you are*
Third	*he/she/it is*	*they are*

Practice

Choose the correct verb to make the sentences agree:

1. Subject-verb agreement is another of those grammatical concepts that (sound / sounds) like something you could never get wrong.

2. Worldwide, nearly one in four people (are / is) Muslim.

3. Corruption and regionalism (have / has) left the public distrustful of the state.

4. Alec and Kate (is / are) the best comedy duo in theater history.

Verb Tense Consistency

One of the most common mistakes in college writing is a lack of consistency in the tense of your verbs. Writers often start a sentence in one tense but ended up in another. Like in that sentence: the first verb *start* is in the present tense, but *ended* is in the past tense. The correct version of the sentence would be "Writers often start a sentence in one tense but end up in another."

These mistakes often occur when writers change their minds halfway through writing the sentence, or when they come back and make changes but only end up changing half the sentence. Maintaining a consistent tense is one of the conventions of standard English, not just within a sentence but across paragraphs and pages. Decide if something happened, is happening, or will happen and then stick with that choice unless a specific sentence logically demands a change.

Read through the following paragraphs to spot the errors in tense.

If you want to pick up a new outdoor activity, hiking is a great option to consider. It's a sport that is suited for a beginner or an expert—it just depended on the difficulty of the hikes you chose. However, even the earliest beginners can complete difficult hikes if they pace themselves and were physically fit.

Not only is hiking an easy activity to pick up, it also will have some great payoffs. As you walked through canyons and climbed up mountains, you can see things that you wouldn't otherwise. The views are breathtaking, and you will get a great opportunity to meditate on the world and your role in it. The summit of a mountain is unlike any other place in the world.

What errors did you spot? Let's take another look at this passage. This time, the tense-shifted verbs have been bolded, and the phrases they belong to have been underlined:

If you want to pick up a new outdoor activity, hiking is a great option to consider. <u>It's a sport that is suited for a beginner or an expert—it just **depended** on the difficulty of the hikes you **chose.**</u> However, even the earliest beginners can complete difficult hikes <u>if they pace themselves and **were** physically fit.</u>

<u>Not only is hiking an easy activity to pick up, it also **will have** some great payoffs.</u> <u>As you **walked** through canyons and **climbed** up mountains,</u> you can see things that you wouldn't otherwise. <u>The views are breathtaking, and you **will get** a great opportunity to meditate on the world and your role in it</u>. The summit of a mountain is unlike any other place in the world.

As we mentioned earlier, you want to make sure your whole passage is consistent in its tense. You may have noticed that the most of the verbs in this passage are in present tense—this is especially apparent if you ignore those verbs that have been bolded. In many academic disciplines, writing in the present tense is the convention. You may well be writing about something that happened in the past: Daniel Defoe wrote *Robinson Crusoe* 300 years ago; Emile Durkheim developed his concept of the division of labor in the late nineteenth century. You, however, are thinking about the significance of Defoe's novel or Durkheim's theory now, so the ideas, and the texts, and your brain are all operating in the present moment. That's why we write, "Defoe elevates socially marginalized protagonists," not "Defoe elevated." Or, "Durkheim focuses on the shift in societies from simple to complex," not "Durkheim focused." But writing in the present tense is a convention, which means it can vary from one discipline to another, so check with your instructors.

Now that we've established that the passage about hiking should be in the present tense, let's address each of the underlined segments:

- It's a sport that is suited for a beginner or an expert—it just **depended** on the difficulty of the hikes you choose.

  ◦ *depended* should be the same tense as *is*; it just **depends** on the difficulty

- if they pace themselves and **were** physically fit.

  ◦ *were* should be the same tense as *pace*; if they pace themselves and **are** physically fit.

- Not only is hiking an easy activity to pick up, it also **will have** some great payoffs.

  ◦ *will have* should be the same tense as *is*; it also **has** some great pay offs

- As you **walked** through canyons and **climbed** up mountains

  ◦ *walked* and *climbed* are both past tense, but this doesn't match the tense of the passage as a whole. They should both be changed to present tense: As you **walk** through canyons and **climb** up mountains.

- The views are breathtaking, and you **will get** a great opportunity to meditate on the world and your role in it.

  ◦ *will get* should be the same tense as *are*; you **get** a great opportunity

Here's the corrected passage as a whole; all edited verbs have been bolded:

If you want to pick up a new outdoor activity, hiking is a great option to consider. It's a sport that can be suited for a beginner or an expert—it just **depends** on the difficulty of the hikes you choose. However, even the earliest beginners can complete difficult hikes if they pace themselves and **are** physically fit.

Not only is hiking an easy activity to pick up, it also **has** some great payoffs. As you **walk** through canyons and **climb** up mountains, you can see things that you wouldn't otherwise. The views are breathtaking, and you **get** a great opportunity to meditate on the world and your role in it. The summit of a mountain is unlike any other place in the world.

Practice

Read the following sentences and identify any errors in verb tense. Write your corrections below:

1. Whenever Maudeline studies for a Biology test, she had made a review list and stick to it.

2. This experiment turned out to be much more complicated than Felipe thought it would be. It ended up being a procedure that was seventeen steps long, instead of the original eight that he had planned.

3. I applied to some of the most prestigious medical schools. I hope the essays I write get me in!

Attributions

CC licensed content, Original

- Text: Verb Tense Consistency. **Provided by**: Lumen Learning. **License**: *CC BY: Attribution*
- Revision and Adaptation. **Authored by**: Gillian Paku. **Provided by**: SUNY Geneseo. **License**: *CC BY: Attribution*

Public domain content

- Hiker At The Mountain Top. **Authored by**: Jean Beaufort. **Provided by**: Public Domain Pictures. **Located at**: http://www.public-domainpictures.net/view-image.php?image=171368&picture=hiker-at-the-mountain-top. **License**: *Public Domain: No Known Copyright*

Differences between Adjectives and Adverbs

Adjectives and adverbs describe things. For example, compare the phrase "the bear" to "the harmless bear" or the phrase "they run" to "they run slowly."

In both of these cases, the adjective (*harmless*) or the adverb (*slowly*) changes how we understand the phrase. When you first read the word *bear*, you probably didn't imagine a harmless bear. When you saw the word *run* you probably didn't think of it as something done slowly.

Adjectives and adverbs modify other words: they direct our understanding of things towards more specificity.

Adjectives and adverbs act in similar but different roles. Adjectives describe nouns and pronouns ("a reactive nanoparticle;" "she is proficient"); adverbs describe all the other parts of speech. Most intuitively, ad*verbs* modify *verbs* ("our solution glowed brightly"), but adverbs can also modify adjectives ("a scarily reactive nanoparticle;" "she is thoroughly proficient").

A lot of the time this difference between adverbs and adjectives can be seen in the structure of the words:

- A **clever** new idea.
- A **cleverly** developed idea.

Clever is an adjective, and *cleverly* is an adverb. This adjective + *ly* construction is a short-cut to identifying adverbs.

While *–ly* is helpful, it's not a universal rule. Not all words that end in *–ly* are adverbs: *lovely, costly, friendly*, etc. (these are adjectives, e.g. a *costly* mistake). Additionally, not all adverbs end in *-ly*: *here, there, together, yesterday, aboard, very, almost*, etc.

Some words can function both as an adjective and as an adverb:

- *Fast* is an adjective in "a **fast** car" (where it qualifies the noun *car*), but an adverb in "he drove fast" (where it modifies the verb *drove*).

- *Likely* is an adjective in "a likely outcome" (where it modifies the noun *outcome*), but an adverb in "we will likely go" (where it modifies the verb *go*).

Attributions

Common Mistakes with Adjectives and Adverbs

Adjectives

If you're a native English speaker, you may have noticed that "the big red house" sounds more natural than "the red big house." The video below explains the order in which adjectives occur in English, using the acronym *DOSA-SCOMP*. DOSA-SCOMP stands for **D**eterminer **O**pinion **S**ize **A**ge **S**hape **C**olor **O**rigin **M**aterial and **P**urpose, and the video defines those concepts:

- https://youtu.be/7sHbB9VQBgo

Practice

Select the adjectives that are in a natural sounding word order for each sentence.

1. A(n) _____ sports car emerged from the 3D printer in Milne Library.

    - beautiful, new, Italian
    - Italian, new, beautiful
    - Italian, beautiful, new

2. The town's _____ barber pole dates from medieval times.

    - red and white, striped, big
    - big, red and white, striped
    - striped, red and white, big

3. We put an _____ tree on stage to represent the protagonist's stunted emotional state.

    - ugly, tiny, artificial
    - artificial, ugly, tiny

- ugly, artificial, tiny

4. The architect rendered his futuristic style ironic by living in a _____ house in the Roemer Arboretum.

- little, charming, mushroom
- mushroom, little, charming
- charming, little, mushroom

Adverbs

Only

The word *only* can mean different things in a sentence, depending on where it's placed. Let's look at a simple sentence:

She loves Economics.

Moving *only* can influence the meaning of this sentence:

- *Only* she loves Economics.
  - No one loves Economics but her.
- She *only* loves Economics.
  - The one thing she does is love Economics.
- She loves *only* Economics.
  - She loves Economics and nothing else.

Only modifies the word that directly follows it. Whenever you use the word *only* make sure you've placed it correctly in your sentence.

Literally

A linguistic phenomenon is sweeping the nation: people are using *literally* as an intensifier. Here are a couple of examples: "It was literally the worst thing that has ever happened to me," or "His head literally exploded when I told him I was going to be late again." Some people love this phrase while it makes other people want to pull their hair out.

According to *Merriam-Webster's Dictionary*, the actual definition of *literal* is as follows:

- involving the ordinary or usual meaning of a word
- giving the meaning of each individual word
- completely true and accurate : not exaggerated[1]

According to this definition, *literally* should be used only when something actually happened (so if his head actually did explode, or it truthfully was the worst thing that ever happened to you). Our cultural usage may be slowly shifting to allow *literally* as an intensifier, but it's best to avoid using *literally* in any way other than its dictionary definition in standard English writing.

Practice

Which of the following sentences use their adverbs according to the conventions of standard English?

1. Daveed often takes things too literally.
2. Tommy literally died when he saw how he did on the midterm.
3. In their vows, they promised to love only each other.
4. Ava is literally the best student at Geneseo.

Mistaking Adverbs and Adjectives

One common mistake with adjectives and adverbs is using one in the place of the other. For example:

- I wish I could dissect the daffodil as neat as Zach can.
    - The word should be *neatly*, an adverb, since it's modifying a verb, *to dissect*.
- That's real nice of Ariana to create the powerpoint.
    - Should be *really*, an adverb, since it's modifying an adjective, *nice*.

Remember, if you're modifying a noun or pronoun, you should use an adjective. If you're modifying anything else, you should use an adverb. We switch out adverbs for adjectives often enough in spoken language, but standard English, which is more formal, is the version required for most college-level writing.

First v. Firstly

Some good news: students often worry about the difference between these two in a situation where either of them is actually correct.

First can be an adjective or an adverb and refers to the person or thing that comes before all others in order, time, amount, quality or importance:

- The **first** person to orbit Earth was Yuri A. Gagarin. (adjective)
- Carrie always arrives **first** at our Geology lab. (adverb) Not "Carrie always arrives **firstly …**"

We often use *first*, especially in writing, to show the order of the points we want to make. When we are making lists, we can use *first* or *firstly*. *Firstly* is more formal than *first*, but not more correct:

- **First(ly)** the sodium chloride is dissolved in the water and heated gently. Second(ly) a dye is

---

1. "Literal." *Merriam-Webster.com*. Merriam-Webster, n.d. Web. 20 June 2016.

added to the solution.

But not: At first, the sodium chloride…

At first means 'at the beginning' or 'in the beginning' and we use it when we make contrasts:

- No one in the study group could figure out the algebraic equation **at first**, but eventually the Math Learning Center tutor provided enough support for them to solve it successfully.

Good v. Well

One of the most commonly confused adjective/adverb pairs is *good* versus *well*. *Good* is an adjective. *Well* is an adverb. Here are a couple of sentence where people often confuse these two:

- The experiment runs good now.
- I'm doing good with this first problem set.

In the first sentence, *good* is supposed to be modifying *runs,* a verb; therefore the use of *good*—an adjective—is incorrect. *Runs* should be modified by an adverb. The correct sentence would read "The experiment runs well now."

In the second sentence, *good* is supposed to be modifying *doing,* a verb. Once again, this means that *well*—an adverb—should be used instead: "I'm doing well with this first problem set."

> **Note:** The sentence "I'm doing good" can be grammatically correct, but only when it means "I'm doing good things," rather than when it is describing how a person is feeling.

Practice

Select the correct modifier for each sentence:

1. Jimmy has to work (real / really) hard to be (successful / successfully).
2. Kate is really (good / well) with quadratic equations. She computes really (good / well).
3. Eli reads (quick / quickly), and he retains the information (good / well).

Attributions

Introduction to Other Parts of Speech

Congratulations on making it this far through the grammar module of INTD 106! Instead of powering though the whole thing in one hit (especially if it is currently 2 a.m.), you might like to take some of your new or refreshed knowledge and try dropping it where it will do most good – into those INTD 105 essays, Geology lab reports, and the courses you are taking where you have something valuable to add to the scholarly conversation and would like to ensure that your thoughts (could) reach as many of your peers as possible. These grammar concepts aren't ends in themselves – they are the means by which you achieve written, academic goals that are meaningful to you as a developing scholar. If you take a break now and try looking for and applying some of these concepts in writing you're currently producing, we promise that the rest of our INTD 106 grammar module will be right here waiting for you when you get back…

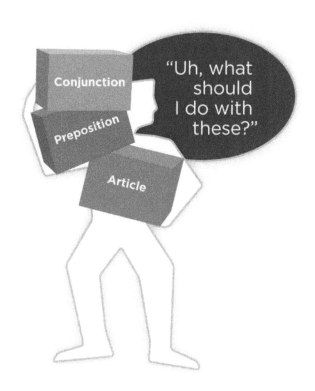

… And welcome back! We're turning now to the little connecting word categories: conjunctions, prepositions, and articles. These small words may not seem as important as verbs, nouns, and adjectives, but they also give our language structure.

- *Conjunctions* connect words and ideas together.
- *Prepositions* indicate relationships.
- *Articles* provide information about nouns.

Attributions

CC licensed content, Original

Conjunctions

Conjunctions are the words that join sentences and phrases, and connect or coordinate other words together. They are difficult to define abstractly, so we will turn quickly to worked examples of four important categories of conjunctions: coordinating conjunctions, adverbial conjunctions, correlative conjunctions, and subordinating conjunctions. As students of INTD 106, INTD 105, and college writing more generally, you'll want to feel competent using conjunctions because they often give shape to the transitional logic that links your ideas into a coherent thesis. The idea of connection – of *join*ing – is at the heart of the term con*junct*ion, so these are the building blocks of controlled complexity in your writing.

Coordinating Conjunctions

The most common conjunctions are *and, or,* and *but.* These are all **coordinating conjunctions**. Coordinating conjunctions are conjunctions that join, or coordinate, two or more equivalent items (such as words, phrases, or sentences). The mnemonic acronym *FANBOYS* stands for the most common coordinating conjunctions: *for, and, nor, but, or, yet,* and *so.*

- **For** presents a reason ("They do not gamble or smoke, for they are ascetics.")

- **And** presents non-contrasting items or ideas ("They gamble, and they smoke.")

- **Nor** presents a non-contrasting negative idea ("They do not gamble, nor do they smoke.")

- **But** presents a contrast or exception ("They gamble, but they don't smoke.")

- **Or** presents an alternative item or idea ("Every day they gamble, or they smoke.")

- **Yet** presents a contrast or exception ("They gamble, yet they don't smoke.")

- **So** presents a consequence ("He gambled well last night, so he smoked a cigar to celebrate.")

Here are some examples of these coordinating conjunctions used in sentences:

- Nuclear-powered artificial hearts proved to be complicated, bulky, **and** expensive.

- In the 1960s, artificial heart devices did not fit well **and** tended to obstruct the flow of venous blood into the right atrium.

- The blood vessels leading to the device tended to kink, obstructing the filling of the chambers **and** resulting in inadequate output.

- Any external injury **or** internal injury put patients at risk of uncontrolled bleeding because the small clots that formed throughout the circulatory system used up so much of the clotting factor.

- The current from the storage batteries can power lights, **but** the current for appliances must be modified within an inverter.

Coordinating conjunctions might seem simple, but, in fact, many undergraduate writers use them imprecisely. They write, "Any external injury **and** internal injury put patients at risk of uncontrolled bleeding…" or, "The current from the storage batteries can power lights, **and** the current for appliances must be modified within an inverter." Presumably, this default to "and" as the coordinating conjunction of choice stems from students' recognition that they want to join related ideas together, but "and" often blurs the precise relationship. If you pile ideas together with "and" *and* don't differentiate logical relationships between items *and* hierarchies, *and* still expect readers to follow your train of thought, you're expecting too much: your sentence sounds as if it is gasping for breath *and* it reads like a list (like this sentence just did). Indeed, a grocery list works fine with "and:" "we need canned tomatoes and pasta and apples and granola bars." You probably don't care whether you pick up the apples first, or the pasta, and the items aren't even ingredients for the same recipe (presumably!). But you really should have a less arbitrary plan for linking ideas together if you want someone to read 5-10 pages of your thoughts about biodiversity or the arts of Oceania. Here's that sentence again with some more precise conjunctions: "If you pile ideas together with "and" *but* don't differentiate logical relationships between items *or* hierarchies, *yet* still expect readers to follow your train of thought, you're expecting too much: your sentence sounds as if it is gasping for breath *and* it reads like a list."

At the bottom of this page, after the discussions of the other categories of conjunctions, is a table of conjunctions divided into the logical categories they serve. It's very useful!

Practice

Are the correct coordinating conjunctions being used in each of the following sentences? Explain your reasoning why or why not:

1. I love algebra or German. They're both a lot of fun.
2. Martin is pretty good at writing, for Jaden is better.
3. Juana had to choose. Would she cut the red wire and the black wire?

As you can see from the examples above, a comma only appears before these conjunctions sometimes. So how can you tell if you need a comma or not? There are three general rules to help you decide.

Rule 1: Joining Two Complete Ideas

Let's look back at one of our example sentences:

The current from the storage batteries can power lights, but the current for appliances must be modified within an inverter.

There are two complete ideas in this sentence. A complete idea has both a subject (a noun or pronoun) and a verb. The subjects have been italicized, and the verbs bolded:

- the *current* from the storage batteries **can power** lights

- the *current* for appliances **must be modified** within an inverter.

Because each of these ideas could stand alone as a sentence, the coordinating conjunction that joins them must be preceded by a comma. Otherwise you'll have a run-on sentence.

> **Note:** Run-on sentences are one of the most common errors in college-level writing. Mastering the partnership between commas and coordinating conjunctions will go a long way towards resolving many run-on sentence issues in your writing. We'll talk more about run-ons and strategies to avoid them in the Punctuation module.

Rule 2: Joining Two Similar Items

So what if there's only one complete idea, but two subjects or two verbs?

- Any external injury or internal injury put patients at risk of uncontrolled bleeding because the small clots that formed throughout the circulatory system used up so much of the clotting factor.

    ◦ The first part of this sentence has two subjects: *external injury* and *internal injury*. They are joined with the conjunction *or*; we don't need any additional punctuation here.

- In the 1960s, artificial heart devices did not fit well and tended to obstruct the flow of venous blood into the right atrium.

    ◦ This sentence has two verbs: *did not fit well* and *tended to obstruct*. They are joined with the conjunction *and*; we don't need any additional punctuation here.

Rule 3: Joining Three or More Similar Items

So what do you do if there are three or more items?

- Anna loves to color-code due dates, Luz loves to get ahead of schedule, and David loves the buzz of an adrenaline-fueled all-nighter.

- Fishing, hunting, and gathering were once the only ways for people to get food.

- Emanuel has a very careful schedule planned for tomorrow. He needs to work, study for his Arabic exam, exercise, eat something substantial, and clean his car.

As you can see in the examples above, there is a comma after each item, including the item just prior to the conjunction. There is a little bit of contention about this, but overall, most styles prefer to keep the additional comma (also called the serial comma). We discuss the serial comma in more depth in Commas.

Starting a Sentence

Many students are taught—and some style guides maintain—that English sentences should not start with coordinating conjunctions.

This video shows that this idea is not actually a rule. And it provides some background for why so many people may have adopted this writing convention:

- https://youtu.be/r8KHIxscCkg

Practice

Are the following sentences correctly punctuated?

1. Ricardo composed one song today and he wants to get three more done by the end of the week.

2. My house mates leave their keys all over the house, and forget where they put them.

3. I wanted to call my friend, but she lost her phone a few days ago.

4. Vesna had already chosen the first presentation slot so I took the second one.

5. Do you want to go to the review session or to the bowling alley?

Adverbial Conjunctions

Adverbial conjunctions link two separate thoughts or sentences. When used to separate thoughts, as in the example below, a comma is required on either side of the conjunction.

> The first artificial hearts were made of smooth silicone rubber, which apparently caused excessive clotting and, **therefore**, uncontrolled bleeding.

When used to separate sentences, as in the examples below, a semicolon is required before the conjunction and a comma after.

- The Kedeco produces 1200 watts in 17 mph winds using a 16-foot rotor; **on the other hand**, the Dunlite produces 2000 watts in 25 mph winds.

- For short periods, the fibers were beneficial; **however**, the eventual buildup of fibrin on the inner surface of the device would impair its function.

- The atria of the heart contribute a negligible amount of energy; **in fact**, the total power output of the heart is only about 2.5 watts.

Adverbial conjunctions include the following words; however, it is important to note that this is by no means a complete list.

therefore	however	in other words
thus	then	otherwise
nevertheless	on the other hand	in fact

Practice

Fill in the missing punctuation marks for the sentences below.

1. My house mate decided to drive to campus __ therefore __ she thought she would arrive earlier than she usually does.

2. She needed to turn left on Park Street. That street __ however __ was under construction.

3. In other words __ she couldn't turn on the street she needed to.

Correlative Conjunctions

Correlative conjunctions are word pairs that work together to join words and groups of words of equal weight in a sentence. This video will define this type of conjunction before it goes through five of the most common correlative conjunctions:

- https://youtu.be/R74Ly00UygU

The table below shows some examples of correlative conjunctions being used in a sentence:

Correlative Conjunction	Example
either…or	You **either** do your work **or** prepare for a trip to the office.
neither…nor	**Neither** the basketball team **nor** the football team is doing well.
not only…but (also)	He is **not only** handsome, **but also** brilliant.
	Not only is he handsome, **but also** he is brilliant.
both…and	**Both** the cross country team **and** the swimming team are doing well.
whether…or	You must decide **whether** you stay **or** you go.
	Whether you stay **or** you go, the film must start at 8 p.m.
just as…so	**Just as** many Americans love basketball, **so** many Canadians love ice hockey.
as much…as	Football is **as much** an addiction **as** it is a sport.
no sooner…than	**No sooner** did she learn to ski, **than** the snow began to thaw.
rather…than	I would **rather** swim **than** surf.
the…the	**The** more you practice dribbling, **the** better you will be at it.
as…as	Football is **as** fast **as** hockey (is (fast)).

Practice

Rewrite the following items. Your new sentences should use correlative conjunctions.

1. She finished packing right when the moving truck showed up.

2. There are two shifts you can work: Thursday night or Saturday afternoon.

3. Chemistry and physics are both complex.

Subordinating Conjunctions

Subordinating conjunctions are conjunctions that join an independent clause and a dependent clause. Here are some examples of subordinating conjunctions:

- The heart undergoes two cardiac cycle periods: diastole, **when** blood enters the ventricles, and systole, **when** the ventricles contract and blood is pumped out of the heart.

- **Whenever** an electron acquires enough energy to leave its orbit, the atom is positively charged.

- **If** the wire is broken, electrons will cease to flow and current is zero.

- I'll be here **as long as** it takes for you to finish.

- She did the favor **so that** he would owe her one.

Let's take a moment to look back at the previous examples. Can you see the pattern in comma usage? The commas aren't dependent on the presence of subordinating conjunctions—they're dependent on the placement of clauses they're in. Let's revisit a couple of examples to figure out the rules:

- The heart undergoes two cardiac cycle periods: diastole, **when** blood enters the ventricles, and systole, **when** the ventricles contract and blood is pumped out of the heart.

  ○ These clauses are both extra information: information that is good to know, but not necessary for the meaning of the sentence. This means they need commas on either side.

- **Whenever** an electron acquires enough energy to leave its orbit, the atom is positively charged.

  ○ In this sentence, the dependent clause comes before an independent clause. This means it should be followed by a comma.

- She did the favor **so that** he would owe her one.

  ○ In this sentence, the independent clause comes before an dependent clause. This means no comma is required.

The most common subordinating conjunctions in the English language are shown in the table below:

after	although	as	as far as	as if		as long as	as soon as
as though	because	before	even if	even though	every time	if
in order that	since	so	so that	than		though	unless
until	when	whenever	where	whereas		wherever	while

- https://youtu.be/IKrRuDWEP68

Practice

All of the commas have been removed from the following passage. Rewrite the passage, adding in the correct punctuation. Identify all of the subordinating conjunctions as well.

Thales came to the silent auction in order to win the chance to be drawn by his favorite artist. Before anyone else could bid Thales went to the bidding sheet and placed an aggressive bid. He knew he would have to come back and check on it while the auction was still open but he felt confident in his ability to win. He was determined to win the auction even if it took all of his money to do so.

Attributions

Practice Activities: Conjunctions

Coordinating Conjunctions

In this practice section, you will combine multiple sentences into a single sentence. For example, look at the sentences "Clint was very skilled at his job. Wade was very skilled at his job." You would combine these two sentences into something like this, using coordinating conjunctions:

- Clint and Wade were both very skilled at their jobs.
- Clint was very skilled at his job, and Wade was too.

When you combine sentences, you can remove repeated information.

1. Wade was really impressed by Clint. Wade was anxious about working with him.
2. Clint thought Wade was annoying. Clint thought Wade was unpredictable. Clint thought Wade was possibly dangerous.
3. In the end, Clint worked well with Wade. In the end, Wade worked well with Clint.

Different Types of Conjunctions

All of the conjunctions have been removed from the following passage. Which conjunctions would best fill the gaps? Explain your reasoning why. The sentences have been numbered to aid you in your comments.

(1) Karni's roommate, Joana, decided to drive to work; _____, Karni rode into the city with her. (2) They needed to turn left on Main Street, _____ that street was under construction. (3) _____ Karni could say anything, _____, Joana had already found an alternate route.

(4) _____ did Karni arrive at work, _____ her boss told her she would be working with her coworker Ian on her next project. (5) Karni was really impressed by Ian's professional accomplishments, _____ she was anxious about working with him. (6) Karni thought Ian was annoying, unpredictable, _____ reckless.

(7) _____, Karni was willing to put aside her opinions to get the job done. (8) She knew Ian would put in his best effort _____ they worked together, _____ she felt she could do no less—_____ he frustrated her. (9) Personal relationships are often _____ important _____ professional skills.

Attributions

CC licensed content, Original

Prepositions

Prepositions are relation words; they can indicate location, time, or other more abstract relationships. Prepositions are noted in bold in these examples:

- The woods **behind** my house are super creepy **at** night.

- She studied **until** three in the morning.

- He was happy **for** them.

A preposition combines with another word (usually a noun or pronoun) called the *complement*. Prepositions are still in bold, and their complements are in italics:

- The woods **behind** *my house* are super creepy **at** *night*.

- She studied **until** *three in the morning*.

- He was happy **for** *them*.

Prepositions generally come before their complements (e.g., **in** England, **under** the table, **of** Jane). However, there are a small handful of exceptions, including **notwithstanding** and **ago**:

- *Financial limitations* **notwithstanding**, Phil paid back his debts.

- He was released *three days* **ago**.

Prepositions of location are pretty easily defined (*near, far, over, under,* etc.), and prepositions about time are as well (*before, after, at, during,* etc.). Prepositions of "more abstract relationships," however, are a little more nebulous in their definition. The video below gives a good overview of this category of prepositions:

- https://youtu.be/RPiAT-Nm3JY

> **Note:** The video said that prepositions are a closed group, but it never actually explained what a closed group is. Perhaps the easiest way to define a closed group is to define its opposite: an open

group. An open group is a part of speech that allows new words to be added. For example, nouns are an open group; new nouns, like *selfie* and *blog*, enter the language all the time (verbs, adjectives, and adverbs are open groups as well).

Thus a closed group simply refers to a part of speech that doesn't allow in new words. All of the word types in this section—prepositions, articles, and conjunctions—are closed groups.

So far, all of the prepositions we've looked at have been one word (and most of them have been one syllable). The most common prepositions are one-syllable words. According to one ranking, the most common English prepositions are *on, in, to, by, for, with, at, of, from, as*.

There are also some prepositions that have more than one word:

- *in spite of* (She won the election in spite of gerrymandering.)
- *by means of* (They filtered the water by means of porous membranes.)
- *except for* (The prices of all commodities spiked except for oil.)
- *next to* (The cell phone tower is next to a busy mall.)

Practice

Identify the prepositions in the following sentences:

1. I love every painting by Vermeer except for *The Girl with the Pearl Earring*.
2. In spite of their cheaper price, batteries were still considered undesirable before the company arranged a safe disposal method.
3. The 1933 Banditry bill was about combating the developing technology of getaways.

Using Prepositions

A lot of struggles with prepositions come from trying to use the correct preposition. Some verbs require specific prepositions. Here's a table of some of the most commonly misused preposition/verb pairs:

different from	comply with	dependent on	think of or about
need of	profit by	glad of	bestow upon

Some verbs take a different preposition, depending on the object of the sentence:

agree with a person	agree to a proposition	part from (a person)	part with (a thing)
differ from (person or thing)	differ from or with an opinion	confide in (to trust in)	confide to (to entrust to)
reconcile with (a person)	reconcile to (a statement or idea)	confer on (to give)	confer with (to talk with)
compare with (to determine value)	compare to (because of similarity)	convenient to (a place)	convenient for (a purpose)

When multiple objects take the same preposition, you don't need to repeat the preposition. For example, in the sentence "I'll read any book by J. K. Rowling or R. L. Stine," both *J. K. Rowling* and *R. L. Stine* are objects of the preposition *by*, so it only needs to appear once in the sentence. However, you can't do this when you have different prepositions, as in the common phrase "We fell out of the frying pan and into the fire." If you leave out one of the prepositions, as in "We fell out of the frying pan and the fire," the sentence is saying that we fell out of the frying pan *and* out of the fire, which would be a preferable fate, but isn't the point of this idiom.

Prepositions in Sentences

You'll often hear about **prepositional phrases** (especially if you and your friends like to read grammar guides). A prepositional phrase includes a preposition and its complement (e.g., "**behind** *the house*" or "a *long time **ago***"). These phrases can appear at the beginning or end of sentences. When they appear at the beginning of a sentence, they typically need a comma afterwards:

- You can drop that off behind the house. Behind the house, there's a covered porch.
- A long time ago, dinosaurs roamed the earth. Pterodactyls ruled the air a long time ago.

Ending a Sentence with a Preposition

- https://youtu.be/NhGQYjXMgsY

As we just learned, it is totally okay to end a sentence with a preposition. And, as we saw, it can often make your writing smoother and more concise to do so.

However, it's still best to avoid doing it unnecessarily. If your sentence ends with a preposition and would still mean the same thing without the preposition, take it out. Consider:

- Where are you at?
- That's not what it's used for.

If you remove *at*, the sentence becomes "Where are you?" This means the same thing, so removing *at* is a good idea. Not only is the preposition redundant, but it also lowers the register of the sentence to colloquial; you might say "Where are you at?" but you shouldn't write it in the fairly formal register of standard English.

On the other hand, if you remove *for*, the next sentence becomes "That's not what it's used," which doesn't make sense.

Another common issue with prepositions is piling too many into a sentence, often including an additional one at the end: "With which acid am I supposed to mix the water with?" Again, this error in standard English tends to occur when students are out of their comfort zone: here, the relationship between the water and some acid isn't clear, or the student is unclear on the instructions, or the student is nervous that something is about to explode, and the language is reflecting that unease.

Practice

Read each sentence and determine if the prepositions are being used correctly. If they are not, re-write the sentence.

1. Do you have any idea why Olivia keeps calling for?

2. You have no idea how much trouble you're in.

3. Luiz agreed with hand his credit card over to the cashier.

4. Last week Ngozi reconciled herself to the new prices and the co-worker she had argued with.

Attributions

CC licensed content, Original

- Revision and Adaptation. **Provided by**: Lumen Learning. **License**: *CC BY-SA: Attribution-ShareAlike*
- Revision and Adaptation. **Authored by**: Gillian Paku. **Provided by**: SUNY Geneseo. **License**: *CC BY: Attribution*

CC licensed content, Shared previously

- Preposition and postposition. **Provided by**: Wikipedia. **Located at**: https://en.wikipedia.org/wiki/Preposition_and_postposition. **License**: *CC BY-SA: Attribution-ShareAlike*
- Prepositions of neither space nor time. **Authored by**: David Rheinstrom. **Provided by**: Khan Academy. **Located at**: https://www.khanacademy.org/humanities/grammar/partsofspeech/the-preposition/v/prepositions-of-neither-space-nor-time. **License**: *CC BY-NC-SA: Attribution-NonCommercial-ShareAlike*
- Terminal prepositions. **Authored by**: David Rheinstrom. **Provided by**: Khan Academy. **Located at**: https://www.khanacademy.org/humanities/grammar/partsofspeech/the-preposition/v/terminal-prepositions-prepositions-the-parts-of-speech-grammar. **License**: *CC BY-NC-SA: Attribution-NonCommercial-ShareAlike*
- Image of box. **Authored by**: Lek Potharam. **Provided by**: The Noun Project. **Located at**: https://thenounproject.com/search/?q=put&i=17426. **License**: *CC BY: Attribution*

Public domain content

- Practical Grammar and Composition. **Authored by**: Thomas Wood. **Located at**: http://www.gutenberg.org/ebooks/22577. **Project**: Project Gutenberg. **License**: *Public Domain: No Known Copyright*

Articles

There are three articles in the English language: *the, a,* and *an.* These are divided into two types of articles: definite (*the*) and indefinite (*a, an*). The definite article indicates a level of specificity that the indefinite does not. "A solar panel" could refer to any solar panel; however, "the solar panel" is referring back to a specific solar panel.

Thus, when using the definite article, the writer assumes the reader knows the identity of the noun's referent (because it is obvious, because it is common knowledge, or because it was mentioned in the same sentence or an earlier sentence). Use of an indefinite article implies that the reader does not have to be told the identity of the referent.

There are also cases where no article is required:

- with generic nouns (plural or uncountable): *cars have accelerators, happiness is contagious,* referring to cars in general and happiness in general (compare *the happiness I felt yesterday,* specifying particular happiness);
- with many proper names: *Sabrina, France, London,* etc.

Watch this quick introduction to indefinite and definite articles and the difference between the two:

- https://youtu.be/TSd0uByBoTo

Indefinite Article

The indefinite article of English takes the two forms *a* and *an.* These can be regarded as meaning "one," usually without emphasis.

Distinction between a and an

You've probably learned the rule that *an* comes before a vowel, and that *a* comes before a consonant. While this is generally true, it's more accurate to say that *an* comes before a vowel *sound*, and *a* comes before a consonant *sound*. Let's look at a couple of examples with *a*:

- *a box*
- *a HEPA filter* (HEPA is pronounced as a word rather than as letters)
- *a one-armed bandit* (pronounced "won. . . ")
- *a eulogy* (pronounced "yoo. . . ")

Let's try it again with *an*:

- *an apple*
- *an EPA policy* (the letter *E* read as a letter still starts with a vowel sound)
- *an SSO* (pronounced "es-es-oh")
- *an hour* (the *h* is silent)
- *an heir* (pronounced "air")

> **Note:** Some speakers and writers use *an* before a word beginning with the sound *h* in an unstressed syllable: *an historical novel, an hotel*. However, where the *h* is clearly pronounced, this usage is now less common, and *a* is preferred.

Practice
Look at the following words. When they require an indefinite article, should it be *a* or *an*?

1. ewe
2. SEO specialist
3. apple
4. URL

Definite Article

The definite article *the* is used when the referent of the noun phrase is assumed to be unique or known from the context. For example, in the sentence "The keen astronomy student was looking at the moon," it is assumed that in the context the reference can only be to one keen astronomy student and one moon.

The can be used with both singular and plural nouns, with nouns of any gender, and with nouns that start with any letter. This is different from many other languages which have different articles for different genders or numbers. *The* is the most commonly used word in the English language.

Practice

Choose the article that should go in each sentence:

1. Every season, locusts eat (a / an / the) entirely new crop.
2. Dani was planning to buy (a / an / the) political science book she had been eyeing as soon as she got paid.
3. (A / An / The) business unit like that will dominate the market.

Word Order

In most cases, the article is the first word of its noun phrase, preceding all other adjectives and modifiers.

> *The* little old red bag held *a* very big surprise.

There are a few exceptions, however:

- Certain determiners, such as *all, both, half, double*, precede the definite article when used in combination (*all the team; both the girls; half the time; double the amount*).

- *Such* and *what* precede the indefinite article (*such an idiot; what a day!*).

- Adjectives qualified by *too, so, as* and *how* generally precede the indefinite article: *too great a loss; so hard a problem; as difficult an exam as I have ever sat; I know how demanding a professor she is.*

Practice

Read the following passage and make any necessary changes to articles. Explain your reasoning for each change.

A Hubble Space Telescope (HST) is a space telescope that was launched into low Earth orbit in 1990 and remains in operation. Although not the first space telescope, Hubble is one of the largest and most versatile, and is well known as both an vital research tool and a public relations boon for astronomy. The HST is named after an astronomer Edwin Hubble.

Hubble's orbit outside the distortion of Earth's atmosphere allows it to take extremely high-resolution images. Hubble has recorded the some of most detailed visible-light images ever, allowing the deep view into space and time.

Attributions

CC licensed content, Original

- Revision and Adaptation. **Provided by**: Lumen Learning. **License**: *CC BY-SA: Attribution-ShareAlike*
- Revision and Adaptation. **Authored by**: Gillian Paku. **Provided by**: SUNY Geneseo. **License**: *CC BY: Attribution*

CC licensed content, Shared previously

- English articles. **Provided by**: Wikipedia. **Located at**: https://en.wikipedia.org/wiki/English_articles. **License**: *CC BY-SA: Attribution-ShareAlike*
- Definite and indefinite articles. **Authored by**: David Rheinstrom. **Provided by**: Khan Academy. **Located at**: https://www.khanacademy.org/humanities/grammar/partsofspeech/the-modifier/v/definite-and-indefinite-articles. **License**: *CC BY-NC-SA: Attribution-NonCommercial-ShareAlike*
- Modification of Hubble Space Telescope (with errors inserted). **Provided by**: Wikipedia. **Located at**: https://en.wikipedia.org/wiki/Hubble_Space_Telescope. **License**: *CC BY-SA: Attribution-ShareAlike*

5. Writing Process

Rhetorical Context

Any piece of writing is shaped by external factors before the first word is ever set down on the page. This rhetorical situation, or rhetorical context, can be presented in the form of a pyramid.

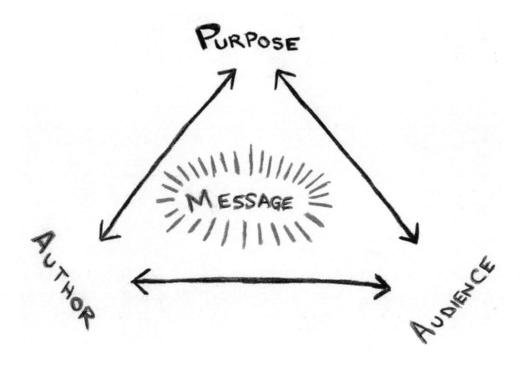

The three key factors—purpose, author, and audience—all work together to influence what the text itself says, and how it says it.

Purpose

Any time you are preparing to write, you should first ask yourself, "Why am I writing?" All writing, no matter the type, has a purpose, or exigence, or stakes: these are all common terms for this concept. Purpose will sometimes be given to you by an instructor—college instructors often ask you to construct a well-reasoned and persuasive argument, and sometimes they give you quite specific questions to address, or sources, evidence, or methods to use. At other times, you will decide your stakes for yourself: this task can seem daunting to an undergraduate student, but part of what you are learning to do at college is not only to understand what others think, but to formulate your own thoughts and pose your own questions about topics whose purpose you yourself find galvanizing or exciting or profound. As the author, it's up to you to make sure that the purpose of your writing is clear not only to yourself, but also—especially—to your audience. If your purpose is not clear, your audience is not likely to receive your intended message. College writing is not just "telling" your reader something; rather, it's conversational in the sense that you are making meaning out of evidence, and offering up your analysis to the broader scholarly community, which means that the community needs to know why what you're saying matters and why your peers should care.

There are, of course, many different reasons to write (e.g., to inform, to entertain, to persuade, to ask questions), and you may find that some writing has more than one purpose. When this happens, be sure to consider any conflict between purposes, and remember that you will usually focus on one main purpose as primary. Try not to imagine your primary purpose as fulfilling an assignment to earn a grade, since that's a generic and pretty uninspiring purpose to apply to everything you write at college; focus instead on academic goals such as persuasion and analysis which will develop you as a thinker and writer, regardless of the particular topic of your essay.

Why Purpose Matters

- If you've ever listened to a lecture or read an essay and wondered "so what?" then you know how frustrating it can be when an author's purpose is not clear. By clearly defining your purpose before you begin writing, it's less likely you'll be that author who leaves the audience wondering.

- If readers can't identify the purpose in a text, they usually quit reading. You can't deliver a message to an audience who quits reading.

- If instructors can't identify the purpose in your text, they might assume you didn't understand the assignment.

Audience

To some extent, naturally, you need to think about the audience you're writing for and adapt your writing approach to their needs, expectations, backgrounds, and interests. Being aware of your audience helps you make better decisions about what to say and how to say it. For example, you have a better idea if you will need to define or explain any terms if you consider that your audience consists of your supportive, but non-Psychology-major friends at a GREAT Day panel (Geneseo's annual public showcase of outstanding student work), rather than of your classmates in a 300-level seminar specializing in developmental psychopathology. Or, you can make a more conscious effort not to say or do anything that would make your audience lose confidence in your judgment when you know that most of your audience will find your— for example, political—argument counterintuitive.

Sometimes you know who will read your writing—for example, if you are writing an email to the supervisor of your internship. Other times you will have to guess who is likely to read your writing—for example, if you are writing an editorial for *The Lamron*. You will often write with a primary audience in mind, but there may be secondary and tertiary audiences to consider as well. In an academic context, although you know that on one level you are writing for your instructor, try to imagine your primary audience as a more broadly academic one. Imagine an educated reader—someone who may not ever have thought about your particular essay topic, but who is intellectually curious enough to become interested in any piece of writing whose purpose is clear and whose level of sophistication moves at an appropriate pace through introductory material and then on to more nuanced, detailed, or complex claims.

Be sophisticated about the role of your audience. The following list suggests some points that might contribute to a profile of your audience, but you should balance those points against the danger of getting trapped by a too concrete, too external sense of what drives your writing. In his classic writing guide, *Writing with Power*, Peter Elbow comments,

> When you attend to audience from the start and let your words grow out of your relationship with it, sometimes you come up with just what you need, and in addition your words have a wonderful integrity or fit with that audience. Everything is on target. But sometimes the effect is opposite. The audience hinders your writing by exerting too much pull on you (or intimidating you). And occasionally when you think too much about audience, your words are too heavy with audience-awareness. Your words feel too much like those of a salesman who is trying too hard to make "audience contact." (194)
>
> [1]

What to Think About

Bearing Elbow's advice in mind, consider these points when analyzing your audience. Creating a profile of your audience can help guide your writing choices.

Background Knowledge or Experience — In general, you don't want to merely repeat what your audience already knows about the topic you're writing about; you want to build on it. On the other hand, you don't want to talk over their heads. Anticipate their amount of previous knowledge or experience based on elements like their profession, level of education, or age. At college, many written assignments expect you to imagine an educated and curious but non-expert reader who will be able to progress rapidly in knowledge if you provide the necessary information: someone just like you. Be careful about assuming that your instructor is your primary audience; undergraduate students often create gaps in logic or knowledge if they work from the assumption that their instructor already knows everything and that they therefore don't need to, or shouldn't, set up any background. Logically, background information should come towards the start of your essay, but not necessarily at the very start where it can read like random facts. Frame background information by how it relates to your thesis.

Expectations and Interests — Your audience may expect to find specific points or writing approaches, especially if you are writing for faculty or a boss. Consider not only what they *do* want to read about, but also what they *do not* want to read about. It is completely appropriate to ask a college instructor about their expectations, especially if you have a specific question, such as whether a relevant personal anecdote would be appropriate, or whether you should be using research materials in your assignment, or graphics, or how they feel about using the first person pronoun ("I").

Attitudes and Biases — Your audience may have predetermined feelings about your topic, which can affect how hard you have to work to win them over or appeal to them. If they expect to disagree with you, they will look for evidence that you have considered their side as well as your own. It's good academic practice to include and treat respectfully such *counterarguments* in any essay, how-

1. Peter Elbow, *Writing with Power* (1981), p. 194

ever, even if you think your audience will share your basic outlook on the topic. Academic arguments are *contestable*, meaning that they aren't just facts arranged in sentences, but rather positions you've taken after considering the evidence.

Demographics — Consider what else you know about your audience, such as their age, gender, ethnic and cultural backgrounds, political preferences, religious affiliations, job or professional background, and area of residence. Think about how these demographics may affect how much background your audience has about your topic, what types of expectations or interests they have, and what attitudes or biases they may have. Don't get caught up in thinking too hard about one particular reader, though: keep that general, educated reader in mind.

Applying Your Analysis to Your Writing

Here are some general rules to apply your thinking about audience to the writing moves you make.[2]

Change the register of the information you currently have. Even if you have the right information, you might be explaining it in a way (a "register") that doesn't make sense to your audience. For example, you wouldn't want to use highly advanced or technical vocabulary in a document for first-grade students or even in a document for a general audience, such as the audience of a daily newspaper, because most likely some (or even all) of the audience wouldn't understand you.

Add examples to help readers understand. Sometimes just changing the register of information you have isn't enough to get your point across, so you might try adding an example. If you are trying to explain a complex or abstract issue, you might offer a metaphor or an analogy to something readers are more familiar with to help them understand. Or, if you are writing for an audience that disagrees with your stance, you might offer examples that create common ground and help them see your perspective.

Change the level of your examples. Once you've decided to include examples, you should make sure you aren't offering examples your audience finds unacceptable or confusing. For example, some instructors find personal stories unacceptable in academic writing, so you might use a metaphor instead. Metaphors, however, may distract your reader from the purpose of your argument if you reserve too much textual space for them. Use them to supplement, not replace, the contents of your argument. There's no magic bullet for appealing to every audience.

Strengthen transitions. You might make decisions about transitions based on your audience's expectations. For example, most instructors expect to find topic sentences, which serve as transitions between paragraphs. In a shorter piece of writing such as a memo to co-workers, however, you would probably be less concerned with topic sentences and more concerned with transition words. In general, if you feel your readers may have a hard time making connections, providing transition words (e.g., "therefore" or "on the other hand") can help lead them.

Write stronger introductions – both for the whole document and for major sections. Academic readers like to get the big picture up front. Offer this vital information in your introduction and thesis statement, and reiterate it in smaller introductions to major sections within your document. In a docu-

2. (Rules adapted from David McMurrey's online text, *Power Tools for Technical Communication*)

ment that doesn't have sections, topic sentences (the first sentences of a paragraph) function much the same way an introduction does – they offer readers a preview of what's coming and how that information relates to the overall document and your overall purpose.

Author

The final unique aspect of anything written down is who it is, exactly, that does the writing. You can harness the aspects of yourself that will make the text most effective to its audience, for its purpose. Tap into your own strengths, but remember also that your ability to manage the conventions of standard English, including essay structure, spelling, and grammar, will inevitably affect how much an academic audience perceives you to be a believable author. The words *author* and *authority* share the same root for a reason.

Analyzing yourself as an author allows you to clarify, either to your audience or just to yourself, why your audience should pay attention to what you have to say, and why they should listen to you on the particular subject at hand. It is more appropriate in some writing scenarios than others to describe yourself explicitly; in many college assignments, you might not even use "I," but having thought deliberately about yourself as the author of a paper on any topic is a valuable academic habit of mind. Again, the motivation you bring to an essay should be more than needing to get a grade to pass the course! A liberal arts education places most students in varying states of knowledge, motivation, and comfort regarding a topic, so use that variety to learn about yourself as an author in different contexts.

Questions for Consideration

- What personal motivations do you have for writing about this topic?

- What background knowledge do you have on this subject matter?

- What personal experiences directly relate to this subject? How do those personal experiences influence your perspectives on the issue? How would you describe yourself demographically?

- What formal training or professional experience do you have related to this subject?

- What skills do you have as a communicator? How can you harness those in this project?

- What should audience members know about you, in order to trust what you have to tell them? How will you convey that in your writing?

Consider, though, that as with Peter Elbow's advice above about imagining a specific audience, forming too concrete a profile of yourself as author can also feel restrictive. The authorial self you project in your standard English, academic, college-level essays is a constructed self, functioning in a specific, constructed space. As another writing theorist, Steven Pinker, says,

> Writing is above all an act of pretense. We have to visualize ourselves in some kind of conversation, or correspondence, or oration, or soliloquy, and put words into the mouth of the little avatar who represents us in this simulated world. [3]

Attributions

CC licensed content, Original

3. Steven Pinker, *The Sense of Style*, p. 28

Thesis Statement

Whether you are writing a short essay or a doctoral dissertation, your thesis statement will be arguably the most complex part to formulate. An effective thesis statement states the purpose of the paper and, therefore, functions to control, assert, and structure your entire argument. Without a sound thesis stated clearly at the beginning of your paper, your writing will sound unfocused, and uninteresting to the reader.

Most college-level writing is analytical, valuing a thesis that arises from close attention to the significance of patterns of evidence that are not stated explicitly. Think of analysis as "value added" reading where you need to move beyond comprehending and summarizing what the text explicitly states.

Start with a question—then make the *answer* your thesis

Regardless of how complicated the subject is, almost any thesis can be constructed by answering a question. This question-and-answer format encourages you to formulate a claim about a topic, rather than just announcing that a topic exists. An academic thesis must be something that can be argued (and argued against), which means it can't simply be a statement of fact, or lack any contestable claim.

> Note that the *question* is not your thesis—the *answer* to the question is your thesis, and that answer is the *starting point* of your essay. Some inexperienced writers pose a question in their introduction and delay answering it clearly until their conclusion. That strategy is not appropriate in most college writing.

- **Question:** "What are the benefits of using computers in a fourth-grade classroom?"
  - ○ **Thesis:** "Computers allow fourth graders an early advantage in technological and scientific education."
- **Question:** "Why is the Mississippi River so important in Mark Twain's *Huckleberry Finn*?"
  - ○ **Thesis:** "The Mississippi River comes to symbolize both division and progress, as it separates the characters and country while still providing the best chance for Huck and Jim to get to know one another."

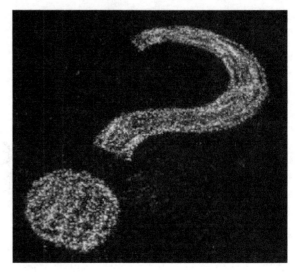

- **Question:** "Why do people seem to get angry at vegans, feminists, and other 'morally righteous' subgroups?"
  - ○ **Thesis:** "Through careful sociological study, we've found that people frequently assume that 'morally righteous' people look down on them as 'inferior,' causing anger and conflict where there generally is none."

Ensure your thesis is provable

Don't get wedded to your draft thesis! The thesis is the end point of your research: you often begin with some sense of your thesis, but you need to be prepared to nuance, alter, or abandon that thesis if your evidence suggests a different answer to the question that prompted your thesis in the first place. A thesis ultimately emerges from your evidence, so an academic thesis is one you must be able to back up *with evidence*.

Resist the urge to formulate a broad thesis: the more specific your thesis, the more obvious it will be to you what kind of evidence will support it—or contradict it—and the more persuasive and logical that evidence will seem to your readers.

Examples of Good Theses:

Note that because a thesis and an introduction form one structural unit, these thesis statements are only part of what each author would need to write to introduce an argument.

- "By owning up to the impossible contradictions within 'experienced innocence,' embracing religious paradox and structuring multiple poems around oxymorons found in the natural world, William Blake forges his own faith, and is stronger for it. Ultimately, the only way for his poems to encourage faith is to temporarily lose it."

- "Although many working people with autism find flexible employment instructions difficult to manage, and they often struggle with social subtleties or even with the everyday office-life annoyances of fluorescent lights and ringing phones, employers should reconceptualize the disability status of those with an autism spectrum disorder to realize the workplace benefits of hyperfocus and reliability."

Bad Theses Examples:

- "The wrong people won the American Revolution." While striking and unique, the claim about who is "right" and who is "wrong" is exceptionally hard to prove, and very subjective.

- "The theory of genetic inheritance is the binding theory of every human interaction." Too complicated and overzealous. The scope of "every human interaction" is just too big. "The binding theory" is too absolute. This desire to make a sweeping claim is a very common symptom of a thesis that's headed for trouble, since the writer can't possibly live up to the promise of that scope in 5-10 pages and will either collapse into banal generalizations or fail to present a coherent body of evidence (is there anything that *wouldn't* count as evidence of "every human interaction"?!?). The good news is that no one expects you to explain the universe in your first year at college; demonstrate instead that you can argue a manageable point well.

- "Paul Harding's novel *Tinkers* is ultimately a cry for help from a clearly depressed author." Unless you interviewed Harding extensively, or had a lot of real-life sources, you have no way of proving what is fact and what is fiction.

This ed.ted.com video on thesis statements (https://www.youtube.com/watch?v=4sx42_C10zw) makes a useful point about topic, claim, and major points as elements of a thesis, although the necessary generalizing results in thesis statements that lack the complexity expected from college-level writers. Notice how the major points are listed and the claims aren't very sophisticated: that's a function of trying to explain thesis statements to a general audience in under two minutes, but the principles of doing more than simply announcing a topic or asserting an opinion are illustrated usefully.

Get the sound right

You want your thesis statement to be identifiable as a thesis statement. You signal its centrality by using logical words like "because," "by," or "therefore"; signal its complexity with logic like "although" or "however"; and signal your right to contribute to the scholarly conversation surrounding your topic by taking a confident, measured tone. The evidence from which your thesis emerges will prove your claim, so it's okay to sound confident about what you're saying. However, every thesis should be open to other perspectives (otherwise, if no one could disagree, there'd be no real motivation to write), so you don't want to sound as if only a fool could possibly think anything other than what you are telling them is true; e.g., "All store owners always argue against any legislation regarding hours of business because of the supreme importance merchants place on profits." Those absolute terms like "all," "always," "any," and "supreme" are too assertive, sounding like bluster rather than confidence. Watch out for such *intensifiers*.

Example thesis statements with confident, logical, but not blustering statement language include:

- "Because William the Conqueror's campaign into England initiated Anglo-Norman intermarriage, that nation developed the elite cosmopolitan culture it would need to eventually build the British Empire."

- "Hemingway challenged the self-satisfied elitism of literature by normalizing simplistic writing and frank tone. However, his deliberate cultivation of short, declarative sentences became its own exclusionary literary standard."

Know where to place a thesis statement

Because of the role thesis statements play, they appear at the beginning of the paper. Although many people look for the thesis at the end of the first paragraph, its location can depend on a number of factors such as how much background you need before you can introduce your thesis, or the length of your paper. More importantly, since your thesis drives your essay, nothing at all in the introduction should be—or seem—irrelevant to it. You might be able to identify one particular sentence as the most concise statement of your thesis, but even the way you present background information should be framed by the particular thesis you want that background to support. Avoid starting your paper with what sound like decontextualized facts ("An electrode is a conductor through which electricity enters or leaves an electrolyte, gas, or vacuum") or sweeping generalizations ("Throughout history, Americans. . . ") as if you need to clear your throat before you introduce the point of *your* paper. Readers are more likely to tolerate the definition of an electrode if they already have the context of a thesis like "Although the automative industry has relied for decades on electrodes to keep drivers safe, . . . " Now your readers will want to know what an electrode is because they know it has something to do with their safety when they get into a car (which they care about, even if they don't yet know that they care about developments in the automotive industry), and because the logic signaled by "although" lets them already know that your thesis is going to build from an understanding of electrodes as the starting point to the significance of something new.

Attributions

The Paragraph

As Michael Harvey writes, paragraphs are, in essence, "a form of punctuation, and like other forms of punctuation they are meant to make written material easy to read."[1] Effective paragraphs are the fundamental units of academic writing; consequently, the thoughtful, multifaceted arguments that your professors expect depend on them. Without good paragraphs, you cannot clearly convey sequential points and their relationships to one another. Each paragraph provides space for a body of evidence that proves a particular aspect of your claim: the paragraph units need to seem focused within themselves, and linked between each other in a specific order that moves readers forward through your paper.

Many novice writers tend to make a sharp distinction between content and style, thinking that a paper can be strong in one and weak in the other, but focusing on paragraphs as organizational units shows how content and style converge in deliberative academic writing. Your professors will view even the most elegant prose as rambling and tedious if there isn't a carefully constructed, cohesive argument unfolding logically across the topic sentences, backed up by the right evidence in the right place at the right time. Paragraphs are the "stuff" of academic writing and, thus, worth our attention here.

Topic Sentences

In academic writing, readers expect each paragraph to open with a sentence or two that captures its main point. They're often called "topic sentences," although the phrase "topic sentence" can make it seem like the paramount job of that sentence is simply to announce the topic of the paragraph, and that it must always be a single grammatical sentence. **A topic sentence expresses the central idea of the paragraph** *in terms of the central thesis of your essay.* And sometimes a question or a two-sentence construction functions as the key to those central concepts.

Topic sentences in academic writing do two closely related things. First, they establish the main point that the rest of the paragraph supports. Second, they situate each paragraph within the sequence of the argu-

1. Michael Harvey, *The Nuts and Bolts of College Writing*, Second Edition (Indianapolis, IN: Hackett Publishing, 2013), 70.

ment, a task that requires both transitioning from the prior paragraph and restating what this particular paragraph adds to the central thesis. Don't be afraid of repetition. **If your topic sentences aren't repeating a key term or concept from your introduction, readers will feel disoriented because you appear to be asking them to think about something new rather than developing an idea they knew to expect.** You are not trying to catch an academic reader unawares! If you do, the reader will get jumpy ("What will the next paragraph ask me to think about?? Bananas? Aircraft carriers? Montenegro?"). Feel free to impress your readers with the elegance, soundness, and complexity of your thinking, but don't subject them to topic sentence jump scares.

Consider these two examples:[2]

- **Version A:**

- Now we turn to the epidemiological evidence.

- **Version B:**

- The epidemiological evidence provides compelling support for the hypothesis emerging from these etiological studies.

Both versions convey a topic; it's pretty easy to predict that the paragraph will be about epidemiological evidence, but only the second version establishes an argumentative point and puts it in context. This topic sentence doesn't just announce the existence of the epidemiological evidence; it shows how epidemiology is telling the same story as etiology. That story, or hypothesis, must be the thesis of this paper (and giving that concrete sense of the stakes is probably the job of the following sentence, because not all ideas fit elegantly into one sentence, and there's no rule that says a topic sentence must be literally only one sentence). Seeing these two ideas connected will come as a relief to your reader, who wants reassurance that all this thinking about epidemiology and etiology will serve a coherent claim. Put another way, while Version A doesn't relate to anything in particular, Version B immediately suggests that the prior paragraph addresses the biological pathway (i.e., etiology) of a disease and that the new paragraph will bolster the emerging hypothesis with a different kind of evidence. As a reader, it's easier now to keep track of how the paragraph about cells and chemicals and such relates to the previous paragraph about populations in different places. Presumably, these two paragraphs occur in this order, and not the reverse order, because readers will move more easily in this argument from etiology to epidemiology than the other way around: topic sentences move the reader through the arc of your thesis in the most logical way possible, which often means that the more familiar or more foundational material structures the earlier paragraphs. **Topic sentences shouldn't give the impression that your paragraphs follow an order no more compelling than "Another thing I want to talk about is…"**

Key Takeaway
There are many possible reasons for ordering your paragraphs in certain ways; whatever reason you choose should be clear to your readers from the transitional logic you provide in the topic sentence(s).

2. Etiology is the cause of a disease—what's actually happening in cells and tissues—while epidemiology is the incidence of a disease in a population.

A point to emphasize about key sentences is that academic readers expect them to be at the beginning of the paragraph, and not at the end. **You don't build up to a topic sentence; you use it to set the scene, and then build up *evidence* to support it.** This placement at the start helps readers comprehend your argument and easily follow the sequence of logic.

Knowing this convention of academic writing can help you both write and read more effectively. When you're reading a complicated academic piece for the first time, you might want to go through reading only the first sentence or two of each paragraph to get the overall outline of the argument. Then you can go back and read all of it with a clearer picture of how each of the details fit in. And when you're writing, you may also find it useful to write the first sentence of each paragraph (instead of a topic-based outline) to map out a thorough argument before getting immersed in sentence-level wordsmithing.

Cohesion and Coherence

With a key sentence established, the next task is to shape the body of your paragraph to be both cohesive and coherent. As Joseph Williams and Joseph Bizup explain, **cohesion is about the "sense of flow" (how each sentence fits with the next), while coherence is about the "sense of the whole" (how all the sentences in a paragraph focus on the same topic).**[3]

For the most part, a text reads smoothly when it conveys a well organized argument or analysis. Focus first and most on your ideas, on crafting an ambitious analysis. The most useful guides advise you to first focus on getting your ideas on paper and then revising for organization and word choice later, refining the analysis as you go. Thus, consider the advice here as if you already have some rough text written and are in the process of smoothing out your prose to clarify your argument for both your reader and yourself.

Cohesion

Cohesion refers to the flow from sentence to sentence. For example, compare these passages:

Version A:

Granovetter begins by looking at balance theory. If an actor, A, is strongly tied to both B and C, it is extremely likely that B and C are, sooner or later, going to be tied to each other, according to balance theory (1973:1363). Bridge ties between cliques are always weak ties, Granovetter argues (1973:1364). Weak ties may not necessarily be bridges, but Granovetter argues that bridges will be weak. If two actors share a strong tie, they will draw in their other strong relations and will eventually form a clique. Only weak ties that do not have the strength to draw together all the "friends of friends" can connect people in different cliques.[4]

Version B:

Granovetter begins by looking at balance theory. In brief, balance theory tells us that if an actor, A, is strongly tied to both B and C, it is extremely likely that B and C are, sooner or later, going to be tied to each other (1973:1363). Granovetter argues that because of this, bridge ties between cliques are always weak ties (1973:1364). Weak ties may not necessarily be bridges, but Granovetter argues that bridges will be weak. This is because if two actors share a strong tie, they will draw in their other

3. Joseph M. Williams and Joseph Bizup. *Style: Lessons in Clarity and Grace* 11th edition (New York: Longman, 2014), pp. 68, 71.?
4. The quotation uses a version of an ASA-style in-text citation for Mark S. Granovetter, "The Strength of Weak Ties," *American Journal of Sociology* 78 (1973): 1360-80.

strong relations and will eventually form a clique. The only way, therefore, that people in different cliques can be connected is through weak ties that do not have the strength to draw together all the "friends of friends."[5]

Version A has the exact same information as version B, but it is harder to read because it is less cohesive. The paragraph in version B feels more cohesive because each sentence begins with old information and bridges to new information. Note that "old" is a relative term: it might be something you've known for years, or it might only be as old as one sentence ago. **You can convey a lot of new information to your readers if you keep presenting and linking what's new to what's familiar, even if none of the material was "old news" to you five minutes earlier.**

The first sentence in this example establishes the key idea of balance theory. The next sentence begins with balance theory and ends with social ties, which is the focus of the third sentence. The concept of weak ties connects the third and fourth sentences and the concept of cliques connects the fifth and sixth sentences. In Version A, in contrast, the first sentence focuses on balance theory, but then the second sentence makes a new point about social ties *before* telling the reader that the point comes from balance theory. The reader has to take in a lot of unfamiliar information

before learning how it fits in with familiar concepts. Version A is coherent, but the lack of cohesion makes it tedious to read.

Key Takeaway

The point is this: if you or others perceive a passage you've written to be awkward or choppy, even though the topic is consistent, try rewriting it to ensure that each sentence begins with a familiar term or concept. If your points don't naturally daisy-chain together like the examples given here, consider numbering them. For example, you may choose to write, "Proponents of the legislation point to four major benefits." Then you could discuss four loosely related ideas without leaving your reader wondering how they relate.

Coherence

While cohesion is about the sense of flow, coherence is about the sense of the whole. For example, here's a passage that is cohesive (from sentence to sentence) but lacks coherence:

---

5. Guiffre. *Communities and Networks*, 98.

> Your social networks and your location within them shape the kinds and amount of information that you have access to. Information is distinct from data, in that it makes some kind of generalization about a person, thing, or population. Defensible generalizations about society can be either probabilities (i.e., statistics) or patterns (often from qualitative analysis). Such probabilities and patterns can be temporal, spatial, or simultaneous.

Each sentence in the above passage starts with a familiar idea and progresses to a new one, but it lacks coherence—a sense of being about one thing. In fact, it feels like an introduction to several main concepts of Communication crammed into one paragraph: this essay, if it were submitted in this form, would quickly overwhelm and exhaust its reader.

Note, though, that good writers often write passages like that when they're free-writing or using the drafting stage to cast a wide net for ideas. A writer weighing the power and limits of social network analysis may free-write something like that example and, from there, develop a more specific plan for summarizing key insights about social networks and then discussing them with reference to the core tenets of social science. As a draft, an incoherent paragraph often points to a productive line of reasoning—you just have to continue thinking it through in order to identify a clear argumentative purpose for each paragraph. With its purpose defined, each paragraph becomes a lot easier to write. Coherent paragraphs aren't just about style; they are a sign of a focused, well developed analysis.

Concluding a Paragraph

Some guides advise you to end each paragraph with a specific concluding sentence—in a sense, to treat each paragraph as a kind of mini-essay—but that's not a widely held convention. Most well written academic pieces don't adhere to that structure. The last sentence of the paragraph should certainly be in your own words (as in, not a quotation or paraphrase of somebody else's ideas about your topic), but as long as the paragraph succeeds in carrying out the task that it has been assigned by its topic sentence, you don't need to worry about whether that last sentence has an air of conclusiveness. For example, consider these paragraphs about the cold fusion controversy of the 1980s that appeared in a best-selling textbook:[6]

> The experiment seemed straightforward, and there were plenty of scientists willing to try it. Many did. It was wonderful to have a simple laboratory experiment on fusion to try after the decades of embarrassing attempts to control hot fusion. This effort required multi-billion dollar machines whose every success seemed to be capped with an unanticipated failure. 'Cold fusion' seemed to provide, as Martin Fleischmann said during the course of that famous Utah press conference, 'another route'—the route of little science.

6. Harry Collins and Trevor Pinch, *The Golem: What You Should Know About Science* 2nd ed. (Cambridge: Canto, 1998), 58.

In that example, the first and last sentences in the paragraph are somewhat symmetrical: the authors introduce the idea of accessible science, contrast it with big science, and bring it back to the phrase "little science." Here's an example from the same chapter of the same book that does not have any particular symmetry:[7]

> The struggle between proponents and critics in a scientific controversy is always a struggle for credibility. When scientists make claims which are literally 'incredible,' as in the cold fusion case, they face an uphill struggle. The problem Pons and Fleischmann had to overcome was that they had credibility as electrochemists but not as nuclear physicists. And it was nuclear physics where their work was likely to have its main impact.

The last sentence of the paragraph doesn't mirror the first, but the paragraph is in great shape, coherently connecting its initial, general claim about credibility to the specific challenge to the credibility of Pons and Fleischmann. In general, don't trouble yourself with having the last sentence in every paragraph serve as a mini-conclusion if it feels forced. Instead, worry about developing each point sufficiently and making your logical sequence clear. Let your topic sentences do most of the work of keeping your essay coherent and giving it forward momentum.

Key Takeaway

Rather than striving for mini-conclusions that might seem to pause your essay too heavily at the end of each paragraph if they are heavy-handed repetitions of the topic sentence, use the topic sentence of the *next* paragraph to bridge that gap of white space between paragraphs by regrouping where you are in your larger argument and clarifying how what you just finished saying relates to where your essay is heading in the coming paragraph. Topic sentences drive an essay forward; mini-conclusions sometimes stall it.

Conclusion: Paragraphs as Punctuation

To reiterate the initial point, it is useful to think of paragraphs as punctuation that organize your ideas in a readable way. Each paragraph should be an irreplaceable node within a coherent sequence of logic. In a successful, coherent college paper, the structure of each paragraph reflects its indispensable role within the overall piece. Make every bit count and have each part situated within the whole.

Attributions

CC licensed content, Original

- Revision and Adaptation. **Provided by**: Lumen Learning. **License**: *CC BY-NC-SA: Attribution-NonCommercial-ShareAlike*
- Revision and Adaptation. **Authored by**: Gillian Paku. **Provided by**: SUNY Geneseo. **License**: *CC BY: Attribution*

CC licensed content, Shared previously

- Cohesion and coherence. **Authored by**: Amy Guptill. **Provided by**: The College at Brockport, SUNY. **Located at**: http://text-

7. Ibid., 74.

Introductions and Conclusions

A key piece of advice many writers either do not ever get or don't believe is that **it's not necessary to write introductions first or to write conclusions last.** Just because the introduction appears first and the conclusion appears last doesn't mean they have to be written that way. Just because you walk into a building through the door doesn't mean the door was built first. And the larger frame for this point about being flexible in your thinking, and in the writing that both reflects and shapes that thinking, is that academic writing is not a "one size fits all" enterprise. INTD 106 does not present a set of rules, especially in this module on the writing process. INTD 105 in conjunction with INTD 106 will not teach you everything you need to know about writing academically in one semester; this advice and the introduction to conventions of standard, academic prose function partly to share knowledge evenly among students who have taken very different paths to Geneseo, but also to give you a basis in the principles of good writing—principles that may well resonate differently for you in your first year than they do in your junior year. If you don't revisit the principles, you won't hear the resonances, so we encourage you to think about yourself as a constantly developing writer.

Introductions

In working toward the overall goal of orienting readers, introductions often

- lay out the stakes for the piece of writing—that is, why the reader should bother reading on. Situate your writing within a larger scholarly conversation.

- articulate a main thesis fully. The detail will generate the key vocabulary that will give coherence to your whole essay, so don't be vague, broad, or coy, promising some really important claim based on really amazing evidence but refusing to say yet what that claim is. Readers don't pick up college essays for the sheer suspense of it all…. The key vocabulary you generate in your introduction will recur in your topic sentences; when your topic sentences follow through logically and predictably on the claim you make in the introduction, your essay is focused. Your readers, far from feeling as if the surprise has been ruined when your essay turns out to support your thesis, will thank you for not confusing them.

- suggest the bodies of evidence that you'll draw on to prove your claim, but DON'T PROVIDE THE EVIDENCE ITSELF. Again, in your introduction, you are generating key terms that you will develop later. Development and evidence are what body paragraphs are for.

- provide background about a topic that will make newcomers feel welcome and confident about reading on.

- locate readers in a specific time and/or place or include some other method to make the ideas seem concrete.

- include an ethical appeal, with which you (explicitly or implicitly) show that you've done your homework and are credible. NOTE TO SELF: don't be grandiose about your appeal. The aim is not to shock and awe your readers into submission with your superior intellect, or, as more often happens, to present some obvious ethical idea that, for all its undeniable validity, doesn't (or shouldn't) come as news to anyone. Too often, student essays collapse under the weight of an idea that may well be really important, but shouldn't be the rhetorical highpoint of your introduction because, frankly, it's obvious. You risk sounding very high-school by announcing the equivalent of, "And thus I shall demonstrate, through this carefully selected evidence, that true love is based on mutual affection, not finances" (or that "we should, in fact, embrace diversity," or that "academic intelligence is not the same as 'street smarts'"). Yes, these things are true, and they are very important ideas to grasp, but they are so true that you risk obscuring the specific ethical appeal in your ideas by collapsing it into broad statements that your reader very probably does not need to hear as if they were "the big reveal."

Conclusions

Conclusions usually

- bookend a story or conversation that started in the introduction.

- reiterate an ethical appeal, with which you (explicitly or implicitly) connect the logic of the argument to a more passionate reason intended to sway the reader, or in which you restate your central stakes in a rhetorically heightened fashion because this is your last chance to make your point.

- issue a call to action.

Ideally, a conclusion will work in tandem with an introduction, having some kind of "call back" element to remind your reader of the powerful opening you provided. Be careful, though, about summarizing your argument in a conclusion. If you stated your thesis clearly in your introduction and unfolded the arc of that thesis via topic sentences that constantly reminded readers where you and they were situated in your argument, then reiterating your argument in its entirety can be a boring waste of a final paragraph.

One related pet peeve of college professors is when students give the clearest statement of their thesis *in the conclusion:* "And now to sum it all up, let me finally tell you what my point was, and how I thought my evidence supported it. And out." To the person who just read through 5-10 pages of college-level material, the summary conclusion is frustrating: generate interest and a sense that you have something coherent and important to say at the *start* of your essay. Then go ahead and write that essay. Then end with an engaged reminder of the stakes of your argument, but NOT with a plodding, abstracted recapitulation of the steps you took along the way. Readers were right there with you for the whole trip, attending to your every twist and turn, looking always for your guidance and direction. If you guided them well, you don't need to tell them where they just were: they know. And really don't expect them to be excited if, instead of guiding them, you blindfolded them and stumbled along (often down what seemed to be detours and dead ends, or in circles), only to graciously present them with a detailed map of the journey they wish they'd known they were taking when they've already arrived (exhausted) at the destination.

Additional, less exasperated advice for conclusions is found in the following video.

- https://youtu.be/2L7aeO9fBzE

Attributions

CC licensed content, Original

- Revision and Adaptation. **Provided by**: Lumen Learning. **License**: *CC BY-NC-SA: Attribution-NonCommercial-ShareAlike*
- Revision and Adaptation. **Authored by**: Gillian Paku. **Provided by**: SUNY Geneseo. **License**: *CC BY: Attribution*

CC licensed content, Shared previously

- Introductions and Conclusions. **Authored by**: Jay Jordan. **Provided by**: The University of Utah University Writing Program. **Project**: Open2010. **License**: *CC BY-NC-SA: Attribution-NonCommercial-ShareAlike*

All rights reserved content

- Writing Grabby Intro Sentences by Shmoop. **Authored by**: Shmoop. **Located at**: https://youtu.be/Rkefst9D6n0. **License**: *All Rights Reserved*. **License Terms**: Standard YouTube License
- Writing a Killer Conclusion. **Authored by**: Shmoop. **Located at**: https://youtu.be/2L7aeO9fBzE. **License**: *All Rights Reserved*. **License Terms**: Standard YouTube License

Higher-Order Concerns for Editing

Introduction

Regardless of writers' levels of experience or areas of expertise, many struggle with revision, a component of the writing process that encompasses everything from transformative changes in content and argumentation to minor corrections in grammar and punctuation. Perhaps because revision involves so many forms of modification, it is the focus of most scientific writing guides and handbooks. Revision can be daunting; how does one progress from initial drafts (called "rough drafts" for good reason) to a polished piece of scholarly writing?

Developing a process for revision can help writers produce thoughtful, polished texts and grow their written communication skills. Consider, then, a systematic approach to revision, including strategies to employ at every step of the process.

A System for Approaching Revision

Generally, revision should be approached in a top-down manner by addressing **higher-order concerns** before moving on to **lower-order concerns**. In writing studies, the term "higher order" is used to denote major or global issues such as thesis, argumentation, and organization, whereas "lower order" is used to denote minor or local issues such as grammar and mechanics.[1] The more analytical work of revising higher-order concerns often has ramifications for the entire piece. Perhaps in refining the argument, a writer will realize that the discussion section does not fully consider the study's implications. Or, a writer will try a new organizational scheme and find that a paragraph no longer fits and should be cut. Such revisions may have far-reaching implications for the text.

Dedicating time to tweaking wording or correcting grammatical errors is unproductive if the sentence will be changed or deleted. Focusing on higher-order concerns before lower-order concerns allows writers to revise more effectively and efficiently.

1. McAndrew DA, Registad TJ. *Tutoring writing: a practical guide for conferences*. Portsmouth (NH): Boynton/Cook; 2001.

Revision Strategies

Bearing in mind the general system of revising from higher- to lower-order concerns, you can employ several revision strategies.

- **Begin by evaluating how your argument addresses your rhetorical situation**—that is, the specific context surrounding your writing, including the audience, purpose, and author, as well as any constraints (the assignment)).[2]

    ◦ For example, you might one day write a medical article describing a new treatment. If the target journal's audience comes from a variety of disciplines, you might need to include substantial background explanation, consider the implications for practitioners and scholars in multiple fields, and define technical terms. By contrast, if you are addressing a highly specialized audience, you may be able to dispense with many of the background explanations and definitions because of your shared knowledge base. You may consider the implications only for specialists, as they are your primary audience. Because this sort of revision affects the entire text, beginning by analyzing your rhetorical situation is effective.

- **Analyze your thesis or main argument for clarity and global coherence**. Do all the key terms you used in your topic sentences appear in your introduction – at least in a suggestive form that means that no paragraph will seem to a reader to come out of the blue? Between the intro and the body, you should be reiterating the key terms of your specific topic, your claim about that topic, and the kinds of evidence you'll employ. Did you say anything as you wrote the paragraphs that has altered your draft thesis in ways that you now need to reflect? Welcome such nuance and complexity: the point of your thesis is to seem insightful, not simple, so develop your thesis rather than cutting complexity—or evidence!

- **Evaluate the global organization of your text by writing a reverse outline**. Unlike traditional outlines, which are written before drafting, reverse outlines reflect the content of written drafts.

    ◦ In a separate document or in your text's margins, record the main idea of each paragraph. Then, consider whether the order of your ideas is logical. This method also will help you identify ideas that are out of place or digressive. You may also evaluate organization by printing the text and cutting it up so that each paragraph appears on a separate piece of paper. You may then easily reorder the paragraphs to test different organizational schemes.

- **Find another reader.** At Geneseo, the Writing Learning Center (WLC) is staffed by students who will, for free, read and discuss your essay with you, one-on-one, for thirty minutes at a time. Those tutors have been employed because of their excellent writing skills, and they are trained to look for all the tips and techniques you are asked to consider in INTD 106 and INTD 105. They not only have the advantage of deep familiarity with college-level writing both in practice and in theory, but they also provide for you something no writers can provide for themselves: a brain that isn't your own. WLC tutors can tell you when they can't follow your logic or were surprised by a term that you didn't prepare them to expect, even though you thought the links or scaffolding were clear. Tutors use other tutors to help them revise their own work; professors use other professors to help them revise their own work. No serious academic at any

2. Bitzer L. "The rhetorical situation." *Philos Rhetoric* 1968; 1 (1): 1-14.

level submits written work that no one else has helped them revise. That's why you practice peer review in class. You can achieve something of the same effect by writing your paper a few days in advance of the deadline, forgetting about it, then pulling it back out and seeing if it still makes sense to you. Or you can bother your friends in the dorm to read what you've written. And also hope that they will take thirty minutes and then give you honest and constructive feedback. Or you can visit your professor's office hours with your draft and some specific questions or issues you would like to discuss. Or you can do all of the above. Just remember that the WLC is open till 11 o'clock most weeknights, and the tutors are friendly and welcoming, and you really should make their acquaintance at the start of your time at Geneseo.

Completing a Post-Draft Outline

The reverse outline mentioned above is also known as a **post-draft outline**. Guidance for how to complete one for an entire essay draft, as well as for an individual problematic paragraph, are found in this presentation.

Attributions

CC licensed content, Original

- Revision and Adaptation. **Provided by**: Lumen Learning. **License**: *CC BY: Attribution*
- Revision and Adaptation. **Authored by**: Gillian Paku. **Provided by**: SUNY Geneseo. **License**: *CC BY: Attribution*

CC licensed content, Shared previously

- Revision Strategies. **Authored by**: Kristin Messuri. **Located at**: http://pulmonarychronicles.com/ojs/index.php?journal=pulmonarychronicles&page=article&op=view&path%5B%5D=263&path%5B%5D=662. **Project**: Pulmonary Chronicles. **License**: *CC BY: Attribution*
- Post-Draft Outline. **Authored by**: Alexis McMillan-Clifton. **Provided by**: Tacoma Community College. **Located at**: http://prezi.com/ilic1tcomvne/?utm_campaign=share&utm_medium=copy&rc=ex0share. **License**: *CC BY: Attribution*
- Image of arrow. **Authored by**: ClkerFreeVectorImages. **Located at**: https://pixabay.com/en/arrow-down-blue-handdrawn-pointing-310601/. **License**: *CC0: No Rights Reserved*

Lower-Order Concerns for Proofreading

Previously we examined higher-order concerns as part of the revision stage of the writing process. Once we move to the proofreading stage, it's time to consider the lower-order concerns. The difference is simple: higher-order concerns are global issues, or issues that affect how a reader understands the entire paper; lower-order concerns are issues that don't *necessarily* interrupt understanding of the writing by themselves.

HOCs	LOCs
Audience	Grammar
Thesis statement	Punctuation
Organization	Citation
Focus	Spelling
Development of ideas	Sentence structure

You may find yourself thinking, "Well, it depends," or, "But what if…?" You're absolutely right to think so. These lists are just guidelines; every writer will have a different hierarchy of concerns. Always try to think in terms of, "Does this affect my understanding of the writing?"

Are HOCs More Important than LOCs?

No, not necessarily. Higher-order concerns tend to interrupt a reader's understanding of the writing, and that's why they need to be addressed first. However, if a lower-order concern becomes a major obstacle, then it naturally becomes a higher priority. Tellingly, many people judge how well others can write by focusing on their mechanics; errors in punctuation and spelling are more obvious to most readers than gaps in logic or underdeveloped thesis statements.

Here are some issues that may be more difficult to categorize as explicitly higher- or lower-order since they may largely depend on the piece writing. If you think, "It depends," make notes about the circumstances under which these issues could be a HOC or a LOC.

- evaluating sources

- citation method

- style

- paragraph structure

- active vs. passive voice

- format

The Importance of ~~Speling~~ Spelling

Word-processing programs usually have a spell-checker, and you should TURN IT ON, but you should still carefully check for correct changes to your words. This is because automatic spell-checkers may not always understand the **context** of a word.

Misspelling a word might seem like a minor mistake, but it can reflect very poorly on a writer. It suggests (however fairly or not) one of two things: either the writer does not care enough about their work to proof-read it, or they do not know their topic well enough to properly spell words related to it. Either way, spelling errors will make a reader less likely to trust a writer's authority.

The best way to ensure that a paper has no spelling errors is to look for them during the proofreading stage of the writing process. You can force yourself not to skim if you read the document backwards, word for word, looking for spelling errors. If the error is actually a typo ("teh" for "the" is common), you may have made the mistake more than once. You can use the find-and-replace function to search the document electronically for all instances of "teh" and correct them with the click of a button.

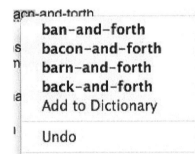

Sometimes, a writer just doesn't know how to spell the word they want to use. This may be because the word is technical jargon or comes from a language other than their own. Other times, it may be a proper name that they have not encountered before. Anytime you want to use a word but are unsure of how to spell it, do not guess. Instead, check a dictionary or other reference work to find its proper spelling. Look back at the original sources for proper nouns.

How to Address Other Lower-Order Concerns

Analyze your use of source material. Check any paraphrases and quotations against the original texts. Quotations should replicate the original author's words, while paraphrases should maintain the original author's meaning but have altered language and sentence structures. For each source, confirm that you have adhered to the preferred style guide for the target journal or other venue.

Consider individual sentences in terms of grammar, mechanics, and punctuation. Many concerns can be revised by isolating and examining different elements of the text. Read the text sentence by sentence, considering the grammar and sentence structure. Remember, a sentence may be grammatically correct and still confuse readers. If you notice a pattern—say, a tendency to misplace modifiers or add unnecessary commas—read the paper looking only for that error. Throughout the writing process and especially at this stage of revision, keep a dictionary, a thesaurus, and a writing handbook nearby (check out the Internet…). This process sounds laborious, and it might well be the first few times you undertake it, but you will learn pretty quickly what your bad habits are, and you can change them at the beginning of your college career. Better to work laboriously through a few five-page papers in your first year and improve your writing than to have to tear apart a senior thesis.

Strategies such as reading aloud and seeking feedback are useful at all points in the revision process. Reading aloud will give you distance from the text and prevent you from skimming over what is actually written on the page. This strategy will help you to identify both higher-order concerns, such as missing concepts, and lower-order concerns, such as typos. If you can't bear to read your own work aloud, you can paste it into Google Translate and have their electronic voice read it for you.

Even more importantly, seeking feedback will allow you to test your ideas and writing on real readers. Seek feedback from readers both inside and outside of your target audience in order to gain different perspectives. Visit Geneseo's Writing Learning Center (WLC) or your professor's office hours.

Proofreading Advice

The following video features two student tutors from the Writing and Reading Center at Fresno City College. In addition to great guidance about proofreading strategies, they also offer insights about what to expect when working with WLC tutors here at Geneseo.

- https://youtu.be/STa5W4gm2qY

Attributions

CC licensed content, Original

- Revision and Adaptation. **Provided by**: Lumen Learning. **License**: *CC BY-SA: Attribution-ShareAlike*
- Revision and Adaptation. **Authored by**: Gillian Paku. **Provided by**: SUNY Geneseo. **License**: *CC BY: Attribution*

CC licensed content, Shared previously

- Image of students. **Authored by**: Anne Petersen. **Located at**: https://flic.kr/p/8NKsze. **License**: *CC BY-NC-ND: Attribution-Non-Commercial-NoDerivatives*
- Writing Center Theory and Pedagogy. **Provided by**: Missouri State University. **Located at**: https://msuwritingcenter.wiki-spaces.com/Writing+Center+Theory+and+Pedagogy. **Project**: MSU Writing Center Wiki. **License**: *CC BY-SA: Attribution-Share-Alike*
- Revision Strategies. **Authored by**: Kristin Messuri. **Located at**: http://pulmonarychronicles.com/ojs/index.php?journal=pulmonarychronicles&page=article&op=view&path%5B%5D=263&path%5B%5D=662. **Project**: Pulmonary Chronicles. **License**: *CC BY: Attribution*

All rights reserved content

- Proofreading. **Authored by**: FCCTutors. **Located at**: https://youtu.be/STa5W4gm2qY?t=17s. **License**: *All Rights Reserved*. **License Terms**: Standard YouTube License

6. Research

Why Is Research Important?

The Pacific Northwest Tree Octopus

A few years ago a little-known animal species suddenly made headlines. The charming but elusive Tree Octopus became the focal point of Internet scrutiny.

If you've never heard of the Pacific Northwest Tree Octopus, take a few minutes to learn more about it on this website, devoted to saving the endangered species:

- http://zapatopi.net/treeoctopus/.

You can also watch this brief video for more about the creatures:

- https://youtu.be/SU-yq_IJhtU

Source Reliability

If you're starting to get the feeling that something's not quite adding up here, you're on the right track. The Tree Octopus website is a hoax, although a beautifully done one. There is no such creature (unfortunately).

It's easy to assume that "digital natives"–people who have grown up using the Internet–are naturally web-savvy. However, a 2011 U.S. Department of Education study that used the Tree Octopus website as a focal point revealed that students who encountered this website completely fell for it. According to an NBC news story by Scott Beaulieu, "In fact, not only did the students believe that the tree octopus was real, they actually refused to believe researchers when they told them the creature was fake."[1]

While this is a relatively harmless example of a joke website, it helps to demonstrate that anyone can say anything they want on the Internet. If you have paid even the slightest attention to politics since 2016, you will have a particularly heightened sense of how dangerous real "fake news" can be in our society, and what a potent charge it is to allege that any given story is or isn't fake. Here's one brief (and lightly edited) excerpt from a CBS *60 Minutes* episode from March 2017 on "Fake News":

"To get an idea of who reads fake news we turned to the Trade Desk, the Internet advertising firm that helps companies steer clear of fraudulent sites. Jeff Green is the CEO.

Jeff Green: *So the first thing that we found out is that it is definitely a phenomenon that affects both sides.*

Scott Pelley: *Liberals and Conservatives.*

Jeff Green: *There is no question they're both affected.*

One fake story Green examined claimed that the Congress was plotting to overthrow President Trump. He was surprised to learn that right-leaning fake news overwhelmingly attracted readers in their 40s and 50s. And he also found fake-news readers on the left were more likely to be affluent and college-educated.

Jeff Green: *That shocked me.*

Scott Pelley: *Why?*

Jeff Green:*I think I thought the same way that many Americans perhaps think, [which] is that fake news was a phenomenon that only tricked the uneducated. Not true. Just not. The data shows it's just not true.*

Green's analysis showed fake news consumers tend to stay in what he calls "Internet echo chambers," reading similar articles rather than reaching for legitimate news.

Jeff Green: *What is most concerning is the amount of influence that they seem to have because the people that spend time in those echo chambers are the ones that vote.*

---

1. http://www.nbcconnecticut.com/news/local/An-Octopus-in-a-Tree-Seems-Real-115497484.html

After the election, Facebook and Twitter recognized the threat to their credibility and changed their programs to make it harder for fakes to proliferate. Both companies declined to be interviewed."[2]

The ability to evaluate what you're looking at is crucial: a good-looking website can be very convincing, regardless of what it says. Such slickness makes irresponsible use of the principles we emphasize here in the INTD 106 modules on grammar and documentation: when writers pay attention to detail in content and form, readers are inclined to give them the benefit of the doubt that the argument itself is careful and accurate. Of course, such trust can be lost if the accuracy is only cosmetic, but a reader has to work a little harder to see beyond a slick surface. The more you research, the more you'll see that sometimes the least professional-looking websites offer the most credible information, and the most professional-looking websites can be full of biased, misleading, or outright wrong information. To help you hone these important skills of evaluation, Milne Library has an extensive Research Guide titled, "Decoding Fake News" (http://libguides.geneseo.edu/newsliteracy) and also hosts a **GOLD workshop** (**G**eneseo **O**pportunities for **L**eadership **D**evelopment) [https://gold.geneseo.edu/currentyearschedule.php] called Fake News, Bias, and Perspective: How to Sort Fact From Fiction (http://libguides.geneseo.edu/FakeNewsGold)

Both the Research Guide and the GOLD workshop touch on the important idea of *confirmation bias*, which is related to what the cognitive scientist Steven Pinker calls "the curse of knowledge" (we discuss that idea in the Writing Process module of INTD 106). Essentially, both confirmation bias and the curse of knowledge remind us how difficult it is to get beyond–or imagine a reader who comes from outside–what we already know.

There are no hard and fast rules when it comes to resource reliability. Each new source has to be evaluated on its own merit, and this module will offer you a set of tools to help you do just that.

USING SOURCES IN RESEARCH

In this module, you'll learn about tips and techniques to enable you to find, analyze, integrate, and document sources in your research. These are skills that will be reinforced in INTD 105, and all INTD 105 sections meet at least once physically in Milne Library, with a Research Instruction Librarian.

Attributions

CC licensed content, Original

- Why Is Research Important?. **Provided by**: Lumen Learning. **License**: *CC BY: Attribution*

- Find, analyze, integrate, document graphic. **Authored by**: Kim Louie for Lumen Learning. **License**: *CC BY: Attribution*

2. This link https://cbsnews.com/news/how-fake-news-find-your-social-media-feeds takes you to a transcript of that CBS 60 Minutes episode from March 2017 on "Fake News." We are not asking you to watch the video—access isn't free. You don't need to read the whole transcript for INTD 106, either, but you're welcome to read it if the topic of fake news interests you.

Preliminary Research Strategies

THE RESEARCH PROCESS

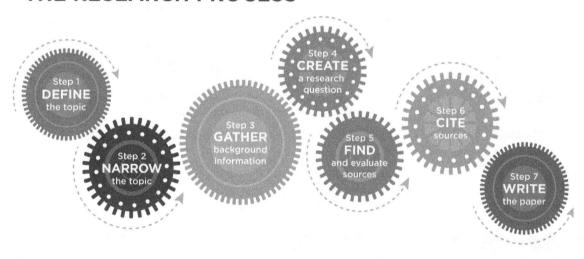

The first step towards writing a research paper is pretty obvious: find sources. Not everything that you find will be good, and those that are good are not always easily found. Instructors are very familiar with the phenomenon whereby a student has left research till the last minute, uses the first result that pops up on Google, and then tries to force a merely tangential source to seem central to the thesis of the student's paper.

It's not pretty.

Having a focused and confident idea of what you're looking for—what will most help you develop your essay and enforce your thesis—will help guide your process.

Example of a Research Process

A good research process should go through these steps:

1. Decide on the topic.

2. Narrow the topic in order to generate more key terms that will narrow search parameters.

3. Create a question that your research will address.

4. Generate sub-questions from your main question.

5. Determine what kind of sources are best for your argument.

6. Create a bibliography as you gather and reference sources.

Each of these is described in greater detail below.

Preliminary Research Strategies

A research plan should begin after you can clearly identify the focus of your argument. First, inform yourself about the basics of your topic (Wikipedia and general online searches are great starting points). Be sure you've read all the assigned texts and carefully read the prompt as you gather preliminary information. This stage is sometimes called **pre-research or prefocus exploration**.

Books, books, books …Do not start research haphazardly—come up with a plan first.

A broad online search will yield thousands of sources, which no one could be expected to read through. To make it easier on yourself, the next step is to narrow your focus. Think about what kind of position or stance you can take on the topic. What about it strikes you as most interesting? Refer back to the prewriting stage of the writing process, which will come in handy here.

Preliminary Search Tips

1. It is okay to start with Wikipedia as a reference, but do not use it as an official source if you have been asked to use peer-reviewed material. Look at the links and references at the bottom of the page for more ideas.

2. Use "Ctrl+F" to find certain words within a webpage in order to jump to the sections of the article that interest you.

3. Use Google Advanced Search to be more specific in your search. You can also use tricks to be more specific within the main Google Search Engine:

    *   Use quotation marks to narrow your search from just tanks in WWII to "Tanks in WWII" or "Tanks" in "WWII".

    *   Find specific types of websites by adding "site:.gov" or "site:.edu" or

“site:.org”. You can also search for specific file types like “filetype:.pdf”.

4. Click on “Search Tools” under the search bar in Google and select “Any time” to see a list of options for time periods to help limit your search. You can find information just in the past month or year, or even for a custom range.

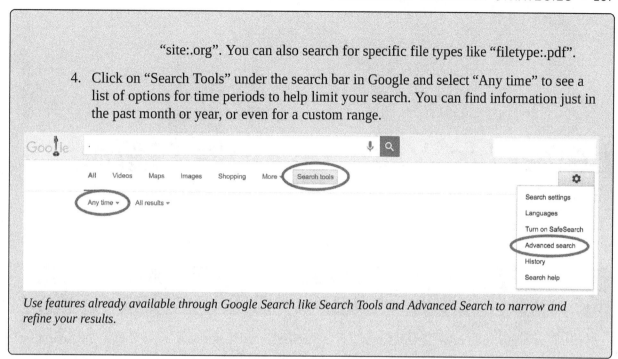

Use features already available through Google Search like Search Tools and Advanced Search to narrow and refine your results.

As you narrow your focus, create a list of questions that you’ll need to answer in order to write a good essay on the topic. The research process will help you answer these questions.

Minerva's Research Tip:
If any part of this process is unfamiliar to you, don't hesitate to make an appointment for a one-on-one Research Consultation. Milne's Librarians are experts at research management practices and know of tools that can assist you with keeping your information organized.

Another part of your research plan should include identifying the type of sources you want to gather. Track your sources in a bibliography list and then jot down notes about the book, article, or document and how it will be useful to your essay. It may seem tedious at first, but as you progress to the writing phase of the paper, this practice will save you a lot of time later—you’ll thank yourself!

Attributions

CC licensed content, Original

- Revision and Adaptation. **Provided by**: Lumen Learning. **License**: *CC BY-SA: Attribution-ShareAlike*
- The Research Process graphic. **Authored by**: Kim Louie for Lumen Learning. **License**: *CC BY: Attribution*
- Revision and Adaptation. **Authored by**: Gillian Paku. **Provided by**: SUNY Geneseo. **License**: *CC BY: Attribution*

CC licensed content, Shared previously

- Organizing Your Research Plan. **Provided by**: Boundless. **Located at**: https://www.boundless.com/writing/textbooks/boundless-writing-textbook/the-research-process-2/organizing-your-research-plan-262/organizing-your-research-plan-51-1304/. **Project**: Boundless Writing. **License**: *CC BY-SA: Attribution-ShareAlike*

Level Up Your Google Game

10 Google Quick Tips

We all know how to Google…but we may not be getting as much out of it as we'd like. The following video walks through ten really useful tips for getting you closer to what you're looking for. Take the time to watch it now: you'll be glad you did!

- https://youtu.be/R0DQfwc72PM

Getting More Out of Google

For a visual representation of additional online search tips, follow this link: https://www.hackcollege.com/blog/2011/11/23/infographic-get-more-out-of-google.html

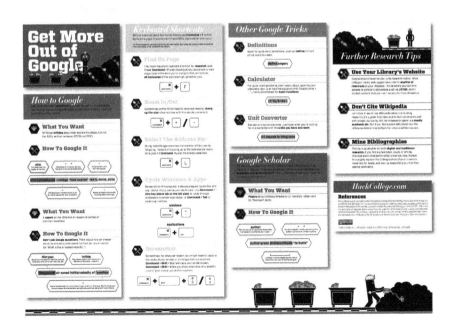

Attributions

Intermediate Research Strategies

Popular vs. *Scholarly* Sources

Research-based writing assignments in college will often require that you use **scholarly sources** in your essay. INTD 105 certainly asks you to be able to locate such sources and to know how to distinguish them from non-scholarly sources like the types of articles found in newspapers or general-interest magazines. Below is a chart listing some of the most common criteria which you can examine to make this determination:

	Popular Source	**Scholarly Source**
Intended Audience	Broad: readers are not expected to know much about the topic already	Narrow: readers are expected to be familiar with the topic beforehand
Author	Journalist: may have a broad area of specialization (war correspondent, media critic)	Subject Matter Expert: often has a degree or other academic qualification in the subject and/or extensive experience on the topic
Research	Includes quotations from interviews. No bibliography.	Includes summaries, paraphrases, and quotations from previous writing done on the subject. Footnotes and citations. Ends with bibliography.
Publication Standards	Article is reviewed by editor and proofreader	Article has gone through a peer-review process, where experts on the field have given input before publication

Still not feeling entirely sure of how to identify and distinguish scholarly vs non-scholarly materials? Go to Milne's Research Guide, **"Distinguish Scholarly vs. Popular Sources,"** (https://libguides.geneseo.edu/scholarlyvspopular) which will link you to videos for a more detailed explanation.

Where to Find Scholarly Sources

The first step in finding scholarly resources is to look in the right place. Sites like Google, Yahoo, and Wikipedia are good for locating popular sources, but if you want something you can cite in a scholarly paper, ***you need to search for it in a scholarly database.*** These are information sources provided and paid for by your tuition dollars, via the library.

Two common scholarly databases are **Academic Search Premier** and **ProQuest**, although many others are also available that focus on specific topics. **Milne Library's website** lists the most commonly used ones on the main page under **"Databases",** and the complete A-Z list of the ~150 resources available to you via Milne Library is found under **"More Databases"** below (red arrows) .

You have another incredible resource at your fingertips: Milne's librarians! For assistance in locating resources, you will find that librarians are extremely knowledgeable and may help you uncover sources you would never have found on your own.

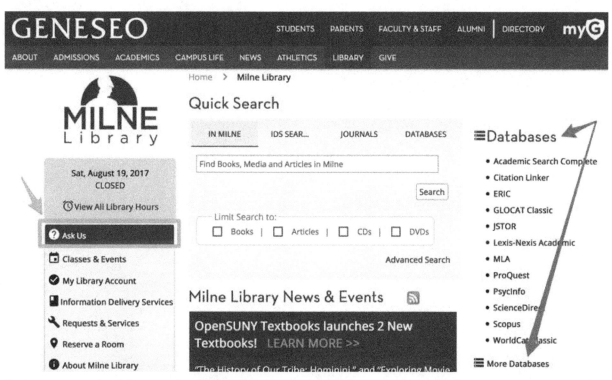

Perhaps your school has a microfilm collection, an extensive genealogy database, or access to another library's catalog. You will not know unless you utilize the valuable skills available to you, so be sure to find out how to get in touch with a research instruction librarian for support!

Simply click on the **"Ask Us"** button (green arrow) on the left side of Milne Library's home page to get started.

Attributions

CC licensed content, Original

- Revision and Adaptation. **Provided by**: Lumen Learning. **License**: *CC BY-SA: Attribution-ShareAlike*
- Finding sources image. **Authored by**: Kim Louie for Lumen Learning. **License**: *CC BY: Attribution*
- Revision and Adaptation. **Authored by**: Gillian Paku. **Provided by**: SUNY Geneseo. **License**: *CC BY: Attribution*

CC licensed content, Shared previously

- Choosing Search Terms for Sources. **Provided by**: Boundless. **Located at**: https://www.boundless.com/writing/textbooks/boundless-writing-textbook/the-research-process-2/finding-your-sources-263/choosing-search-terms-for-sources-53-540/. **Project**: Boundless Writing. **License**: *CC BY-SA: Attribution-ShareAlike*

Google Scholar

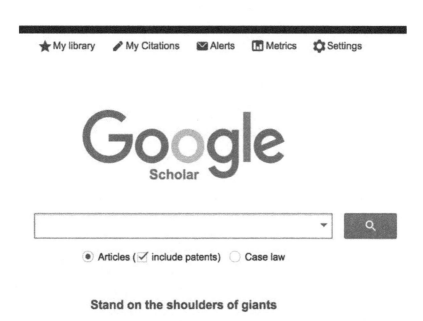

An increasingly popular search engine for locating articles is **Google Scholar.** At first glance, it appears and functions very much like a regular "Google search." However, behind the scenes, it filters your results with the aim to include the vast majority of *scholarly* resources openly available via the Internet. While it has some limitations (like not including a list of which journals they include in their searches), it's a very useful tool if you want to cast a wide net, and it's getting better all the time.

Here are three tips for using Google Scholar effectively:

1. **Include your topic field (e.g. economics, psychology, French, etc.) as one of your keywords**. If you just put in "crime," for example, Google Scholar's search engine will return all sorts of stuff from sociology, psychology, geography, and history. If your paper is on crime in French literature, your best sources may be buried under thousands of papers from other disciplines. A set of search terms like "crime French literature modern" will get you to relevant sources much faster.

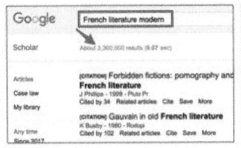 

2. **Don't EVER pay out-of-pocket for an article**. When you click on links to articles in Google Scholar, you may end up on a publisher's site that tells you that you can download the article for $20 or $30. ***Don't do it!*** Milne Library provides you access to virtually all the published academic literature through their award-winning **IDS** (Information Delivery Services.) **Always look for the "Get It" button.** that's the easiest way to request the items that you need. Having said that, there are many systems working behind the scenes to make it that easy and sometimes the may function incorrectly. Should that happen, capture the work you've done and find a librarian to help you; write down the key information (authors' names, title, journal title, volume, issue number, year, page numbers) and get help.

3. **Use the "cited by" feature**. Finding one great hit on Google Scholar is great, but that is only the beginning. Follow along with the tutorial example, below and see the power of this search engine.

1. Begin with good search terms for locating resources relevant to your topic. 2. The search on "Crime economics" yields 1.4 million results, but glancing at the results we notice "The economics of crime deterrence: A survey of theory and evidence" by Cameron.	
3. Looking more closely at this citation, we notice that it was published in 1988. That's nearly 30 years ago, and we want something a little more recent. Fortunately, when we look below the first couple of sentences about the article, we see a link to "Cited by 445". 4. Clicking this link will run the search for the 445 articles that have cited Cameron's paper, many of which will have related theses.	

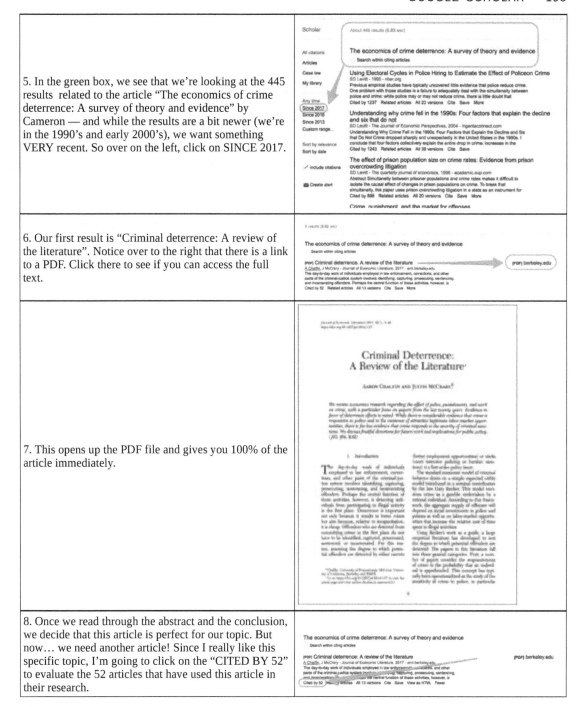

5. In the green box, we see that we're looking at the 445 results related to the article "The economics of crime deterrence: A survey of theory and evidence" by Cameron — and while the results are a bit newer (we're in the 1990's and early 2000's), we want something VERY recent. So over on the left, click on SINCE 2017.	
6. Our first result is "Criminal deterrence: A review of the literature". Notice over to the right that there is a link to a PDF. Click there to see if you can access the full text.	
7. This opens up the PDF file and gives you 100% of the article immediately.	
8. Once we read through the abstract and the conclusion, we decide that this article is perfect for our topic. But now… we need another article! Since I really like this specific topic, I'm going to click on the "CITED BY 52" to evaluate the 52 articles that have used this article in their research.	

Using Google Scholar

Watch this video to get a better idea of how to utilize Google Scholar for finding articles. While this video shows specifics for setting up an account with Eastern Michigan University, the same principles apply to other colleges and universities. Ask Milne's librarians if you have more questions.

- https://youtu.be/oqnjhjISHFk

Attributions

CC licensed content, Original

- Revision and Adaptation. **Provided by**: Lumen Learning. **License**: *CC BY-NC-SA: Attribution-NonCommercial-ShareAlike*
- Revision and Adaptation. **Authored by**: Gillian Paku. **Provided by**: SUNY Geneseo. **License**: *CC BY: Attribution*

CC licensed content, Shared previously

- Secondary Sources in Their Natural Habitats. **Authored by**: Amy Guptill. **Provided by**: The College at Brockport, SUNY. **Located at**: http://pressbooks.opensuny.org/writing-in-college-from-competence-to-excellence/chapter/4/. **License**: *CC BY-NC-SA: Attribution-NonCommercial-ShareAlike*

All rights reserved content

- Using Google Scholar. **Authored by**: EMU Library. **Located at**: https://youtu.be/oqnjhjISHFk. **License**: *All Rights Reserved*. **License Terms**: Standard YouTube License

How to Search in a Library Database

As we learned earlier, the strongest articles to support your academic writing projects will come from scholarly sources. Finding exactly what you need becomes specialized at this point, and requires a new set of searching strategies beyond even Google Scholar.

For this kind of research, you'll want to utilize library databases, which allow you to search scholarly journals. Many journals are sponsored by academic associations. Most of your professors belong to some big, general one (such as the Modern Language Association, the American Psychological Association, or the American Physical Society) and one or more smaller ones organized around particular areas of interest and expertise (such as the Association for the Study of Food and Society or the International Association for Statistical Computing).

Finding articles in databases

Milne Library invests a lot of time and care into making sure you have access to the sources you need for your writing projects. Our Research Instruction Librarians have created research guides that point you to the best databases for the specific discipline or subject and, sometimes even for a specific course. Librarians are eager to help you succeed with your research—it's their job and they love it!—so don't be shy about asking.

Scholarly databases like the ones Milne Library subscribes to work differently than search engines like Google and Yahoo because they offer sophisticated tools and techniques for searching that can improve your results.

Databases may look different but they can all be used in similar ways. Most databases can be searched using **keywords** or **fields**. In a keyword search, you want to search for the main concepts or synonyms of your keywords. A field is a specific part of a record in a database. Common fields that can be searched are *author, title, subject,* or *abstract.* If you already know the author of a specific article, entering their "Last Name, First Name" in the author field will pull more relevant records than a keyword search. This will ensure all results are articles written by the author and not articles about that author or with that author's name. For example, a keyword search for "Albert Einstein" will search anywhere in the record for Albert Einstein and reveal 12, 719 results. Instead, a field search for Author: "Einstein, Albert" will show 54 results, all written by Albert Einstein.

Practice: Keyword Search

1. Identify the keywords in the following research question: "How does repeated pesticide use in agriculture impact soil and groundwater pollution?"

2. When you search, it's helpful to think of synonyms for your keywords to examine various results. What synonyms can you think of for the keywords identified in the question above?

Sometimes you already have a citation (maybe you found it on Google Scholar or saw it linked through another source), but want to find the article. Everything you need to locate your article is already found in the citation.

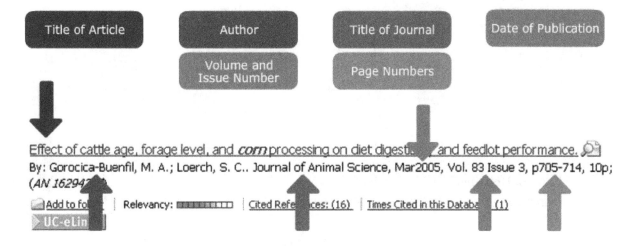

CC-BY-NC-SA image from UCI Libraries Begin Research Online Workshop Tutorial.

Many databases, including the library catalog, offer tools to help you narrow or expand your search. Take advantage of these. The most common tools are Boolean searching and truncation.

Boolean Searching

Boolean searching allows you to use AND, OR, and NOT to combine your search terms. Here are some examples:

1. **"Endangered Species" AND "Global Warming"** When you combine search terms with AND, you'll get results in which BOTH terms are present. Using AND limits the number of results because all search terms must appear in your results.

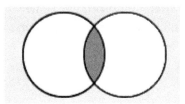

"Endangered Species" AND "Global Warming" will narrow your search results to where the two concepts overlap.

2. **"Arizona Prisons" OR "Rhode Island Prisons"** When you use OR, you'll get results with EITHER search term. Using OR increases the number of results because either search term can appear in your results.

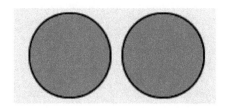

"Arizona Prisons" OR "Rhode Island Prisons" will increase your search results.

3. **"Miami Dolphins" NOT "Football"** When you use NOT, you'll get results that exclude a search term. Using NOT limits the number of results.

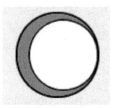

"Miami Dolphins" NOT "Football" removes the white circle (football) from the green search results (Miami Dolphins).

Truncation

Truncation allows you to search different forms of the same word at the same time. Use the root of a word and add an asterisk (*) as a substitute for the word's ending. It can save time and increase your search to include related words. For example, a search for "Psycho*" would pull results on *psychology, psychological, psychologist, psychosis,* and *psychoanalyst.*

Attributions

CC licensed content, Original

- Revision and Adaptation. **Authored by**: Gillian Paku. **Provided by**: SUNY Geneseo. **License**: *CC BY: Attribution*

CC licensed content, Shared previously

- Bowman Library Research Skills Tutorial, Boolean search images. **Provided by**: Menlo College. **Located at**: http://www.menlo.edu/library/research/tutorial/#module3. **License**: *CC BY-NC-SA: Attribution-NonCommercial-ShareAlike*
- Begin Research Tutorial. **Authored by**: UCI Libraries. **Provided by**: University of California, Irvine. **Located at**: http://www.lib.uci.edu/sites/tutorials/BeginResearch/public/articles.html. **License**: *CC BY-NC-SA: Attribution-NonCommercial-ShareAlike*

Lumen Learning authored content

- Revision and Adaptation. **Provided by**: Lumen Learning. **License**: *CC BY-NC-SA: Attribution-NonCommercial-ShareAlike*

Primary, Secondary, and Tertiary Sources

When searching for information on a topic, it is important to understand the value of primary, secondary, and tertiary sources.

> **Primary sources** allow researchers to get as close as possible to original ideas, events, and empirical research. Such sources may include creative works, first-hand or contemporary accounts of events, and the publication of the results of empirical observations or research.

> **Secondary sources** analyze, review, or summarize information in primary resources or other secondary resources. Even sources presenting facts or descriptions about events are secondary unless they are based on direct participation or observation. Moreover, secondary sources often rely on other secondary sources and standard disciplinary methods to reach results, and they provide the principal sources of analysis about primary sources.

> **Tertiary sources** provide overviews of topics by synthesizing information gathered from other resources. Tertiary resources often provide data in a convenient form or provide information with context by which to interpret it.

The distinctions between primary, secondary, and tertiary sources can be ambiguous. An individual document may be a primary source in one context and a secondary source in another. Encyclopedias are typically considered tertiary sources, but a study of how encyclopedias have changed on the Internet would use them as primary sources.

Different discipline areas may also classify sources differently…

In the Humanities & Social Sciences

In the humanities and social sciences, primary sources are the direct evidence, original documents, or first-hand accounts of events without secondary analysis or interpretation. A primary source is a work that was created, or written contemporarily with the period or subject being studied. Secondary sources analyze or interpret historical events or creative works.

Primary sources examples

- Diaries

- Interviews

- Letters

- Original works of art

- Photographs

- Speeches

- Works of literature

A **secondary source** contains commentary on or discussion about a primary source. The most important feature of secondary sources is that they offer an *interpretation* of information gathered from primary sources.

Secondary sources

- Journal articles

- Monographs (a book written on a single subject or an aspect of it)

- Edited collections of scholarly articles on a topic

- Biographies

- Dissertations

A **tertiary source** presents summaries or condensed versions of materials, usually with references back to the primary and/or secondary sources. They can be a good place to look up facts or get a general overview of a subject, but they rarely contain original material.

Tertiary sources

- Dictionaries

- Encyclopedias

- Handbooks

- Indexes, abstracts, bibliographies (used to locate a secondary source)

Examples

Subject	Primary	Secondary	Tertiary
Art	Painting	Critical review of the painting	Encyclopedia article on the artist
History	Civil War diary	Book on a Civil War Battle	List of battle sites
Literature	Novel or poem	Essay about themes in the work	Biography of the author
Political science	Geneva Convention	Article about prisoners of war	Chronology of treaties

In the Sciences

In the sciences, primary sources are documents that provide full descriptions of the original research. For example, a primary source would be a journal article where scientists describe their research on the genetics of tobacco plants. A secondary source would be an article commenting or analyzing the scientists' research on tobacco.

Primary sources

- Conference proceedings
- Interviews
- Journals
- Lab notebooks
- Patents
- Preprints
- Technical reports
- Theses and dissertations

These are where the results of original research are usually first published in the sciences. This makes them the best source of information on cutting edge topics. However the new ideas presented may not be fully refined or validated yet.

Secondary sources

- Monographs
- Reviews
- Textbooks
- Treatises

These tend to summarize the existing state of knowledge in a field at the time of publication. Secondary sources are good to find comparisons of different ideas and theories and to see how they may have changed over time.

Tertiary sources

- Compilations
- Dictionaries
- Encyclopedias
- Handbooks
- Tables

These types of sources present condensed material, generally with references back to the primary and/or secondary literature. They can be a good place to look up data or to get an overview of a subject, but they rarely contain original material.

Examples

Subjects	Primary	Secondary	Tertiary
Agriculture	Conference paper on tobacco genetics	Review article on the current state of tobacco research	Encyclopedia article on tobacco
Chemistry	Chemical patent	Book on chemical reactions	Table of related reactions
Physics	Einstein's diary	Biography on Einstein	Dictionary of relativity

Attributions

CC licensed content, Original

- Revision and Adaptation. **Authored by**: Gillian Paku. **Provided by**: SUNY Geneseo. **License**: *CC BY: Attribution*

CC licensed content, Shared previously

- Primary, Secondary, and Tertiary Sources. **Provided by**: Virginia Tech University Libraries. **Located at**: http://www.lib.vt.edu/help/research/primary-secondary-tertiary.html. **Project**: Introduction to Academic Research. **License**: *CC BY-NC-SA: Attribution-NonCommercial-ShareAlike*

Tools for Evaluating Sources

You will need to evaluate each source you consider using by asking two questions:

- Is this source trustworthy?
- Is this source suitable?

Not every suitable source is trustworthy, and not every trustworthy source is suitable.

Determining Suitability

Your task as a researcher is to determine the appropriateness of the information your source contains for your particular research project. It is a simple question, really: will this source help me answer the research questions that I am posing in my project? Will it help me learn as much as I can about my topic? Will it help me write an interesting, convincing essay for my readers?

Need a good way to evaluate a source? Take a look at its "craap"!

The CRAAP method is a way to determine the validity and relevance of a source. CRAAP stands for

- **C**: Currency. When was the information published?
- **R**: Relevance. How relevant to your goals is the information?
- **A**: Authority. How well does the author of the information know the information?
- **A**: Accuracy. How reliable is the information?
- **P**: Purpose. Why does this information exist in this way?

Watch the two-minute video below to reinforce these ideas.

If the source you're looking at is fairly current, relevant, and accurate, it's probably a good source to use. Depending on the aim of your paper, you'll be looking for an authority and purpose that are unbiased and informative. Currency can depend on your topics: it might mean within the past year for some topics, but for others, it might be within the past twenty years. The state of some fields changes very rapidly, but even in fields that seem historically bounded (e.g., Medieval Spanish literature), currency has a lot to do with whether the topic you're researching is currently hot. If ten scholars have revolutionized thinking about ecocriticism in medieval Spanish literature in the past two years, currency will be affected. You can get a sense of how hot a topic is by ordering the results in a database search chronologically from the most recent (often the default system for a scholarly database), or you can ask your instructor.

- https://youtu.be/_M1-aMCJHFg

Attributions

CC licensed content, Original

- Revision and Adaptation. **Provided by**: Lumen Learning. **License**: *CC BY: Attribution*
- Revision and Adaptation. **Authored by**: Gillian Paku. **Provided by**: SUNY Geneseo. **License**: *CC BY: Attribution*

CC licensed content, Shared previously

- Evaluating Sources. **Provided by**: iWriting. **Located at**: https://iwriting.wikispaces.com/Evaluating+sources. **License**: *CC BY-SA: Attribution-ShareAlike*
- How Library Stuff Works: How to Evaluate Resources (the CRAAP Test). **Authored by**: McMaster Libraries. **Located at**: https://youtu.be/_M1-aMCJHFg. **License**: *All Rights Reserved*. **License Terms**: Standard YouTube License

Using Sources in Your Paper

Within the pages of your research essay, it is important to properly reference and cite your sources to avoid plagiarism and to give credit for original ideas.

There are three main ways to put a source to use in your essay: you can quote it, you can summarize it, and you can paraphrase it.

Quoting

 Direct quotations are words and phrases that are taken directly from another source, and then used word-for-word in your paper. If you incorporate a direct quotation from another author's text, you must put that quotation or phrase in quotation marks to indicate that it is not your language.

When you write direct quotations, it's a good idea to use the source author's name in the same sentence as the quotation to introduce the quoted text and to indicate the source in which you found the text. Think of this habit in terms of INTD 105's model of academic writing as joining a conversation: it's a social norm to introduce yourself or a speaker before you or they contribute to a conversation. You should then include the page number or other relevant information in parentheses at the end of the phrase (the exact format will depend on the formatting style of your essay: later modules of INTD 106 cover documentation styles).

Summarizing

Summarizing involves condensing the main idea of a source into a much shorter overview. A summary outlines a source's most important points and general position, but, in academic writing, such summaries seldom appear in a vacuum. Typically, you summarize a source in such a way that it serves the thesis of your own writing. Finding the balance between highlighting the connections to your own thesis and remaining faithful to the original context and emphasis of your source is not easy: many students err either in the direction of too much unfocused summary ("And the next point this author makes is that. . ."), which can distract readers from their own point, or in the direction of a failure to represent the original context accurately, which often happens when they choose a source that is only tangentially related to their topic (because they picked the first hit in the result list without checking its CRAAP rating. . .) and attempt to present it as if it were a highly relevant source, wresting it from its original concerns. Many students are good at summarizing sources as an exercise in itself, but find summarizing at the college level, where you need to connect the summary to your own key terms, much more challenging.

When summarizing a source, it is still necessary to use a citation to give credit to the original author. You must reference the author or source in the appropriate citation method at the end of the summary; again, the author will often appear in the body of the summary, but each instance will depend on context, the conventions of the academic field, and other variables.

Paraphrasing

When paraphrasing, you may put any part of a source (such as a phrase, sentence, paragraph, or chapter) into your own words. You may find that the original source uses language that is more clear, concise, or specific than your own language, in which case you should use a direct quotation, putting quotation marks around those unique words or phrases you don't change.

It is common to use a mixture of paraphrased text and quoted words or phrases, as long as the direct quotations are inside quotation marks.

Providing Context for Your Sources

Whether you use a direct quotation, a summary, or a paraphrase, it is important to distinguish the original source from your ideas, and to explain how the cited source fits into your argument. While the use of quotation marks or parenthetical citations tells your reader that these are not your own words or ideas, you should follow the quotation with a description, in your own terms, of what the quotation says and why it is relevant to the purpose of your paper. You should not let quoted or paraphrased text stand alone in your paper, but rather, should integrate the sources into your argument by providing context and explanations about how each source supports your argument.[1]

Sources that are not properly integrated into your paper are like "bricks without mortar: you have the essential substance, but there's nothing to hold it together, rendering the whole thing formless" (Smith).

It can be tempting to hand over your essay to other voices, especially to voices that have already received academia's stamp of approval by being peer-reviewed and published. Students often expect that such voices will stand alone, proving their own argument's validity through sheer weight of authority. It's important to remember, however, that your professors are not evaluating the authority of a peer-reviewed argument so much as they evaluating *your* ability to manage an academic conversation. When you thrust a quotation onto the center stage of your essay and then scurry off-stage yourself, you're missing the opportunity to manage the moment. Here's an example of a poorly executed quotation from INTD 105's most

1. Smith, Matt. "Putting It All Together: Thesis Synthesis." Web log post. Walden University Writing Center, 12 Apr. 2013. Web. 04 Apr. 2016.

commonly assigned writing handbook, *They Say / I Say;* authors Gerald Graff and Cathy Birkenstein describe what follows as a "typical hit-and-run quotation by a writer responding to an essay by the feminist philosopher Susan Bordo, who laments that media pressures on young women to diet are spreading to previously isolated regions of the world like the Fiji islands" (44-45).

> Susan Bordo writes about women and dieting. "Fiji is just one example. Until television was introduced in 1995, the islands had no reported cases of eating disorders. In 1998, three years after programs from the United States and Britain began broadcasting there, 62 percent of the girls surveyed reported dieting." I think Bordo is right. Another point Bordo makes is that…

The authoritative claim by Bordo, complete with statistics and dates, is presented as if these facts in the hands of this established scholar are the final word on "women and dieting," as the hugely broad and unfocused first sentence suggests. Even its introductory verb, "writes about," is bland and unhelpful: Bordo is lamenting what happened in Fiji, not "writing about" it. The writer makes no attempt to remind the reader what their own thesis is (hopefully more than a statement that "women and dieting" is a topic – what is this writer arguing about women and dieting? Is the writer's essay focused on media influences? On Pacific islands? On eating disorders? On girls? If it's a standard five-page essay, the answer should not be "all of the above," so the reader needs guidance.) The inadequate comment, "I think Bordo is right," abdicates the writer's responsibility to restate a source so that it clearly comments on the writer's own thesis. Saying "she's right" puts all the responsibility of connecting Bordo's comments to the writer's thesis on the reader. We all assume that Bordo's facts and figures are "right," but in an analytical essay, the facts and figures are not as important as the interpretation those elements support, and on that crucial question of how exactly the quotation from Bordo supports this writer's thesis, our writer is silent. Instead, the writer rushes off to another point Bordo made, clearly hoping that Bordo will carry the essay herself.

Attributions

CC licensed content, Original

- Revision and Adaptation. **Provided by**: Lumen Learning. **License**: *CC BY-SA: Attribution-ShareAlike*
- Revision and Adaptation. **Authored by**: Gillian Paku. **Provided by**: SUNY Geneseo. **License**: *CC BY: Attribution*

CC licensed content, Shared previously

- Incorporating Your Sources Into Your Paper. **Provided by**: Boundless. **Located at**: https://www.boundless.com/writing/textbooks/boundless-writing-textbook/the-research-process-2/understanding-your-sources-265/understanding-your-sources-62-8498/. **Project**: Boundless Writing. **License**: *CC BY-SA: Attribution-ShareAlike*

Public domain content

- Image of bricks. **Authored by**: Tasja. **Located at**: https://commons.wikimedia.org/wiki/File:Berg_van_stenen.jpg. **License**: *Public Domain: No Known Copyright*
- quotation marks. **Authored by**: Cuahl. **Provided by**: Wikipedia. **Located at**: https://en.wikipedia.org/wiki/Wikipedia:Wikipedia_Signpost/2009-04-13/Dispatches#/media/File:Cquote2.svg. **License**: *Public Domain: No Known Copyright*

Using Multiple Sources

Sources are a great help for understanding a topic more deeply. But what about when sources don't quite agree with one another, or challenge what you have experienced yourself?

This is where your skill of **synthesis** comes into play as a writer. *Synthesizing* includes comparison and contrast, but also allows you to combine multiple perspectives on a topic to reach a deeper understanding.

This video explains the process of synthesis in action. Note the emphasis on creating your own frame for the material you synthesize, not simply pasting the sources one after the other and expecting your *reader* to perform the intellectual work of synthesis for you.

- https://youtu.be/7dEGoJdb6O0

Attributions

CC licensed content, Original

- Video: Using Multiple Sources. **Provided by**: Lumen Learning. **License**: *CC BY: Attribution*
- Revision and Adaptation. **Authored by**: Gillian Paku. **Provided by**: SUNY Geneseo. **License**: *CC BY: Attribution*

All rights reserved content

- Synthesizing Information. **Authored by**: GCFLearnFree.org. **Located at**: https://youtu.be/7dEGoJdb6O0. **License**: *All Rights Reserved*. **License Terms**: Standard YouTube License

Academic Dishonesty

Academic Honesty

For the purposes of INTD 106 and INTD 105, where our focus is on helping new academic writers join existing intellectual conversations confidently by using appropriate conventions and strategies, **academic honesty** arises from following the guidelines and understanding the principles we discuss in these courses. Your instructors and the Geneseo community want you to succeed at what are often new skills, playing out in a new environment. Sometimes, misunderstandings, cultural differences, or mistakes occur to upset the ideal situation, and academia has terminology for those situations. Essentially, **academic dishonesty** or **academic misconduct** is any type of cheating that occurs in relation to a formal academic exercise. It can include

- **Plagiarism**: The adoption or reproduction of original creations of another author (person, collective, organization, community or other type of author, including anonymous authors) without due acknowledgment.

- **Fabrication**: The falsification of data, information, or citations in any formal academic exercise.

- **Deception**: Providing false information to an instructor concerning a formal academic exercise—e.g., giving a false excuse for missing a deadline or falsely claiming to have submitted work.

- **Cheating**: Any attempt to obtain assistance in a formal academic exercise (like an examination) without due acknowledgment.

- **Bribery or paid services**: Giving assignment answers or test answers for money.

- **Sabotage**: Acting to prevent others from completing their work. This includes cutting pages out of library books or willfully disrupting the experiments of others.

- **Professorial misconduct**: Professorial acts that are academically fraudulent equate to academic fraud and/or grade fraud.

- **Impersonation**: assuming a student's identity with intent to provide an advantage for the student.

Watch this video to deepen your understanding about the importance of practicing academic honesty.

- https://youtu.be/JylxFnk7btU

Attributions

CC licensed content, Original

- Revision and Adaptation. **Provided by**: Lumen Learning. **License**: *CC BY-SA: Attribution-ShareAlike*
- Revision and Adaptation. **Authored by**: Gillian Paku. **Provided by**: SUNY Geneseo. **License**: *CC BY: Attribution*

CC licensed content, Shared previously

- Academic Dishonesty. **Provided by**: Wikipedia. **Located at**: https://en.wikipedia.org/wiki/Academic_dishonesty. **License**: *CC BY-SA: Attribution-ShareAlike*
- What is Academic Honesty?. **Authored by**: NEIU Ronald Williams Library. **Located at**: https://youtu.be/JylxFnk7btU. **License**: *CC BY: Attribution*

Defining Plagiarism

Plagiarism is the unauthorized or uncredited use of the writings or ideas of another in your writing. While it might not be as tangible as auto theft or burglary, plagiarism is still a form of theft.

Examples of plagiarism include:

- Turning in someone else's paper as your own

- Asking someone else to give you the answer to an INTD 106 quiz question, then representing that answer as your own effort

- Using the exact words of a source without quotation marks and/or a citation

- Taking an image, chart, or statistic from a source without telling where it originated

- Copying and pasting material from the Internet without quotation marks and/or a citation

- Including another person's idea without crediting the author

In the academic world, plagiarism is a serious matter because ideas in the forms of research, creative work, and original thought are highly valued. Geneseo has strict rules about what happens when someone is caught plagiarizing. The penalty for plagiarism is severe – everything from a failing grade for the plagiarized work or a failing grade for the class to expulsion from the college.

You might not be aware that plagiarism can take several different forms. We will outline some here, but refer you also to Milne Library's sophisticated discussions of and workshops on plagiarism, which you can **register for on this page.** (https://www.geneseo.edu/library/library-workshops) (Note that completing this module of INTD 106 is *not equivalent* to completing Milne's workshop, nor sufficient to earn Geneseo GOLD credit.)

The most well known, **intentional or purposeful plagiarism**, is handing in an essay written by someone else and representing it as your own, copying your essay word for word from a magazine or journal, or downloading an essay from the Internet.

A much more common and less understood phenomenon is **unintentional or accidental plagiarism**. Accidental plagiarism is the result of improperly paraphrasing, summarizing, quoting, or citing your evidence in your academic writing. Generally, writers accidentally plagiarize because they simply don't know or they fail to follow the rules for giving credit to the ideas of others in their writing.

Both intentional and unintentional plagiarism are against academic rules and can result in harsh punishments. Ignoring or not knowing the rules of how to not plagiarize and properly cite evidence might be an *explanation*, but it is not an excuse.

A GENERAL GUIDE TO UNDERSTANDING WRITTEN PLAGIARISM

Are my own words being used?

YES

NO

Is it my idea?

Are you using quotation marks or placing it in a block quote?

YES   NO

YES   NO

Yay! You're not plagiarizing!

Yay! You're not plagiarizing!

You're plagiarizing!

You're paraphrasing

Go quote it!

Brought to you by

EasyBib

Now what?

ADD A CITATION AND BIBLIOGRAPHY!

How to Recognize Plagiarism. Indiana University Bloomington's School of Education. 2005. Web. <https://www.indiana.edu/~istd/overview.html>.

Attributions

CC licensed content, Original

CC licensed content, Shared previously

Avoiding Plagiarism

How to Avoid Plagiarizing

Tip #1: Make Sure You Are Very Certain about What Is and Is Not Plagiarism

- https://youtu.be/t5dRz6ZEkj8

Tip #2: Give Yourself Plenty of Time to Complete an Assignment

Running out of time on an assignment is a main cause of plagiarism. Rushing to meet a deadline can result in carelessness (leading to unintentional plagiarism—see the next tip) and the desire to find a quick, easy solution such as copying someone else's work. Don't give in to that temptation! Plagiarism is a serious academic offense, and the chance of being caught, which is high, is not worth the risk. Software helps identify plagiarism, but your professors have also read thousands of essays and they are both very familiar firsthand with many research sources and very competent at picking up when the voice of an essay changes from "undergraduate" to "published expert."

Avoid this situation entirely by starting your assignment ahead of the last-minute panic schedule and planning out when you will complete each phase of the writing process. Even if your teacher does not require you to turn in materials for each stage of the writing process (i.e., brainstorming, creating a thesis statement, outlining, drafting, revising, etc.), set your own personal deadlines for each step along the way and make sure to give yourself more than enough time to finish everything. Pulling an all-nighter might be an iconic undergraduate experience, but it does nothing for the quality of your work.

Tip #3: Document Everything

Plagiarism isn't always a conscious choice. Sometimes it can be unintentional, typically resulting from poor documentation of your sources during the research phase. For example, sometimes students will write down an idea from a source using words identical to or very close to those in the original, but then when they go to write their paper forget that the material was not already in their own words. Adopting good research habits can prevent this type of plagiarism.

Print, photocopy, take a photo of, or scan the relevant pages of every source you are using, including the title and copyright pages, since they have the information you need for a bibliographic citation. Your phone can be a helpful tool if you aren't near a copying machine. When taking notes by hand (or typed into a file), list the bibliographic information for each source you use. Make sure to put quotation marks around any wordings taken directly from the source, and note the page where you found it, and remember to put everything else into your own words right away, so there is no danger of forgetting that something is a quotation. Documenting where all of your ideas, information, quotations, and so on come from is an important step in avoiding plagiarism.

Tip #4: Don't Include Too Much Material Taken from Other Sources

Tips for integrating sources into your research.

Writing assignments are about your ideas, your interpretations, and your ability to synthesize information. You should use relevant sources to support your ideas using evidence such as quotations, paraphrases, and summaries, as well as statistics and other data, but don't lose sight of the fact that *your* argument is central! Including too much material from other sources can result in a paper that feels like it has been pasted together from a variety of authors, rather than a cohesive essay. Such papers also run a much higher risk of setting off plagiarism warnings in TurnItIn or other plagiarism-detecting software. Try to find a balance: use enough evidence from credible sources to enter the conversation and prove your points, but don't let the ideas of others crowd or take the place of your own thoughts.

Tip #5: When in Doubt, Give a Citation

There are certain types of information—typically referred to as *common knowledge*—that don't require a citation when you include them in your writing. These are facts that are widely known and can be easily found in a number of sources. They are not ideas that originated with one particular source. Examples include scientific facts (for example, that solid, liquid, and gas are three states of matter), general historical information (for example, that George Washington was the first US president), or even information commonly known to certain groups of people but not others, if the certain group is your audience (for example, most musicians know that a C major triad includes the notes C, E, and G, even though many non-musicians would have no idea what a C major triad is).

For everything else, you need to include a citation, regardless of whether you are quoting directly from the source, paraphrasing it, or giving a summary. If you are at all unsure whether something qualifies as common knowledge or not, give a citation. You can also consult a more experienced figure in your field, such as your instructor, to find out if something counts as common knowledge or not.

In academic writing, the **"Quotation Sandwich" approach** is useful for incorporating other writers' voices into your essays. It gives meaning and context to a quotation, and helps you avoid plagiarism. This 3-step approach offers your readers a deeper understanding of how the quotation relates to your essay's goals.

1. **Step 1**: Provide context for the source. If you haven't used it yet in the essay, tell us the source's title and author (if known), and any other information that's relevant, like the purpose of the organization that published it, for instance.

2. **Step 2**: Provide the quotation itself. Be sure to format correctly and use quotation marks around exact language.

3. **Step 3**: Provide a summary and analysis of what the quotation says, and how it relates to the subject matter of your essay and your thesis.

Attributions

CC licensed content, Original

- Revision and Adaptation. **Provided by**: Lumen Learning. **License**: *CC BY-NC-SA: Attribution-NonCommercial-ShareAlike*
- Integrating sources image. **Authored by**: Kim Louie for Lumen Learning. **License**: *CC BY: Attribution*
- Revision and Adaptation. **Authored by**: Gillian Paku. **Provided by**: SUNY Geneseo. **License**: *CC BY: Attribution*

CC licensed content, Shared previously

- Plagiarism. **Provided by**: CUNY Academic Commons. **Located at**: http://bacwritingfellows.commons.gc.cuny.edu/plagiarism/. **License**: *CC BY-NC-SA: Attribution-NonCommercial-ShareAlike*

All rights reserved content

- What is Plagiarism?. **Authored by**: Virtual High School. **Located at**: https://youtu.be/t5dRz6ZEkj8. **License**: *All Rights Reserved*. **License Terms**: Standard YouTube License

7. MLA Documentation

Why Is MLA Documentation Important?

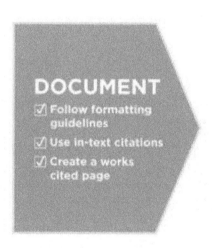

DOCUMENT
☑ Follow formatting guidelines
☑ Use in-text citations
☑ Create a works cited page

The term "documentation" tends to elicit the same response as the term "grammar." Students who have been asked to complete exercises in documentation since middle school sometimes think of documentation as nothing but a set of arbitrary rules enforced by people with a petty delight in finding misplaced commas. Yes, documentation does require attention to detail, and yes, those details are written down in reference guides that don't make great bedtime reading, but they are no more taxing than the rules that govern, for example, behavior at the dinner table: Is it okay to cross chopsticks? What about licking them? In which settings is it unsophisticated to split the bill? And is your own sense of whether something really matters the only sense that counts, or do you have obligations to meet others' expectations?

As with many somewhat demanding tasks, learning some of the philosophy and background behind documentation gives more meaning to the "rules."

"MLA," for example, stands for Modern Language Association. This is a professional organization for scholars of language and literature, broadly conceived; they hold conventions, give scholarships, provide a network, and support scholars. The MLA, like many other academic organizations, also publishes a scholarly journal and has done so for decades. In years before computers were common, the editors of this journal required typed submissions for publication to follow a common formatting template.

Professors who were following this format to write their own work recognized the value of having some standard of uniform appearance, an easily understood set of abbreviations ("vol." for "volume," "3.1.45-47" to signal lines forty-five to forty-seven of the first scene of the third act of a play), and attention to the same elements of the source material (the difference between the author and the translator of a work; the publisher of a text; the date of publication). They started asking their students to follow the same format when they typed essays for class projects.

Fast forward to now, and we have a set of guidelines for how the first page of an essay should look, what margins and font are appropriate, and what information a Works Cited entry for a blog post should contain. Not all humanities instructors use MLA, and you should always follow their individual style preferences, but the ultimate goal for MLA formatting and citation standards is to provide everyone with a common template to draw from.

While MLA standards may feel like unbreakable rules when you're wondering whether the period goes before or after the parentheses, it's helpful to remember that they were created to serve a common need, with your interests in mind. Here's 2016 MLA Executive Director Rosemary Feal on the most recent *MLA Handbook*, the eighth edition (which deserves a feather boa and some love):

> I am especially pleased to present the eighth edition of the *MLA Handbook*, because it it embodies so many of the values that define the association: a commitment to sharing ideas, a belief in scholarship as the work of a broad community, and a recognition that, while methods and media may change, basic principles of research stay the same. Designed in consultation with students, teachers, and researchers, this edition gives users more freedom to create references to fit their audiences. The recommendations continue to represent the consensus of teachers and scholars but offer a greater flexibility that will better accommodate new media and new ways of doing research.[1]

Here, too, is Kathleen Fitzpatrick, the Director of Scholarly Communication for the MLA, on what she sees as the philosophy of the eighth edition:

> With the eighth edition, we shift our focus from a prescriptive list of formats [how do you cite an article? a tweet? a YouTube video] to the overarching purpose of source documentation: enabling readers to participate fully in the conversations between readers and their sources. … We hope that this reorientation will convey what we believe to be the most important aspect of academic writing: its engagement with the reader, which obliges the author to ensure that the reader has all the information necessary to understand the text at hand without being distracted from it by the citations."[2]

Viewed this way, as expressed by people who want to help and not hamper students, accurate documentation is very much in line with INTD 105's emphasis on academic writing as a conversation between scholars. We all assess information based on where it comes from; I assess the statement that "my house mate is terrible" differently when it comes from a trusted friend than when it comes from someone whose judgment I have no reason to value. Documentation clarifies the source of academic comments, lets your readers assess and follow up with the source if they'd like to, and gives you a standardized form in which to communicate that important information.

1. (vii-viii, Preface to the eighth edition)
2. (xii, Preface to the eighth edition)

Attributions

CC licensed content, Original

Introduction to MLA Documentation

MLA style is one of the most common citation and formatting styles you will encounter in your academic career. Any piece of academic writing can use MLA style, from a one-page paper to a full-length scholarly book. It is the most common documentation style for humanities subjects.

The importance of using citations is explained in the following video. Note that this video is not focused on MLA, and that the in-text citations and Works Cited pages it displays are not in MLA style. The point is to reinforce the concept of citation as vital to academic conversation (and it's *plagiarism*, by the way, not *plagarism*!):

- https://youtu.be/IMhMuVvXCVw

The Purpose of MLA Style

The MLA style guide aims to accomplish several goals:

1. to ensure consistent use of the English language in academic writing
2. to ensure consistent formatting and presentation of information, for the sake of clarity and ease of navigation
3. to ensure proper attribution of ideas to their original sources, for the sake of intellectual integrity

Citation Resources

There are many fantastic resources out there that can make the formatting and citation process easier. Some common style guides are found at:

- The Purdue Online Writing Lab: this is a popular resource that concisely explains how to properly format and cite in various academic styles.

- EasyBib: in addition to having a style guide, this website allows you to paste in information from your research and will create and save citations for you.

Reference management websites and applications can also assist you in tracking and recording your research. Most of these websites will even create the works cited page for you! Some of the most popular citation tools are:

- Zotero
- RefME
- BibMe

The New Edition

The newest edition of the *MLA Handbook*, the eighth edition, was released in April 2016. This is the text we are basing this module on, but you should be aware that some instructors may still use the seventh edition of the handbook. It is valid to ask your instructors what their personal preference is, and of course you should use whichever version they ask you to: regardless of the exact conventions, following any documentation style is an exercise in attention to detail and respect for your discipline.

While the overall principles of creating a works cited page and using in-text citations remain the same, there are a few key changes and updates in the eighth edition that make the citation process easier for our modern uses. For example, the guidelines now state that you should always include a URL of an internet source; you can use alternative author names, such as Twitter handles; you no longer need to include the publisher (in some instances); and you don't need to include the city where a source was published. These new changes allow for a more streamlined citation process that will work with a wide variety of source locations such as *YouTube* videos, songs, clips from TV episodes, websites, periodicals, books, academic journals, poems, or interviews.

MLA Document Formatting

Overall Structure of an MLA Paper

Your MLA paper should include the following basic elements:

1. Body
2. Works Cited

General MLA Formatting Rules

- **Font**: Your paper should be written in 12-point text. Whichever font you choose, MLA requires that regular and italicized text be easily distinguishable from each other. Times and Times New Roman are often recommended. Avoid fonts that make a noticeable difference to the number of words on a page. Your instructor has graded thousands of student essays and can tell immediately when a student has written four pages but then changed the Times font to a larger one so that the essay squeaks onto the fifth page. It's not a good look.

- **Line Spacing**: All text in your paper should be double-spaced. That includes the biographical details of your name and class and date, the title, all block quotations, and the entire Works Cited page. Really. Everything is double-spaced. See comment above for how easy it is for your instructor to tell that you have adjusted line spacing in any section.

- **Margins**: All page margins (top, bottom, left, and right) should be set at one inch. All text should be left-justified except for the title, which is centered. The default page layout on most word processing programs works fine.

- **Indentation**: The first line of every paragraph should be indented 0.5 inches. Don't skip a line between paragraphs or before and/or after quotations.

- **Page Numbers**: Create a right-justified header 0.5 inches from the top edge of every page. Note that a header is separate from the main page: you can see the "header and footer" under the "View" tab on your document. This header should include your last name, followed by a space and the page number. Your pages should be numbered with Arabic numerals (1, 2, 3…) and should start with the number 1 on your title page. Most word-processing programs have the ability to automatically add the correct page number to each page so you don't have to do this by hand.

- **Use of Italics:** In MLA style, you should italicize (rather than underline) the titles of books, plays, or other standalone works. You should also italicize (rather than underline) words or phrases you want to lend particular emphasis—though you should do this rarely.

- **Sentence Spacing**: Include just one single space after a period before the next sentence, as in this example from William Deresiewicz's *Excellent Sheep*: "Status is a funny thing. Money gets you stuff, at least. Status doesn't get you much except the knowledge that you have it" (113).

- **The first page:** Like the rest of your paper, everything on your first page should be double-spaced. The following information should be left-justified in regular font at the top of the first page (in the main part of the page, not the header):

  ○ on the first line, your first and last name (helpful hint: use your preferred first name if that's how the instructor knows you)

  ○ on the second line, your instructor's name (helpful hint: use your instructor's preferred name, which often includes an honorific like "Dr." or "Professor")

  ○ on the third line, the name of the class

  ○ on the fourth line, the date

- **The title:** After the header, the next double-spaced line should include the title of your paper. This should be centered, and it should not be bolded, underlined, or italicized (unless it includes the name of a book, in which case just the book title should be italicized). All significant words are capitalized: the first word, the last word, nouns, pronouns, verbs, adjectives, adverbs and subordinating conjunctions. Unless they are the first or last word of a title, do not capitalize articles, prepositions, coordinating conjunctions, or the "to" in the infinitive construction of a verb, e.g. "Locke's Capacity Contract: How to Construct Idiocy." It can be difficult to resist the urge to use typography to signal that your title is significant, or witty, or simply not part of the body of your essay, but we're confident that you can control that urge. On the topic of titles, note that the title of your essay is not the name of the assignment. Don't call your essay "Assignment 1 on Global Contemporary Art." Come up with a title that describes your individual response to the assignment prompt, not the assignment prompt itself.

- **The Oxford Comma:** The Oxford comma (also called the serial comma) is the comma that comes after the second-to-last item in a series or list. For example: "The UK includes the countries of England, Scotland, Wales, and Northern Ireland." In the previous sentence, the comma immediately after "Wales" is the Oxford comma. In general writing conventions, whether the Oxford comma should be used is actually a point of fervent debate among passionate grammarians. However, it's a requirement in MLA style, so double-check all your lists and series to make sure you include it!

MLA Formatting

Watch this video to review all of the basic formatting recommendations:

- https://youtu.be/4edLWc-elyQ

Attributions

CC licensed content, Original

- Revision and Adaptation. **Provided by**: Lumen Learning. **License**: *CC BY-SA: Attribution-ShareAlike*
- Revision and Adaptation. **Authored by**: Gillian Paku. **Provided by**: SUNY Geneseo. **License**: *CC BY: Attribution*

CC licensed content, Shared previously

- Overall Structure and Formatting of an MLA Paper. **Provided by**: Boundless. **Located at**: https://www.boundless.com/writing/textbooks/boundless-writing-textbook/writing-a-paper-in-mla-style-humanities-255/introduction-to-mla-style-299/overall-structure-and-formatting-of-an-mla-paper-301-16889/. **Project**: Boundless Writing. **License**: *CC BY-SA: Attribution-ShareAlike*
- How to Format Your Paper in MLA Style. **Authored by**: Memorial University Libraries. **Located at**: https://youtu.be/4edLWc-elyQ?t=58s. **License**: *CC BY: Attribution*
- MLA: The Works Cited Section. **Authored by**: Boundless. **Located at**: https://www.boundless.com/writing/textbooks/boundless-writing-textbook/writing-a-paper-in-mla-style-humanities-255/mla-citations-and-references-303/mla-the-works-cited-section-319-16905/. **Project**: Boundless Writing. **License**: *CC BY-SA: Attribution-ShareAlike*

MLA Works Cited Page Formatting

In MLA style, all the sources you cite parenthetically throughout the text of your paper are listed together in full in the Works Cited section, which comes after the main text of your paper.

Formatting the Works Cited Section

- **Page numbers:** Just like the rest of your paper, the top of the page should retain the right-justified header with your last name and the page number. Don't number your Works Cited page "1," which often happens if you create it as a separate document then forget to merge it with your essay.

- **Title:** On the first line, the title of the page—"Works Cited"—should appear centered, and not italicized or bolded.

- **Spacing:** Like the rest of your paper, this page should be double-spaced and have 1-inch margins (don't skip an extra line after the title or between citations!).

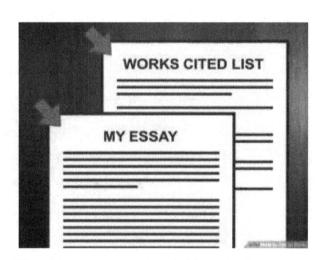

When citing an essay, you include information in two places: in the body of your paper and in the Works Cited that comes after it. The Works Cited is just a bibliography: you list all the sources you used to write the paper. The citation information you include in the body of the paper itself is called the "in-text citation."

- **Alphabetical order:** Starting on the next line after the page title, your references should be listed in alphabetical order by author. Multiple sources by the same author should be alphabetized by their titles within the same group. After the first full listing of the author's name, the following entries have three hyphens in place of the name rather than writing it out in full each time.

- **Hanging indents:** Each reference should be formatted with what is called a *hanging indent*. This means that the first line of each reference should be flush with the left margin (i.e., not indented), but the rest of that reference should be indented 0.5 inches further. It's basically the reverse of a normal paragraph, where the first line is indented and the rest are left-justified. Here, every line *after* the first is indented. A startling number of students fail to master hanging indention, but any word-processing program will let you format this automatically so you don't even have to do it by hand. In Microsoft Word, for example, you simply highlight your citations, click on the small arrow right next to the word "Paragraph" on the home tab, and in the popup box choose "hanging indent" under the "Special" section. Click "OK," and you're done.

Take a look at the example below, match your own Works Cited page to it, and, again, resist the urge to add your own special formatting flourishes. Remember, too, that this page follows the eighth edition of the MLA Handbook, which came out in April 2016. If you have a tried and trusted model from recent high school days, you might need to update it now. One quick way to check the difference is to look at how page numbers in a printed document are formatted. In older editions of the *MLA Handbook*, pages were *not* signaled by the abbreviation "pp." (see the Coontz entry below for an example of this new abbreviation in action).

Freeman 8

Works Cited

Buchanan, Wyatt. "More Same-Sex Couples Want Kids: Survey Looks at Trends among Homosexuals." *SF Gate*, Hearst Communications, 25 Apr. 2006, www.sfgate.com/bayarea/article/NATION-More-same-sex-couples-want-kids-Survey-2499131.php.

Coontz, Stephanie. "Not Much Sense in Those Census Numbers." *Uncommon Threads: Reading and Writing about Contemporary America*, edited by Robert D. Newman et al., Longman, 2003, pp. 146-48.

"Developments in the Law: The Law of Marriage and Family." *Harvard Law Review*, vol. 116, no. 7, 2003, pp. 1996-2122. *JSTOR*, www.jstor.org/stable/1342754.

Hymowitz, Kay S. "The Incredible Shrinking Father." *City Journal*, Spring 2007, www.city-journal.org/html/17_2_artificial_insemination.html.

Marcotty, Josephine, and Chen May Yee. "New World of Fertility Medicine Is a Big-Money Marketplace." *Seacoastonline.com*, Local Media Group, 30 Oct. 2007, www.seacoastonline.com/article/20071030/PARENTS/71029007.

A correctly formatted Works Cited page, according to the eighth edition of the MLA Handbook.

Attributions

Creating MLA Works Cited Entries

Because of the wide variety of source formats, MLA 8 now requires that researchers follow a simple set of guidelines to create appropriate citations (instead of looking up one of the fifty-nine types of sources inside the previous handbook and following the instructions). Although there are still distinct rules you need to follow to create a citation, the rules are less rigid and allow for you to look for the main components of a citation and construct it yourself. This means you will need to think about the source and its information, select the appropriate components, and organize it in a logical and useful manner.

Regardless of the source type, you are now asked to locate the same "core elements" from your sources and place them in a standard order in order to create citations. These core elements are explained in detail below. **Note that you do not need to memorize every step of this process**, but should take this opportunity to understand how citations are created. You can always return to this page, to the MLA handbook, the MLA Style Center, or to other online resources to help you create the citations you need for your paper. Click through the following slides to learn more about each component and to see examples of MLA citations.

You can also download the presentation here: https://s3-us-west-2.amazonaws.com/oerfiles/Composition/Waymaker+English/MLA+8.pdf

Watch this video to see examples of how to identify the core elements needed in a citation (note that the video is not produced by Milne Library, so you should contact Milne librarians for additional help, not the librarians at Marquette University in Milwaukee!):

- https://youtu.be/lSekgYAdQcU

MLA In-Text Citations

Because the use of in-text citations will be so integral to your writing processes, being able to instantly craft correct citations and identify incorrect citations will save you time during writing and will help you avoid having unnecessary points taken off for citation errors.

Here is the standard in-text citation style according to MLA guidelines:

"Quotation" (Author's Last Name Page Number).

Take a moment to carefully consider the placement of the parts and punctuation of this in-text citation. Note that there is no punctuation indicating the end of a sentence inside of the quotation marks—closing punctuation should instead *follow the parentheses*. There is also *no punctuation* between the author's last name and the page number inside of the parentheses. The misplacement of these simple punctuation marks is one of the most common errors students make when crafting in-text citations.

Include the right information in the in-text citation. Every time you reference material in your paper, the name of the author whose information you are citing must be clear to the reader. You must include a page number that tells the reader where, in the source, they can find this information. The most basic structure for an in-text citation looks like this: (Smith 123).

So, let's say we have the following quotation, which comes from page one hundred of Elizabeth Gaskell's *North and South*: "Margaret had never spoken of Helstone since she left it."[1]

The following examples show **incorrect** MLA formatting:

"Margaret had never spoken of Helstone since she left it." (Gaskell 100)	*Incorrect because the period falls within the quotation marks*
"Margaret had never spoken of Helstone since she left it" (Gaskell, 100).	*Incorrect because of the comma separating the author's last name and the page number*
"Margaret had never spoken of Helstone since she left it" (Elizabeth Gaskell 100).	*Incorrect because the author's full name is used instead of just her last name*
"Margaret had never spoken of Helstone since she left it" (*North and South* 100).	*Incorrect because the title of the work appears, rather than the author's last name; the title should only be used if no author name is provided*

The following example shows **correct** MLA formatting:

> "Margaret had never spoken of Helstone since she left it" (Gaskell 100).

However, there are exceptions to the above citation guideline, and for most writing you do in undergraduate assignments, because you typically have a clear central focus and relatively few outside sources, the exception will occur more often than the standard. Consider the following format of an in-text citation, which is also formed correctly.

> Elizabeth Gaskell's narrator makes it clear that "Margaret had never spoken of Helstone since she left it" (100).

The difference between this citation format and the format of the first example is that, unlike the first example, this citation does not list the author's last name inside the parentheses. This change is because the last name is included in the quotation's introduction, which makes the identity of the author clear to the reader. Including the author's last name again inside of the parenthesis would be redundant and is not required for MLA citation. Ideally, it should always be clear to your reader where a quotation is coming from before you quote it. If you think of academic writing in the terms INTD 105 encourages—that is, as a conversation—it should strike you as odd to have commentary coming either from someone who has not been introduced (would you break into a real-life conversation between others that way?) or from a voice whose origin isn't quite clear. Certainly, if the source's name is in the *signal phrase* (the introduction to the quotation), repeating it in the citation is redundant, but think more broadly, too, about context. If this essay is about Gaskell's novel, and you've been discussing Margaret and/or Helstone all along, or at least for this whole paragraph, then you will not need to tell your reader here that you're quoting from Gaskell's book. That's the default understanding, and the page number will, by default, refer to Gaskell's novel. In short, if you find yourself introducing a source's name for the first time in a citation after you have already quoted from that source, consider whether you can move that source information into the main body of your writing. Page numbers, on the other hand, belong in citations, not in your sentences.

---

1. Gaskell, Elizabeth. North and South. Oxford UP, 1973.

The same rule about inclusion of the author's last name applies for paraphrased information, as well, as shown in the following example:

> Elizabeth Gaskell's narrator makes it clear that her protagonist does not speak of her home once she is in Milton (100).

In this paraphrase, the author's last name precedes the paraphrased material, but as in the case of quotation integration, if the author's last name is not described in the paraphrase then it is required inside the parentheses before the page number.

When and How to Create MLA In-Text Citations

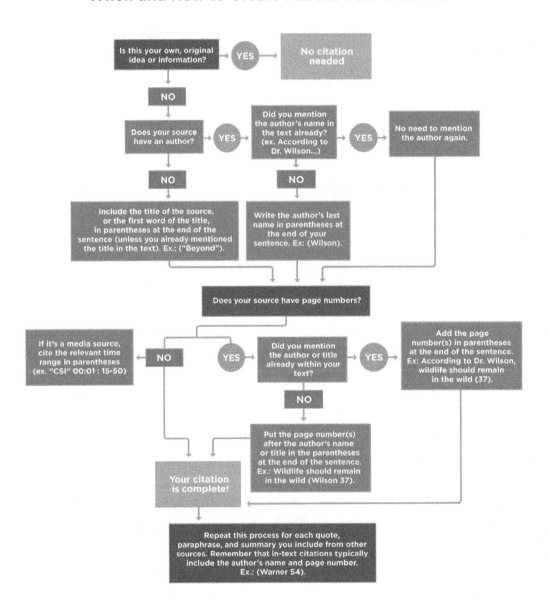

Being more compliant with MLA in-text citation guidelines will become easier if you review these examples and the citation rules on which they rely.

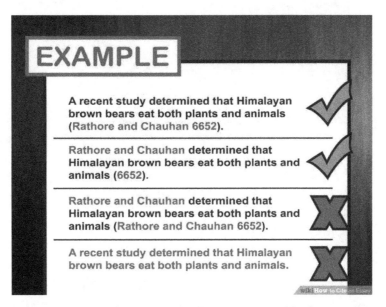

In-text citations are often parenthetical, meaning you add information to the end of a sentence in parentheses. But if you include that necessary information in the language of the sentence itself, you should not include it again in the parenthetical citation. This example shows you proper uses of in-text citations.

Attributions

CC licensed content, Original

- MLA In-text citations graphic. **Authored by**: Kim Louie for Lumen Learning. **License**: *CC BY: Attribution*
- Revision and Adaptation. **Authored by**: Gillian Paku. **Provided by**: SUNY Geneseo. **License**: *CC BY: Attribution*

CC licensed content, Shared previously

- In-Text Citations in MLA 8th Edition. **Authored by**: EasyBib. **Located at**: http://www.easybib.com/guides/citation-guides/mla-8/in-text-citations/. **License**: *CC BY-NC-SA: Attribution-NonCommercial-ShareAlike*
- Image and Caption of How to Cite Sources . **Provided by**: Wikihow. **Located at**: http://www.wikihow.com/Cite-Sources. **License**: *CC BY-NC-SA: Attribution-NonCommercial-ShareAlike*
- Formatting In-text Citations (MLA). **Authored by**: Jennifer Yirinec and Lauren Cutlip. **Provided by**: Writing Commons. **Located at**: http://writingcommons.org/open-text/writing-processes/format/mla-format/444-formatting-in-text-citations-mla. **License**: *CC BY-NC-ND: Attribution-NonCommercial-NoDerivatives*

MLA Block Quotations

When to Use a Block Quotation

A typical quotation is enclosed in double quotation marks and is part of a sentence within a paragraph of your paper. However, if you want to quote more than four lines of prose (or three lines of verse) from a source, you should format the excerpt as a block quotation, rather than as a regular quotation within the text of a paragraph. Such quotations have some of their own documentation conventions: a block quotation will begin on its own line, it will not be enclosed in quotation marks, and its in-text citation will come after the ending punctuation, not before it.

> For example, if you wanted to quote the entire first paragraph of Lewis Carroll's *Alice in Wonderland*, you would begin that quotation on its own line and format it as follows:
>
> > Alice was beginning to get very tired of sitting by her sister on the bank, and of having nothing to do: once or twice she had peeped into the book her sister was reading, but it had no pictures or conversations in it, "and what is the use of a book," thought Alice, "without pictures or conversations?" (Carroll 98)
>
> The full reference for this source would then be included in your Works Cited section at the end of your paper.

Formatting Block Quotations

The entire block quotation should be indented one inch from the left margin. Watch the video below to see how to do this quickly in Word using the ruler bar at the top of a document. The first line of the excerpt should not be further indented, unless you are quoting multiple paragraphs—in which case the first line of each quoted paragraph should be further indented 0.25 inches. Like the rest of your paper, a block quotation in MLA style should be double-spaced. Note that for poetry or drama or other genres where the typographical layout on the page is complex or significant, you should reproduce that layout in your own block quotation.

Block Quotations

Watch this video: www.youtube.com/watch?v=OvDzIkha1JI from Imagine Easy Solutions for more information on formatting block quotations. The author's advice about using block quotations sparingly is important. Again, think of INTD 105's model of academic writing as conversation: it can be tempting to hand over your paper to the voice of someone who has already been published, but your professor is more interested in your developing skill at entering the conversation than in the sources (which professors are quite capable of reading for themselves!).

Attributions

CC licensed content, Original

- Revision and Adaptation. **Provided by**: Lumen Learning. **License**: *CC BY-SA: Attribution-ShareAlike*
- Revision and Adaptation. **Authored by**: Gillian Paku. **Provided by**: SUNY Geneseo. **License**: *CC BY: Attribution*

CC licensed content, Shared previously

- MLA: Block Quotations. **Authored by**: Catherine McCarthy. **Provided by**: Boundless. **Located at**: https://www.boundless.com/writing/textbooks/boundless-writing-textbook/writing-a-paper-in-mla-style-humanities-255/mla-structure-and-formatting-of-specific-elements-302/mla-block-quotations-310-16896/. **Project**: Boundless Writing. **License**: *CC BY-SA: Attribution-ShareAlike*

Sample MLA-Style Paper

Amanda Wentworth

Dr. Herzman

ENGL 494

23 February 2018

Alisoun's Absolutes: Using Contradictions for Control

Using carefully crafted and conscious contradictions throughout "The Wife of Bath's Prologue," Chaucer establishes the Wife as one of the most complex and manipulative characters in his fifteenth-century Middle English work, *The Canterbury Tales*. Chaucer uses this series of contradictions to build the inconsistent argument that the Wife uses to defend herself against how her fellow pilgrims might negatively perceive her along their journey to the pilgrimage site at Canterbury. Her prologue shows that the Wife is obsessed with control, not only over her various past husbands, but also over any "readers" who encounter her. While the Wife begins her prologue by championing "experience" over "auctoritee" (1), she continuously works to establish herself as an authority on marriage, turning herself into a text to be read in her physical appearance as well as in her words. This prologue is a reactionary tale, in line with those preceding it that respond to perceived "attacks" on the teller's personal character; the Wife responds, however, to a much more hypothetical attacker. Alisoun is fighting with what she imagines her attackers might say and is consequently forced to produce an unstable argument that warps common interpretation of the existing authority on marriage. The Wife's use of the apostle Paul's writings on virginity and marriage is a tricky feature of her argument, and Chaucer uses her interpretation of Paul's "conseille" (66) to reinforce that she is fixated on control and "absolutes."

Just as Chaucer's portrait of the Wife in his *General Prologue* to the larger *Canterbury Tales* characterizes her as fixated on appearances, he expands on this fixation in her prologue, where he reveals her inability to see beyond absolutes. While the Wife's prologue is amusingly shocking in its depiction of her point of view and history, it is nothing that Chaucer did not prepare us for in her portrait. The characters in *The Canterbury Tales* are developed linearly; their portraits in *The General Prologue* set the foundation for how we can perceive them throughout the rest of the poem. Chaucer establishes the Wife as a bawdy and flashy member of this pilgrimage and goes to great lengths to characterize her as obsessed with appearances, which is something that she seeks to maintain absolute control over. From her attire to her status in her local parish, the Wife carefully constructs how she would like to be seen by onlookers, or, by her "readers." Chaucer extends this characterization into her prologue, exploring the foundation of this initial concern—appearances—with a more explicit demonstration of her compulsion for control in general. It is, therefore, not surprising that the primary narrative structure of the Wife's prologue is argumentative; Alisoun does everything in her power to beat her criticizers to the punch and refute them, thereby immediately establishing her control over the situation.

The Wife's numerous references to Paul and to the New Testament in general illuminate her firm resolve to live on one, versus the other, side of the "virtue spectrum," and reaffirm her inability to imagine a reality outside of total absolutes. While Alisoun directly confronts a potential critique of her behavior—that she should not "wedded be but ones" (13)—she goes on to ask for a specific number of times that it would be permissible for her to marry. The Wife needs to know this "nombre diffinicioun" (25) in order to feel obligated to abate her search for a husband after each one passes; she needs an absolute commandment condemning her behavior. If Alisoun is not provided with a specific and concrete ruling, she tends to take what is suggested, or seen as an ideal, and go exponentially in the opposite way. Since God "of no nombre mencion made" (32), what should stop the Wife from "octogamye" (33)? As she occasionally reminds people that she is on the lookout for her "sixte" husband, it is clear that she would remarry to infinity if given the opportunity, and the life span. Furthermore, according to the Wife, because Jesus was not speaking to everyone when he bade them to sell their belongings and live in poverty while following him, and only to "hem that wolde lyve parfitly" (111), she is clearly excused from living in any semblance of this perfection; so, again, the Wife chooses to live exponentially in the other direction. When given an ambiguous, nonspecific piece of Christian dogma that allows for interpretation or choice, the Wife is compelled to react to it in an absolute way; this is a manifestation of the obsessive need for control with which Chaucer is characterizing the Wife, building on the characterization in her portrait. In her portrait in *The General Prologue*, Chaucer tells us that Alisoun always had to be the first wife in her "parisshe" (449) to give "the offrynge" (450) or else she would have no more "charitee" (452) to give; the Wife wants everything or nothing.

Understandably, therefore, the Wife cannot accept the non-absolute nature of the apostle Paul's "counseillyng" (67) on virginity and marriage, using its non-definitiveness as her "indulgence" (84) for remarrying. When Paul "speketh of maydenhede" (64) he admits to having no precepts or rules, but that he would, simultaneously, like everyone to be "swich as he" (81), namely, a virgin. A common interpretation of this counsel would be that Paul is encouraging people to try and live up to an ideal, so that, if they fall short, they are still better than they would have been otherwise; he is, in part, advocating for moderation. The Wife, however, does not process the idea of moderation very well, and so latches on to the interpretation that if Paul does not explicitly condemn marriage, then she should marry without limit.

Wentworth 4

Chaucer uses the contradictions in "The Wife of Bath's Prologue" to illustrate the control that she is constantly seeking to obtain. We get a clearer sense of how eager the Wife is for control later in the prologue, as she explicitly details how she gained and maintained control over at least the first three of her husbands. The Wife's misinterpretation of the apostle Paul's writings on virginity and marriage illuminates the way in which Alisoun's need for control is inextricably tied to her adherence to absolutes, and demonstrates the layered characterization Chaucer develops for this unorthodox Wife.

Wentworth 5

Works Cited

Chaucer, Geoffrey. *The General Prologue. The Riverside Chaucer*, edited by Larry Dean Benson

and F. N. Robinson, Oxford UP, 2008, pp. 23-36.

---. "The Wife of Bath's Prologue." *The Riverside Chaucer*, edited by Larry Dean Benson and F.

N. Robinson, Oxford UP, 2008, pp. 105-16.

Attributions

CC licensed content, Original

8. APA Documentation

Why Is APA Documentation Important?

American Psychological Association (APA) style is a method of formatting and referencing works in research papers and manuscripts. This style is most commonly practiced by academics within the social sciences, including the fields of education, psychology, political science, and economics. APA style provides writers with a consistent formula for acknowledging the works of others by using parenthetical in-text citations and a page listing all references. Additionally, APA style makes use of specific guidelines concerning the structure, content, and order of each page of a research paper or manuscript. Adhering to the uniform standards of APA style will enhance your paper's organization and allow readers to review your work with greater clarity.

Not all social science instructors use APA, and you should always follow their individual style preferences, but the ultimate goal for APA formatting and citation standards is to provide everyone with a common template to draw from. If you're still inclined to dismiss documentation as overly zealous attention to comma placement, it might help to think about the philosophy behind documentation styles, which is essentially to give students clear tools with which to enter academic conversation. Editors want you to have the tools of the trade, so spending a few minutes on documentation styles—and the plural is important because a liberal arts education such as Geneseo's asks you to recognize that academic disciplines have differing conventions—is in line with INTD 105's emphasis on academic writing as a process in which students are introduced to the conventional moves that structure this variety of writing, have opportunities to practice the moves and improve at them, and know where to find resources to refresh their memories when they need these skills in future classes.

Let's be frank about the number of details that go into a correctly formatted APA document! Yes, there are a lot of details, and yes, it's time-consuming to check that you're attending to all those details while you're constructing your argument. Try thinking about it the same way you would approach assembly instructions for something like a futon: if you eyeball the hardware and all those flat-pack pieces of wood, and decide that it really doesn't matter whether you differentiate 3-inch from 3.5-inch bolts, or whether you assemble Part C before Part D when Part D is the one in your hand right now, you know in your heart of hearts exactly what will happen to your futon! When you're holding a buckled armrest or find yourself suddenly collapsing to the floor in the middle of the night, you'll appreciate that yes, it would have been better to read the manual closely the first time (or to have read it at all…) instead of displaying a warped futon or having to unpick your mistakes now when you're tired and it's dark and you really have better things to be doing with your time. The authors of APA style have made their documentation conventions as clear as possible, but there's no escaping the fact that sometimes, you just have to put in some careful work.

The APA articles and templates on this website were developed in accordance with the 6th edition of the *Publication Manual of the American Psychological Association*. Consult the *Publication Manual* (6th ed.) for more details about formatting and organizing your document.

Attributions

CC licensed content, Original

- Revision and Adaptation. **Authored by**: Gillian Paku. **Provided by**: SUNY Geneseo. **License**: *CC BY: Attribution*

CC licensed content, Shared previously

- APA. **Provided by**: Writing Commons. **Located at**: http://writingcommons.org/open-text/writing-processes/format/apa-format. **License**: *CC BY-NC-ND: Attribution-NonCommercial-NoDerivatives*
- Image of APA 6th Edition. **Authored by**: The COM Library. **Located at**: https://flic.kr/p/xPfx4B. **License**: *CC BY-NC-ND: Attribution-NonCommercial-NoDerivatives*

APA Order of Major Sections

Careful adherence to these conventions is likely to make a good initial impression on the reader, while carelessness may have the opposite effect. When the major sections of a paper are carefully arranged in the appropriate order, the reader may be more inclined to show an interest in the paper's ideas.

How should the major sections of an APA-style paper be arranged?

- **Title Page**: acts as the first major section of the document
    - Presents a running head and begins the document's pagination
    - Includes the paper's full title centered in the upper half of the page
    - Contains the name(s) of the writer(s) and their institutional affiliation
- **Abstract**: acts as the second major section of the document
    - Presents a single-paragraph summary of the paper's contents
    - Contains approximately 150 to 250 words
    - Includes select keywords for easy access by researchers
- **Main Body**: acts as the third major section of the document
    - Presents a report of the writer's (or writers') research and findings
    - Includes four sections (typically): the Introduction, Method, Results, and Discussion
    - Provides the reader with pertinent information about the paper's topic
- **References page**: acts as the fourth major section of the document
    - Presents a compilation of the sources cited in the paper
    - Provides a comprehensive list of works that appear as in-text citations in the paper
    - Details the full source information for each entry

APA Title Page Formatting

Placement

As the first major section of the document, the title page appears as the first page.

Components

The title page is comprised of a few key elements:

- Running head (or shortened title) and label
- Page number
- Full title of the paper
- Author byline: first name(s), middle initial(s), and last name(s)
- Affiliated institution(s) or organization(s)
- Author note (optional)

Follow your instructor's directives regarding additional lines on the title page. Some professors require further information, including the date of submission, course number or title, or name of the professor.

General Format

Like the rest of the paper, the title page should be double-spaced and typed in Times New Roman, 12-point font. The margins are set at 1" on all sides.

How should the running head be formatted on the title page?

The running head and label is flush (i.e., not indented) with the upper left-hand corner of the title page, while the page number is flush with the upper right-hand corner of the page. The label "Running head" should only appear on the title page; on all other pages, simply include the shortened title of the paper. All letters of the running head should be capitalized and should not exceed 50 characters, including punctuation, letters, and spaces.

Example of a correctly formatted running head on the title page:

Running head: EFFECTS OF NUTRITION ON MEMORY

*Note: The title page is distinct in that the shortened title of this page is preceded by the label "Running head" followed by a colon; **no other page**of the document features this label.*

How should the full title of the paper be formatted?

The full title of the paper is centered in the upper half of the page, and the first letter of each major word is capitalized. The paper's title should be a maximum of 12 words and fill one or two lines; avoid using abbreviations and unnecessary words. Do not format the title with bold, italics, underlining, or quotation marks.

How should the author byline be formatted?

The author byline is comprised of the author's or authors' first name(s), middle initial(s), and last name(s); this line follows after the full title of the research paper. Note that two authors are separated by the word *and*, but more than two authors' names are separated by commas, with 'and' before the last author's name.

What should the institutional affiliation include?

Following the author byline is the institutional affiliation of the author(s) involved with the research paper. Include the name of the college or university you attend, or the name of the organization(s) that provided support for your research.

Any additional lines of information requested by your professor may be situated after the institutional affiliation. If your instructor requires you to include an author's note, position it in the lower half of the title page.

Attributions

APA Abstract Page

Placement

The abstract acts as the second major section of the document and typically begins on the second page of the paper. It follows directly after the title page and precedes the main body of the paper.

The abstract is a succinct, single-paragraph summary of your paper's purpose, main points, method, findings, and conclusions, and you usually compose it after the rest of your paper has been completed.

General Format

How should the abstract page be formatted?

The abstract's length should be a minimum of 150 words and a maximum of 250 words; it should be confined within a single paragraph. Unlike in other paragraphs in the paper, the first line of the abstract should not be indented five spaces from the left margin.

Like the rest of the paper, the pages of the abstract should be double-spaced and typed in Times New Roman, 12-pt. The margins are set at 1" on all sides. While the running head is flush with the upper left-hand corner of every page, the page number is flush with the upper right-hand corner of every page. Note that all letters of the running head should be capitalized and should not exceed fifty characters, including punctuation, letters, and spaces.

The title of the abstract is simply "Abstract," and the word "Abstract" should be centered at the top of the page; there is no extra space between the title and the paragraph. Avoid formatting the title with bold, italics, underlining, or quotation marks, or mislabeling the abstract with the title of the research paper.

When writing the abstract, note that the APA recommends using two spaces after sentences that end in a period; however, sentences that end in other punctuation marks may be followed by a single space. Additionally, the APA recommends using the active voice and past tense in the abstract, but the present tense may be used to describe conclusions and implications. Acronyms or abbreviated words should be defined in the abstract.

How should the list of keywords be formatted?

According to your professor's directives, you may be required to include a short list of keywords to enable researchers and databases to locate your paper more effectively. The list of keywords should follow after the abstract paragraph, and the word *Keywords* should be italicized, indented five spaces from the left margin, and followed by a colon. There is no period at the end of the list of keywords.

Attributions

CC licensed content, Original

- Revision and Adaptation. **Authored by**: Gillian Paku. **Provided by**: SUNY Geneseo. **License**: *CC BY: Attribution*

CC licensed content, Shared previously

- Formatting the Abstract Page (APA). **Authored by**: Jennifer Janechek. **Provided by**: Writing Commons. **Located at**: http://writingcommons.org/open-text/writing-processes/format/apa-format/1100-formatting-the-abstract-page-apa-sp-770492217. **License**: *CC BY-NC-ND: Attribution-NonCommercial-NoDerivatives*

APA First Main Body Page Formatting

Beginning at the top of a new page, the main body of the research paper follows the abstract and precedes the References page. Comprised of the Introduction, Method, Results, and Discussion subsections, the main body acts as the third major section of the document and typically begins on the third page of the paper.

General Format

Like the rest of the paper, the pages of the main body should be double-spaced and typed in Times New Roman, 12-pt. The margins are set at 1" on all sides. While the running head is flush with the upper left-hand corner of every page, the page number is flush with the upper right-hand corner of every page. Note that all letters of the running head should be capitalized and should not exceed fifty characters, including punctuation, letters, and spaces.

- https://youtu.be/dYRZh-llIBo

The full title of the paper is centered directly above the introduction with no extra space between the title and the first paragraph. Avoid formatting the title with bold, italics, underlining, or quotation marks. The first letter of each major word in the title should be capitalized. Unlike other sections of the main body, the introduction does not require a heading or label.

When writing each paragraph, note that the APA recommends using two spaces after sentences that end in a period; however, sentences that end in other punctuation marks may be followed by a single space.

APA Headings and Subheadings

How should section and subsection headings be formatted in APA style?

A research paper written in APA style should be organized into sections and subsections using the five levels of APA headings. APA recommends using subheadings **only when the paper has at least two subsections within a larger section**. Notice how sections contain at least two smaller subsections in the example below:

Method

Design

Participants

Demographic.

Characteristics.

Starting with the first level of heading, the subsections of the paper should progressively use the next level(s) of heading without skipping any levels. Major sections of the paper's main body, including the Method, Results, and Discussion sections, should always be formatted with the first level of heading. However, keep in mind that the Introduction section, which is preceded by the full title of the paper, should be presented in plain type. Any subsections that fall under the major sections are formatted with the next level of heading.

Note that all paragraphs of the main body, including those that fall under subsections of a larger section, still maintain the pattern of indentation, use Times New Roman font, 12-pt., and are double-spaced. There are no extra lines or spaces between paragraphs and headings.

How are the five levels of APA-style headings formatted?

Format each of the five levels of APA-style headings as demonstrated in the example below. Note that while the example features headings titled "First Level," "Second Level," and so on, each heading in your paper should be named according to the section it describes.

First Level

The first level of heading is bolded and centered, and the first letter of each word in the heading is capitalized. The paragraph text should be typed on the following line and indented five spaces from the left.

Second Level

The second level of heading is bolded and situated flush left, and the first letter of each word in the heading is capitalized. The paragraph text should be typed on the following line and indented five spaces from the left.

Third level

The third level of heading is bolded, indented five spaces from the left, and followed by a period. Capitalize only the first letter of the first word in the heading and of proper nouns. The first paragraph following this heading should be typed on the same line as the heading.

Fourth level

The fourth level of heading is bolded, italicized, indented five spaces from the left, and followed by a period. Capitalize only the first letter of the first word in the heading and of proper nouns. The first paragraph following this heading should be typed on the same line as the heading.

Fifth level

The fifth level of heading is italicized, indented five spaces from the left, and followed by a period. Capitalize only the first letter of the first word in the heading and of proper nouns. The first paragraph following this heading should be typed on the same line as the heading.

Remember that taking time at the beginning of your college career to format correctly will turn what can seem like a complicated string of directions into meaningful actions that are generally easier to perform than to read about. They will become easier each time you do them as you move from closely following each step initially to remembering and then knowing some of them. You don't have to become an APA expert, able to indent fifth-level headings at a single key stroke, because the resources are always available here or in the style manual for you to follow; however, you'll save yourself time and frustration if you can become confident about at least some of the details.

All rights reserved content

APA In-Text Citations

An essential component of a research paper, in-text citations are a way of acknowledging the ideas of the author(s) of a particular work.

Each source that appears as an in-text citation should have a corresponding detailed entry in the References list at the end of the paper. Including the required elements in every citation allows other researchers to easily track the references used in a paper and locate those resources themselves. Such referencing is a crucial element of joining the scholarly conversation on a topic; not only are you acknowledging by name the other interlocutors in your conversation, but your readers also need the option to be able to go straight to those other voices and assess their content and contexts for themselves.

There are three pieces of information that should be included in a citation after quoting another writer's work: the author's last name, the year of publication, and the page number(s) of the quoted material, all of which are separated by commas. The page number should follow a lower-case letter '*p*' and a period.

- Basic structure: (Author, Year of Publication, p. 142)
  - **Example**: (Kutner, 2003, p. 451) [1]

If the quoted material was taken from more than one page, use two lower-case letter '*p*' s.

- Basic structure: (Author, Year, of Publication, pp. 194-196)
  - **Example**: (Kutner, 2003, pp. 451-452) [1]

How should multiple authors of a single source be cited?

There are a few guidelines to follow when citing multiple authors for a single source. Separate the names of the source's authors by using commas. Depending on the location and instance of the citation, an ampersand (&), the word *and*, or the term *et al*. may also need to be used.

When should an ampersand be used?

Ampersands (&) should only be used in parenthetical in-text citations. An ampersand separates the last and second-to-last author of a cited work.

- **Example:** Research has demonstrated that "synesthesia appears quite stable over time, and synesthetes are typically surprised to discover that other people do not share their experiences" (Niccolai, Jennes, Stoerig, & Van Leeuwen, 2012, p. 81). [1]

When should the word *and* be used?

The word *and* should only be used in a sentence or paragraph; do not use it in a parenthetical in-text citation. The last and second to last author of a cited work are separated by the word *and*.

- **Example:** Niccolai, Jennes, Stoerig, and Van Leeuwen (2012) observed that "synesthesia appears quite stable over time, and synesthetes are typically surprised to discover that other people do not share their experiences" (p. 81). [1]

When should the term *et al.* be used?

When citing a single work with many authors, you may need to substitute some of the authors' names with the term *et al.* The term *et al.* should not be italicized in your paper, and a period should be placed after the word *al* as it is an abbreviated term. Follow these guidelines regarding the usage of *et al.*:

Use et al.:

- The first time and every time you cite a source with at least six authors.
  - **Example:** The in-text citation of *Zoonoses: Infectious diseases transmissible from animals to humans*, a book authored by Krauss, Weber, Appel, Enders, Isenberg, Schiefer, Slenczka, von Graevenitz, and Zahner, would appear as follows: [2]
    - (Krauss et al., 2003, p. 91)
    - As Krauss et al. (2003) observed, …
- Every following time (after the first instance) that you cite a source with at least three authors.
  - **Example:** Citing the article "Modality and variability of synesthetic experience" by Niccolai, Jennes, Stoerig, & Van Leeuwen would appear as follows: [1]
    - The first instance: (Niccolai, Jennes, Stoerig, & Van Leeuwen, 2012, p. 81)
    - Every following instance: (Niccolai et al., 2012)

Avoid using et al.:

- The first time you cite a source with up to five authors.
  - Instead, list all of the authors at their first mentioning.
- To cite a work that only has two authors.
  - Instead, always list the two authors' names in every citation (separated by either an ampersand or the word *and*, depending on the location in your parenthesis or your sentence)

Attributions

APA References Page Formatting

Placement

The References page is located at the end of the main body of the paper and begins at the top of a new page. Appendices, footnotes, and additional materials should follow after the References page.

General Format

Like the rest of the paper, the References page should be double-spaced and typed in Times New Roman, 12-pt. The running head should appear flush with the upper left-hand corner of the page, and the page number should appear at the upper right-hand corner of the page.

The title of the References page is capitalized and centered at the top of the page without any formatting, including bold, italics, underlining, or quotation marks. Avoid mislabeling the References page as "Works Cited," "Sources," or "Bibliography."

Entries

Each entry should be formatted with a hanging indent: the first line of each citation should be flush with the left margin while each subsequent line of the citation is indented five spaces from the left margin. Alphabetize the entries in the References page based on the authors' last names, or on the first word of a work's title, if a work does not name any authors. Though it will vary from source to source, the general structure of a print book citation is as follows:

Author Last Name, Initials. (Year of publication). *Title of the work.* Publication city: Publishing Company.

Electronic sources generally require more information than print sources, such as a uniform resource locator (URL), a digital object identifier (DOI), or the date the source material was accessed.

Creating APA References Entries

- https://youtu.be/gGtkh_-9OC0

Following is a list of sample citations for commonly used sources. Consult the current edition of the *Publication Manual of the American Psychological Association* (6th ed.) for a complete list of guidelines for formatting entries on the References page. Hopefully, you'll notice that APA documentation style differs from MLA documentation style in a number of details; you signal your scholarly attention to detail and your willingness to join an established community of scholars when you take the time to format the documentation styles of your various academic disciplines correctly.

Print Examples

Single-Authored Book

Hoppensteadt, F. C. (1997). *An introduction to the mathematics of neurons: Modeling in the frequency domain.* New York, NY: Cambridge University Press.

Book with Multiple Authors

Two or more authors

Pandi-Perumal, S. R., Cardinali, D. P., & Chrousos, G. (2007). *Neuroimmunology of sleep.* New York, NY: Springer.

Seven or more authors

Krauss, H., Weber, A., Appel, M., Enders, B., Isenberg, H. D., Schiefer, H. G., . . . Zahner, H. (2003). *Zoonoses: Infectious diseases transmissible from animals to humans.* Washington, DC: ASM Press.

Book by an Association or Organization

American Psychological Association. (2010). *Publication manual of the American Psychological Association* (6th ed.). Washington, DC: Author.

Article or Chapter in an Edited Collection

Riding, R. (2001). The nature and effects of cognitive style. In Sternberg, R. J., & Zhang, L.-F. (Eds.), *Perspectives on thinking, learning, and cognitive styles* (pp. 47-72). Mahwah, NJ: Lawrence Erlbaum.

Collected Content in an Edited Book

Single editor

Gray, W. D. (Ed.). (2007). *Integrated models of cognition systems.* New York, NY: Oxford University Press.

Multiple editors

Reynolds, W. M., & Johnston, H. F. (Eds.). (1994). *Handbook of depression in children and adolescents.* New York, NY: Plenum Press.

Article in Print Periodical

With DOI

Marsh, J. K., & Ahn, W. (2012). Memory for patient information as a function of experience in mental health. *Journal of Applied Cognitive Psychology, 26*(3), 462-474. doi:10.1002/acp.2832

Without DOI

Murphy, V. M. (1960). Anxiety: Common ground for psychology and sociology. *The American Catholic Sociological Review, 21*(3), 213-220.

Electronic Examples

Book in Electronic Form

Levitin, D. J. (2002). *Foundations of cognitive psychology: Core readings.* Retrieved from http://ehis.ebscohost.com

Article in Online Periodical

With DOI

Oruç, I., Krigolson, O., Dalrymple, K., Nagamatsu, L. S., Handy, T. C., & Barton, J. S. (2011). Bootstrap analysis of the single subject with event related potentials. *Journal of Cognitive Neuropsychology, 28*(5), 322-337. doi:10.1080/02643294.2011.648176

Without DOI

Niccolai, V., Jennes, J., Stoerig, P., & Van Leeuwen, T. M. (2012). Modality and variability of synesthetic experience.*The American Journal of Psychology, 125*(1), 81-94. Retrieved from JSTOR database at http://www.jstor.org/

Article from a Webpage

By Multiple Authors

Vorvick, L. J., Longstreth, G. F., & Zieve, D. (2011, January 10). E. coli enteritis. Retrieved from http://www.nlm.nih.gov/medlineplus/ency/article/000296.htm

By an Organization/Group

Centers for Disease Control and Prevention. (2012). Lead. Retrieved from http://www.cdc.gov/niosh/topics/lead/

Unknown Author, Unknown Date

Water, carbon and nitrogen cycle. (n.d.) Retrieved from http://www.etap.org/demo/biology_files/lesson6/instruction4tutor.html

Attributions

APA Block Quotations

When should a block quotation be used?

In APA, a block quotation is an extract consisting of more than forty words from another author's work. Block quotations should be used in moderation—typically when using another writer's words is the most effective way of illustrating an idea. Avoid using block quotations excessively as this practice gives the reader the impression that you are inexperienced in the subject or are simply filling pages to meet a word-count requirement. Remember that the conversational model of academic writing encouraged by INTD 105 centers on *your* ability to join and facilitate a scholarly conversation, not on the voices of others who are already fully admitted to that conversation by virtue of having published peer-reviewed work on a topic.

How should a block quotation be formatted?

While a short quotation is enclosed in quotation marks and integrated into the surrounding paragraph, a block quotation is an independent paragraph that is indented five spaces from the left margin. This type of quotation should be double-spaced like the rest of the paper, but it should not be enclosed in quotation marks. In a block quotation, the parenthetical in-text citation should follow directly after the end punctuation of the final sentence. Note the placement order of the quotation marks, parentheses, and period.

Let's look at two examples. One tangential question you might have when you read them is about the word *sic*: *sic* is a word that you, as the editor of someone else's quoted material, add to a quotation to signal your awareness that there's something erroneous in the quotation (here, it's the clearly accidental "gaining obtaining" phrase) but to reassure readers that the quotation is nonetheless accurate even though the spelling or logic might make them think otherwise. Additionally, *sic* signals clearly that the error was in the original and didn't occur in your copying. Although we're italicizing *sic* here because it's the word under discussion, it is actually an English word (from a Latin root), so you don't italicize it when you use it. You do, however, put it within square editorial brackets, not within the rounded parentheses you use to enclose citation information. Don't mix up square and rounded parentheses; the difference is not aesthetic, but rather signals in both APA and MLA that the material enclosed in square brackets is something the editor (you) has added to the source material. You can use it to include your own clarifications to cited material, which is often necessary when you remove a quotation from its original context, and suddenly it's no longer clear what an "it" or a "this" refers to.

One researcher outlines the viewpoints of both parties:

> Freedom of research is undoubtedly a cherished ideal in our society. In that respect research has an interest in being free, independent and unrestricted. Such interests weigh against regulations. On the other hand, research should also be valid, verifiable, and unbiased, to attain the overarching goal of gaining obtaining [sic] generalisable knowledge. (Simonsen, 2012, p. 46)

Note that although the block quotation is formatted as a separate block of text, it is preceded by an introductory phrase or sentence(s) followed by a colon. If the author's name and the year of publication appear in the introductory sentence, the parenthetical in-text citation at the end of the paragraph should simply include the page number(s) of the original text, as shown in this example:

Simonsen (2012) outlines the two opposing viewpoints:

> Freedom of research is undoubtedly a cherished ideal in our society. In that respect research has an interest in being free, independent and unrestricted. Such interests weigh against regulations. On the other hand, research should also be valid, verifiable, and unbiased, to attain the overarching goal of gaining obtaining [sic] generalisable knowledge. (p. 46)

Attributions

CC licensed content, Original

CC licensed content, Shared previously

Sample APA-Style Paper

New Literacies: Learning Beyond the Classroom

Daisy M. Anderson

SUNY Geneseo

Abstract

This paper considers the effects of expanding traditional teaching methods to utilize new literacies in the classroom by discussing the results of research published in four articles focused on this topic. While the study conducted by Hungerford-Kresser, Wiggins, and Amaro-Jiménez (2011) outlines the undesirable consequences of using various online media in the classroom, specifically due to limited teacher supervision, their study, as well as one done by Casey (2013), underscores the positive effects of student-prompted rather than teacher-prompted discussion. Alexander and Bach (2013) found that online media also allows discussion and learning to extend beyond in-class time, giving both students and teachers time to prepare for class. Larson (2009) points out that not all students or classrooms have access to the resources for this kind of learning, while simultaneously praising the opportunity online media provides socially anxious students to more readily participate in discussions. This paper accounts for these results, arguing that engaging with new literacies in the classroom can help students succeed by developing their individual critical thinking, creating an environment that is more inclusive of less social students, and teaching students and teachers valuable modern-day skills.

Keywords: new literacies, online media, social media, online discussion

New Literacies: Learning Beyond the Classroom

Using new literacies in the classroom can intimidate any educator, especially those unfamiliar with new literacies themselves. Incorporating social media, online media, and new technologies can prove difficult with hit-and-miss results, as seen in *Learning from Our Mistakes: What Matters When Incorporating Blogging in the Content Area Literacy Classroom* by Holly Hungerford-Kresser, Joy Wiggins, and Carla Amaro-Jiménez. In this study, the researchers found that many students found the use of blogs useless and boring (2011, p. 30). Another study by Gail Casey found that students were more likely to behave inappropriately in an online community than in the classroom (2013, p. 64). However, with our society constantly pushing forward technologically as it does, these new literacies may become a vital part of students' education. In fact, more than half of all U.S. institutions have incorporated computer-based information sharing into their courses (Hungerford-Kresser et al., 2012, p. 327). Traditional teaching methods place limits on where and when learning occurs, may not reach students who struggle to learn in a crowded environment, and do not take advantage of the technological skills that students use on a daily basis outside of school. New literacies create an opportunity for learning and individual critical thinking by expanding the learning environment outside of the classroom, making that environment more inclusive of less social students, and teaching students and teachers valuable modern-day skills.

Most students spend hours each day online in some form. With the popularity of Facebook, Twitter, Pinterest, and many other social media outlets on the rise, a new source of learning is increasingly available to students both inside and outside of the classroom. Social-media users absorb all kinds of information as they surf the web, read text-messages, watch videos, and read updates on social media. Keeping this in mind, educators can take advantage of this intake of information and teach students to use these technologies to learn content relevant to the classroom. By expanding the learning process into everyday life, teachers also give students the opportunity to take more leadership over their own learning. According to Hungerford-Kesser et al. (2012), the online message-board, for example, allows students to facilitate discussion with or without the guidance of a teacher (p. 327). If students participate in online discussions outside of class, they will have the chance to discuss their thoughts without the crutch of knowing that an instructor will guide the conversation or take over if the communications come to a halt. This absence of the teacher outside of the classroom may prove difficult for some students, but will strengthen their independence and individual thinking skills in the end. Casey's study found that by incorporating a social network into a classroom, students were able to support each other's learning both inside and outside of the classroom (2013, p. 64). Casey also found that students felt more relaxed coming to class when their out-of-school interests were brought into the classroom (2013, p. 66). Similarly, John Alexander and Dorothe Bach (2013) found that "the blogs helped the instructors and students prepare for class and allowed the discussion to naturally extend beyond in-class time." (p. 27). However, limitations on the ability of new literacies to expand learning beyond the classroom exist. As pointed out by Lotta Larson (2009), not all students and classrooms will have access to the resources necessary for this type of learning. In Casey's (2013) study, she found that teachers may struggle to control the behavior of students as they interact online (p. 64). The asynchronicity of the message-board creates a distance between the teacher and student so that inappropriate behavior potentially goes unchecked until the teacher and students return to the classroom. However, teachers can correct these behaviors in class and prevent them from occurring again, and therefore these do not cause major setbacks in the learning process. Despite the fact that not all students will have access to new literacies, the use of these literacies can expand the learning environment for the students and teachers that do have the opportunity to use them.

Both inside and outside of the regular school day, new literacies can benefit students who struggle to partake in the crowded classroom environment. Participating in a discussion with twenty other pairs of eyes on the speaker can cause anxiety and discourage some students from sharing their thoughts, but the use of online communications creates a protective distance between the speaker and his or her peers. As Larson (2009) discusses, a traditional-style classroom discussion may not provide adequate thinking time for socially anxious students, students with substandard literacy skills, and students who struggle linguistically. The online message-board format, however, gives these students the time that they need to process their thoughts and think through their responses before expressing their ideas to the class, thereby encouraging them to participate (p. 647). This situation benefits not only the shy students, but their peers. In the traditional setting, the other students will not encounter their quieter peers' input, which limits the learning of the entire class. With the online message-board, students can not only think through their own answers, but also the answers of other students. They can go back, reread, and keep every detail of the discussion within reach. While this new literacy benefits the students who struggle socially, working online can create different kinds of struggles for students. For example, Larson (2009) found that one student, who was known to participate often in class, rarely participated in the online discussion. His teacher found that this student struggled with typing and became frustrated when trying to take part online, while he had no trouble speaking up in class. However, the situation was easily rectified when the student was given extra time to type (p. 642).

Although the difficulties with learning new literacies play an important role in their place in the classroom, teachers and students can use this as a learning opportunity. New literacies stem from activities that surround students outside of the classroom. The use of the internet and social media permeates through developed societies today (Casey, 2013). The modern workplace often depends on technology that strongly relates to and overlaps with new literacies. Students will benefit immensely by learning the skills necessary to utilize these literacies early on. For example, the student who struggled to type could not avoid typing forever, even if the classroom stopped using the message-board system. Future classes, careers, and social situations would require him to type and express his ideas on the computer or phone. The skills required to utilize new literacies go beyond typing, as new literacies include animation, video, and user-generated visualizations of information (Casey, 2013, p. 65). Teachers, too, can learn new skills by the integration of new literacies into their classrooms. In fact, Casey (2013) found that many students in the classroom were already comfortable with blogging before it was brought into their course, and those who did not consider themselves "tech savvy" felt more comfortable with blogs by the end of the course (p. 331). Teachers may not possess the skills that their students learn by using new technologies on their own outside of the classroom, and may have just as much to learn from the incorporation of new literacies. By bringing new literacies into the classroom, teachers give themselves a new skill set that they can use to discuss and learn with other teachers. They can apply this knowledge to their students, thereby benefiting both themselves and their classes through the use of new literacies.

Using social media, animation, videos, and other new literacies in the classroom is not a perfect system. Not all students and teachers can access the necessary tools to use new literacies, educators may struggle to monitor online behavior, and the introduction of these literacies brings up new obstacles for both students and staff. However, in the schools where these literacies exist, they benefit the learning of students by bringing learning outside of the classroom, creating a socially comfortable environment for all students, and developing new skills that students will need in the future. Because of this, the provision of the funding and materials needed for disadvantaged schools and students to gain access to these new literacies should be considered in order to avoid hindering these students' abilities to keep up with today's technology-rich environment.

References

Alexander, J., & Bach, D. (2013). Creating classroom community with reflective blogs. *International Journal of Technology, Knowledge & Society, 9*(2), 17-29.

Casey, G. (2013) Interdisciplinary literacy through social media in the mathematics classroom: An action research study. *Journal of Adolescent & Adult Literacy, 57*(1), 60-71. DOI:10.1002/JAAL.216

Hungerford-Kresser, H., Wiggins, J., & Amaro-Jimenez, C. (2012). Learning from our mistakes: What matters when incorporating blogging in the content area literacy classroom. *Journal of Adolescent & Adult Literacy, 55*(4), 326-335. DOI:10.1002/JAAL.00039

Larson, L. (2009). Reader response meets new literacies: Empowering readers in online learning communities. *The Reading Teacher, 62*(8), 638-648. DOI:10.1598/RT.62.8.2

Attributions

9. Chicago/Turabian Documentation

Introduction to Chicago/ Turabian Style

When to Use Chicago/Turabian Style

Chicago style, created by the University of Chicago, is the primary citation style used for papers in history.

> ### Key Takeaways
>
> - Chicago style is another of the most common citation and formatting styles.
> - Chicago style is based on *The Chicago Manual of Style*.
> - Turabian style is based on Kate L. Turabian's *A Manual for Writers of Research Papers, Theses, and Dissertations,* which is very similar to Chicago style but with an emphasis on student writing.
> - Chicago style provides guidelines for grammar, formatting, and citing your sources.
> - There are two subsets of Chicago/Turabian style which cite their research sources differently: Author–Date and Notes and Bibliography.

Chicago style is a citation and formatting style you may encounter in your academic career. Any piece of academic writing can use Chicago style, from a one-page paper to a full-length book. It is used by most historical journals and some social science publications. If you are writing a paper for a history class, it is likely your professor will ask you to write in Chicago style.

The Chicago Manual

The *Chicago Manual of Style* (abbreviated in writing as Chicago style, CMS, or CMOS) is a style guide for American English published since 1906 by the University of Chicago Press. Its sixteen editions have specified writing and citation styles widely used in publishing, particularly in the book industry (as opposed to newspaper publishing, where AP style is more common). Chicago style deals with many aspects of editorial practice. It remains the basis for the *Style Guide of the American Anthropological Association* and the *Style Sheet* for the Organization of American Historians. Many small publishers throughout the world adopt it as their style.

The Turabian Manual

"Turabian style" is named after the book's original author, Kate L. Turabian, who developed it for the University of Chicago. Except for a few minor differences, Turabian style is the same as Chicago style. However, while Chicago style focuses on providing guidelines for publishing in general, Turabian's *Manual for Writers of Research Papers, Theses, and Dissertations* focuses on providing guidelines for student papers, theses, and dissertations.

The Purpose of Chicago/Turabian Style

Chicago/Turabian style offers writers a choice of several different formats, because it is used in a wide variety of academic disciplines. It allows the mixing of formats, provided that the result is clear and consistent.

The most recent edition of *The Chicago Manual of Style* permits the use of both in-text citation systems ("Author–Date" style, which is usually used in the social sciences) or footnotes and endnotes (this is called "Notes and Bibliography" style, which is usually used in the humanities).

Grammar and Formatting

Chicago style includes many basic grammatical rules. For example, Chicago style does use the Oxford comma, which some other citation styles (e.g., AP style) do not. Other examples include rules about what punctuation should be included inside a quotation and when to use what type of dash. For instance, Author–Date citations are usually placed just *inside* a mark of punctuation.

Citations

As mentioned above, the most recent editions of *The Chicago Manual of Style* permit the use of either in-text citation systems or footnotes and endnotes. It can give information about in-text citation by page number or by year of publication; it even provides for variations in styles of footnotes and endnotes, depending on whether the paper includes a full bibliography at the end.

Overall Structure and Formatting of a Chicago/Turabian Paper

Every paper written in Chicago/Turabian style has the same basic structural elements.

Key Takeaways
Key Points
• A Chicago/Turabian-style paper should include a title page, a body, a references section,

and, in some cases, endnotes.

- Chicago/Turabian style provides specific guidelines for line spacing (your paper should be double-spaced), margins (1–1.5 inches), and page numbering.

- Use the Oxford comma, and only use one space following periods.

- Listen to your professor's specific guidelines if they want you to use a table of contents.

Key Terms

- **footnote**: A short piece of text, often numbered, placed at the bottom of a printed page to add a comment, citation, or reference to a designated part of the main text.

Overall Structure of a Chicago Paper

Your Chicago paper should include the following basic elements:

1. Title page
2. Body
3. References (if using the Author–Date method)
4. Bibliography (if using the notes and bibliography method)

General Formatting Rules

Typeface

Your paper should be written in a legible font such as Times New Roman, and 12-point size is recommended.

Line Spacing

All text in your paper should be double-spaced except for block quotations and image captions. On your citations page, each citation should be single-spaced, but there should be a blank line between each citation.

Margins

All page margins (top, bottom, left, and right) should be at least 1 inch and no more than 1.5 inches. All text, with the exception of headers, should be left-justified.

Indentation

The first line of every paragraph and footnote should be indented 0.5 inches.

Page Numbers

Page numbers in Arabic numerals (1, 2, 3...) should appear right-justified in the header of every page, beginning with the number 1 on the first page of text. Most word-processing programs have the ability to automatically add the correct page number to each page so you don't have to do this by hand.

General Grammar Rules

The Oxford Comma

The Oxford comma (also called the serial comma) is the comma that comes after the second-to-last item in a series or list. For example:

The UK includes the countries of England, Scotland, Wales, and Northern Ireland.

In the above sentence, the comma immediately after "Wales" is the Oxford comma.

In general writing conventions, whether the Oxford comma should be used is actually a point of fervent debate among passionate grammarians. However, it's a requirement in Chicago style, so double-check all your lists and series to make sure you include it!

Capitalization After Colons

In most cases, the first word after a colon should not be capitalized:

I know exactly what happened: he stole the cookies.

However, if what follows a colon is a series of multiple sentences, or a quotation, you *do* need to capitalize the first word after the colon: For example:

I know exactly what happened: He stole the cookies. She snatched the cupcakes. You took the brownies.

Sentence Spacing

It used to be convention to type two spaces after every period—for example:

"Roosevelt's White House imposed certain rules. The president was never lifted in public. He was never seen in public seated in a wheelchair."

This convention was developed when typewriters were in use; the space on a typewriter was quite small, so two spaces were needed to emphasize the end of a sentence. However, typewriters, and therefore this practice, are now obsolete—in fact, using two spaces after sentences is now generally frowned upon. Chicago style in particular includes an explicit rule to use only single spaces after periods:

"Roosevelt's White House imposed certain rules. The president was never lifted in public. He was never seen in public seated in a wheelchair."

A Note on the Table of Contents

Chicago style does not provide guidelines for tables of contents for individual papers themselves. If your professor asks you to include a table of contents in your paper, they will give you their own guidelines for formatting.

Attributions

Chicago/Turabian: Structure and Formatting of Specific Elements

Chicago/Turabian: Title Page

A paper in Chicago/Turabian style has a title page that follows specific formatting rules.

Key Takeaways

Key Points

- Your title page should include the title of your paper, your name, the name of your course, and the date the paper is due.
- All the information on your title page should be centered horizontally.
- The title of your paper should be written in all capital letters.

Key Terms

- **dissertation**: a formal research paper that students write in order to complete the requirements for a doctoral degree.

Title Page

The following information should be centered horizontally on the title page:

1. a third of the way down the page, the title of your paper in all capital letters;
2. on the next line, the subtitle of your paper (if you have one);

3. two-thirds of the way down the page, your name;

4. on the next line, the name of your course; and

5. on the next line, the due date of the paper.

These elements should not be bolded, underlined, or italicized. Note that the requirements may be different for doctoral theses or dissertations.

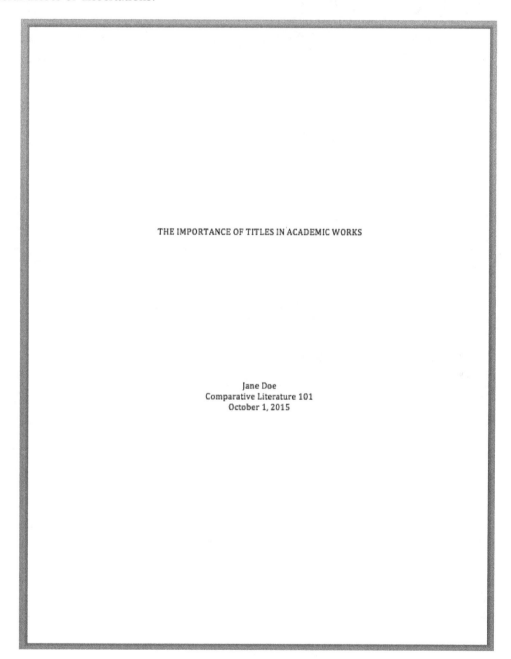

THE IMPORTANCE OF TITLES IN ACADEMIC WORKS

Jane Doe
Comparative Literature 101
October 1, 2015

Chicago-style title page: A title page introduces the title of your paper—and you, its author!

Chicago/Turabian: Headings

In Chicago style, headings are used to organize your writing and give it a hierarchical organization.

Key Takeaways

Key Points

- In Chicago style, headings are used to organize your writing and give it a hierarchical organization.
- There can be up to five levels of headings in your paper. Some use title case; some use sentence case.

Key Terms

- **hierarchical**: Arranged according to importance.

In Chicago style, headings are used to organize your writing and give it a hierarchical organization. Chicago style has specific rules for formatting headings (up to five levels) within your paper:

HEADERS IN CHICAGO STYLE
Level 1: Centered, Bold or *Italics*, Title Case, On Its Own Line
Level 2: Centered, Standard Type, Title Case, On Its Own Line
Level 3: Left-justified, Bold or *Italics*, Title Case, On Its Own Line
Level 4: Left-justified, standard type, sentence case, on its own line
Level 5: Left-justified, bold or *italics*, sentence case, NOT on its own line, ending with period.

If a heading is said to be in title case, that means you should format it as though it were the title of a book, with the first letters of most major words capitalized (e.g., A Study of Color-Blindness in Dogs).

If a heading is said to be in sentence case, that means you should format it as though it were a normal sentence, with only the first letter of the first word (and of any proper nouns) capitalized (e.g., A study of color-blindness in dogs).

You should always use heading levels in this order, beginning with Level 1. So, if you have a paper with two levels of headings, you would use Level 1 formatting for the higher level and Level 2 formatting for the lower level. Similarly, if you have a paper with five levels of headings, you would use Level 1 formatting for the highest level and Level 5 formatting for the lowest level.

Chicago/Turabian: Block Quotations

In Chicago style, format quotations of more than five lines as block quotations.

Key Takeaways

- A typical quotation is part of a sentence within a paragraph in your paper; however, for longer quotations (more than five lines), format the excerpt as a block quotation.
- A block quotation begins on its own line, is not enclosed in quotation marks, and has its in-text citation after the final punctuation.
- Block quotations are not double-spaced, unlike the rest of your Chicago style paper.

When to Use a Block Quotation

A typical quotation is enclosed in double quotation marks and is part of a sentence within a paragraph of your paper. However, if a quotation takes up more than five lines in your paper, you should format it as a block quotation rather than as a regular quotation within the text of a paragraph. Most of the standard rules for quotations still apply, with the following exceptions: a block quotation will begin on its own line (skip a line before and after the block quotation), it will not be enclosed in quotation marks, and its in-text citation will come after the ending punctuation, not before it.

For example, if you wanted to quote the first two sentences of Thomas Paine's "Common Sense," you would begin that quotation on its own line, indent every line, and format it as follows:

> Perhaps the sentiments contained in the following pages, are not YET sufficiently fashionable to procure them general favour; a long habit of not thinking a thing wrong, gives it a superficial appearance of being right, and raises at first a formidable outcry in defense of custom. But the tumult soon subsides.

The full reference for this source would then be included in your References section at the end of your paper.

Spacing and Alignment

Each line of the block quotation should be indented from the left margin the same distance as the first lines of your regular body paragraphs. Unlike the rest of your paper, it should be single-spaced. And as with series and lists, to better visually distinguish a block quotation from the surrounding text, be sure to leave an extra (blank) line between the last line of the block quotation and the first line of the following paragraph.

8

Getz-Gentle's work has inspired harsh criticism. The attribution feuds that have developed as a result of her books are symptomatic of a larger argument about archaeological methodology as a whole. The questions that anyone picking sides must answer are as follows: What is "evidence?" What evidence should anyone have for certain before making an inference? What *can* anyone know for certain about times as far-off as the Bronze Age? What is the value of an attribution? What is the value of connoisseurship? What is the value of archaeological context?

Renfrew, Cherry, and the camp of archaeologists maintain that archaeological context is paramount. Cherry writes a scathing response to *Sculptors of the Cyclades* in his article, "Reflections on Attribution Studies in Aegean Prehistory." Colin Renfrew, probably the only person on the planet who comes close to knowing as much about these sculptures as Getz-Gentle, does not get quite as snippy as Cherry does, but he expresses concern with her methods in his book *The Cycladic Spirit*. He writes,

> These queries are certainly not intended to call into doubt the value of many of Getz-Preziosi's observations nor to question the very great importance of the issues that she has raised…But the majority of the claims rest on highly subjective perceptions and, once again, the dearth of well-documented contexts for these pieces has deprived us of much of the information that we would need for a more adequate interpretation.[6]

It's clear that these archaeologists are of the mind that without context, these pieces are essentially meaningless—or at least, dangerous to derive meaning from. Gill, who may be more impartial than Renfrew and Cherry, wrote that "[Getz-Gentle] may feel that this concern for the archaeology of the corpus is a distraction which blocks her search for the career of artists."[7] However, he acknowledges that Getz-Gentle's "expertise sinks in the

---

6. Renfrew, 1991, 110.

7. Gill, 2002, 214.

Block quotations: This block quotation is correctly formatted according to Chicago/Turabian style.

Chicago/Turabian: Tables and Figures

Chicago/Turabian style has specific rules for formatting tables and figures.

> ### Key Takeaways
>
> - Chicago/Turabian specifies two methods for presenting information visually: tables and figures.
> - A table is a chart that presents numerical information in a grid format.
> - A figure, by the Chicago/Turabian definition, is any visual that is not a table.
> - Using a table or a figure as a visual aid can help you strengthen a claim you're making.

When you need to summarize quantitative data, words can only go so far. Sometimes, using a chart, graph, or other visual representation can be useful in proving your point. However, it's important to make sure you incorporate this extra information in a way that is easy to understand and in line with the conventions set forth in Chicago/Turabian style.

Chicago/Turabian specifies two methods for representing information visually: tables and figures.

Tables

A table is a chart that presents numerical information in a grid format. In Chicago/Turabian style, you must present a table immediately following the paragraph in which you mentioned it. When you mention a table in the text of your paper, make sure you refer to it by its number (e.g., "Table 1") rather than with a phrase like "the table below" or "this table."

Formatting

Format your tables as simply as possible. Do not use bold or italicized text, and do not overuse borders. Generally, you should have only three horizontal lines in your table: one immediately above and one immediately below the column headings, and one at the bottom of the table, to help separate it from the surrounding text. However, Chicago style does allow two exceptions: you may use an additional horizontal line if (1) you need to separate added numbers from their total, or (2) if you have multiple levels of column headings within a table.

Title and Source

Every table should appear flush with the left margin. Immediately above the table, provide its number, followed by a colon, followed by a short but descriptive title:

- Table 1: Frog populations in the Willamette River from 2009-2014

Immediately below the table, write the word "Source" (or or "Sources") in italics, followed by a colon, and then provide the source(s) of the information in the table. Include the same information, with the same formatting, as in a parenthetical citation —i.e., the author 's last name and the page number. End this line with a period:

- *Source*: Rottweiler 67.

Be sure to also include the full citation for this source in your References or Bibliography section. Neither the title nor the source line should be double-spaced.

Past experiments exploring syndromal assessments have involved aversive-event rates, $p(E)$, and conditional probabilities of aggressive reactions, $p(A|E)$, of either .25 or .75 (Wright et al., 2001). Related work using an experimental paradigm to study behavior change has involved a simultaneous increase or decrease from .25 to .75 or .75 to .25 in both $p(E)$ and $p(A|E)$ (Alpert, 2011; Hartley et al., 2012). The use of such extreme "baseline reaction rate" conditions—either .25 or .75—is a problem with regard to ecological validity; these previous studies do not realistically model actual changes in child behavior (see table 2).

Table 2. ANOVA Results for Baseline and Phase for Aversive-Event Rate Measures

Measure	Source	F	p	η^2
Aversive-event rate	Baseline	0.67	.518	.05
	Phase	3.63	.067	.12
	Phase * Baseline	1.29	.291	.09

Source: Catherine McCarthy et al., "Assessment of Child Behavior Change", *Brown Journal of Psychology*, May 2011.

This measure asked subjects to evaluate how the target child's aggressive behavior changed over time. I expected to find a main effect for baseline, with subjects detecting less change in the .00-baseline condition, and that all conditions would detect increases in aggression over time. I performed a one-way between-subjects ANOVA to compare subjects' perception of change in the target child's aggressive behavior as a function of the child's baseline reaction rate. Subjects did indeed detect the targets in the .00 and .25 conditions as increasing over time in aggressive behavior, but they detected no change in the .50 condition.

Sample table: This table is formatted correctly according to Chicago/Turabian formatting rules.

Figures

Treat a figure much as you would treat a table, with two exceptions: (1) you should present a figure immediately after you have referenced it in the text, and (2) all information about the figure, including its number ("Figure 1") and title ("Frogs in the Willamette River, 2012") should appear on the line immediately *below* the figure. The source information should appear on the next line.

23

This measure asked subjects to evaluate how the target child's aggressive behavior changed over time. I expected to find a main effect for baseline, with subjects detecting less change in the .00-baseline condition, and that all conditions would detect increases in aggression over time. I performed a one-way between-subjects ANOVA to compare subjects' perception of change in the target child's aggressive behavior as a function of the child's baseline reaction rate. Subjects did indeed detect the targets in the .00 and .25 conditions as increasing over time in aggressive behavior, but they detected no change in the .50 condition (see figure 3).

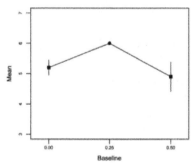

Figure 3. Perceptions of change in target child's aggression
Source: Catherine McCarthy et al., "Assessment of Child Behavior Change", *Brown Journal of Psychology*, May 2011.

This additional condition was run after Study 1 was completed to bridge a methodological gap between Study 1 and Study 2. Specifically, the reaction-baseline values used in Study 1 were .00, .25, and .50. Guided by the results of Study 1, in Study 2, I will hold reaction baseline constant and manipulate aversive-event rate. However, it is impossible to have a baseline event rate of .00 and still have aggressive reactions to

Sample figure: This figure is formatted correctly according to Chicago/Turabian formatting rules.

Attributions

Chicago/Turabian: Citations and References Notes and Bibliography (NB) System

Chicago/Turabian (NB): The Bibliography Section

In Chicago NB style, the sources you cite in your paper are listed at the end in the bibliography.

Learning Objectives
Arrange the bibliography in a Chicago/Turabian NB paper

Key Takeaways
Key Points   • In Chicago/Turabian style, there are two approaches to formatting your citations: the Author Date system or the Notes and Bibliography (NB) system.   • If you are using NB, you will need a bibliography at the end of your paper, in which all the sources you cite throughout the text of your paper are listed together.   • The bibliography has its own special formatting rules, including hanging indentation.   • In each citation style, formatting differs slightly based on source type; for example, you would format a citation differently if your source was an online book vs. a physical text-book.   • There are different citation styles for types of sources, including books, online resources,

journals, and many others.

In Chicago/Turabian papers using the Notes and Bibliography (NB) citation system, all the sources you cite throughout the text of your paper are listed together and in full in the bibliography, which comes after the main text of your paper. (If you are using the Author Date citation system, this will be called the References section.)

Formatting the Bibliography

The top of the bibliography page, as the rest of your paper, should still include the page number in the right header. On the first line, the title of the page—"Bibliography"—should appear centered and not italicized or bolded. After the page title, leave two blank lines before your first citation.

Unlike the rest of your paper, this page should not be double-spaced: leave a blank line between each citation, but the citations themselves should not be double-spaced. Your citations should be in alphabetical order by the first word in each citation (usually the author's last name).

Each citation should be formatted with what is called a hanging indent. This means the first line of each reference should be flush with the left margin (i.e., not indented), but the rest of that reference should be indented one inch from the left margin. Any word-processing program will let you format this automatically so you don't have to do it by hand. (In Microsoft Word, for example, you simply highlight your citations, click on the small arrow right next to the word "Paragraph" on the home tab, and in the popup box choose "hanging indent" under the "Special" section. Click OK, and you're done.)

19

Bibliography

Broodbank, Cyprian. "The Spirit is Willing". Review of *The Cycladic Spirit* by C. Renfrew. *Antiquity*. Volume 66. Oxford: Thames & Hudson, 1992.

Cherry, John F. "Beazley in the Bronze Age? Reflections on Attribution Studies in Aegean Prehistory." In *Aegeum* Volume 8. *Aegean Bronze Age Iconography: Shaping a Methodology*. Liege: University of Liege, 1992.

Getz-Gentle, Pat. *Personal Styles in Early Cycladic Sculpture*. Madison: University of Wisconsin Press, 2001.

Getz-Preziosi, Pat. *Sculptors of the Cyclades*. Ann Arbor: University of Michigan Press, 1987.

Gill, David. Review of *Personal Styles in Early Cycladic Sculpture*, by P. Getz-Gentle. Bryn Mawr Classical Review. Accessed October 31, 2015. http://bmcr.brynmawr.edu/2014/2014-07-12.html.

Renfrew, Colin. *The Cycladic Spirit: Masterpieces from the Nicholas P. Goulandris collection*. New York: H. N. Abrams, 1991.

Bibliography: *This is an example of a correctly formatted bibliography in Chicago/Turabian NB style.*

Constructing a Citation

The first step in building each individual citation is to determine the type of resource you are citing, since in each citation style formatting differs slightly based on source type. Some common types are a book, a chapter from a book, a journal article, an online book or article, an online video, a blog post, and personal communication such as an email or an interview you conducted. (You'll notice that "website" is not a category by itself. If the information you found is online, you want to determine if you're looking at an online book, an online article, or some other type of document.) The most important information to have for citing a source will always be the author names, the title, and the publisher information and year of publication.

As an example, let's look in detail at the process of citing three particular sources in Chicago style: Joseph Conrad's *Heart of Darkness* (i.e., a book by one author), Project Gutenberg's online text of the same book (i.e., an online book), and an online journal article about the book.

Print Sources

Author Name

You always want to start with the author information. You should present the author information in the following order and format: the author's last name (capitalized), a comma, the author's first name (capitalized), the author's middle initial (if given), and then a period:

- Conrad, Joseph.

Title of Source

Next, you should include the title of the source in title case. For a book or other standalone source, the title is italicized; otherwise it should be enclosed in quotation marks.

- *Heart of Darkness.*

City of Publication

Next, you want to provide the location of the publisher's office. The location is generally a city, such as "London" or "New York, NY."

- London:

Publisher Name

Next, provide the publisher's name, followed by a comma:

- Everyman's Library,

Date of Publication

After the publisher information, you provide the year in which the source was published, followed by a period.

- 1993.

All together, then, the citation looks like this:

- Conrad, Joseph. *Heart of Darkness*. London: Everyman's Library, 1993.

Online Sources

Now let's take a look at the citation for the online version of the same book, available online through the publisher Project Gutenberg (gutenberg.org). Treat the online version of a print book exactly the same as a print book, but with an indication of where you found it online.

- Conrad, Joseph. *Heart of Darkness*. *Project Gutenberg*, 2006. https://www.gutenberg.org/files/219/219-h/219-h.htm.

Journal Articles and Multiple Authors

- NooriBerzenji, Latef S., and Marwan Abdi. "The Image of the Africans in *Heart of Darkness* and *Things Fall Apart*." *Interdisciplinary Journal of Contemporary Research in Business* 5, no. 4 (2013): 710–726.

Much of this citation will look familiar to you now that you know the basics. Again, we start with the author information. If the source has multiple authors, the citation rules are a little different. The first author will be listed with their surname first (Conrad, Joseph) but subsequent authors will be listed with their first names first (Joseph Conrad). Use the word "and" (not an ampersand,&") before the last author. Here we have only two authors, but if we had five, the "and" would come before the fifth author's last name, after the comma following the fourth author's name.

The date of publication and title are formatted the same. Note that even though Chicago style says that the article title should not be italicized, the book titles *within* the article title are still italicized.

The new information here begins with citing the journal this article is from. Include the title of the journal in italicized title case (all major words capitalized, as in the title of a book):

- *Interdisciplinary Journal of Contemporary Research in Business*

Then include the journal volume:

- 5

If an issue number is provided in addition to the volume number, as it is here, add a comma after the volume number, the abbreviation "no.", and the issue number:

- 5, no. 4

Next, list the year of the article's publication in parentheses, followed by a colon:

- (2013):

Finally, list the page numbers of the article, followed by a period [note that the dash between the first and second numbers is an en-dash (–), NOT a hyphen (-) or em-dash (—)]:

- 710–726.

Multiple Publications by the Same Author

If you are referencing multiple publications by (or group of authors) that were published in the same year, there is a special rule for denoting this. You should first order those articles alphabetically by source title in the bibliography. But then, replace the author's name in all entries except the first one with an em-dash (—).

- Achenbach, Thomas. "Bibliography of Published Studies Using the ASEBA." *Achenbach System of Empirically Based Assessment,* 2012. http://www.aseba.org/asebabib.html.

- —. "School-Age (Ages 6–18) Assessments." *Achenbach System of Empirically Based Assessment,* 2012. http://www.aseba.org/schoolage.html.

Chicago/Turabian (NB): How to Reference Different Types of Sources

In Chicago/Turabian NB style, there are different formats for citations in your bibliography depending on the type of source you are citing.

Learning Objectives

List the ways to cite different source types in a Chicago/Turabian bibliography

Key Takeaways

Key Points

- If you are using the Notes and Bibliography (NB) method of Chicago/Turabian style, you will need a bibliography at the end of your paper.

- In your bibliography, you will have to create a citation for every source you used in your paper; these citations will be formatted differently depending on the type of source.

- There are different citation styles for books, depending on how many authors they have.

- There are different citation styles for articles, depending on where you found them.

Key Terms

- **bibliography**: A section of a written work containing citations, not quotations, of all the sources referenced in the work.

Now that you know the different components of a book citation in Chicago/Turabian Notes and Bibliography (NB) style and how the citation should be formatted, you will be able to understand the citation formats for other source types. Here are some example citations for the most common types of resources you will use.

Book by One Author

Doyle, Arthur. *The Memoirs of Sherlock Holmes.* Mineola: Dover Publications, Inc., 2010.

Book by Multiple Authors

Two or More Authors

(Write out all author names.)

Dubner, Stephen, and Steven Levitt. *Freakonomics: A Rogue Economist Explores the Hidden Side of Everything.* New York: Harper Perennial, 2005.

Brown, Theodore, H. Eugene Lemay, Bruce Bursten, Catherine Murphy, Patrick Woodward, and Matthew Stoltzfus. *Chemistry: The Central Science.* London: Prentice Hall, 2015.

Book with Author and Editor

Lovecraft, Howard Phillips. *Tales.* Edited by Peter Straub. New York: Library of America, 2005.

Article in a Journal with Continuous Pagination

Rottweiler, Frank, and Jacques Beauchemin. "Detroit and Sarnia: Two foes on the brink of destruction." *Canadian/American Studies Journal* 54 (2012): 66–146.

Article in a Journal Paginated Separately

Rottweiler, Frank, and Jacques Beauchemin. "Detroit and Sarnia: Two foes on the brink of destruction." *Canadian/American Studies Journal* 54, no. 2 (2012): 66–146.

Article in an Internet-Only Journal

Marlowe, Philip, and Sarah Spade. "Detective Work and the Benefits of Colour Versus Black and White." *Journal of Pointless Research* 11, no. 2 (2001): 123–124. Accessed October 31, 2015. http://www.jpr.com/stable/detectiveworkcolour.htm.

Page on a Web Site

Pavlenko, Aneta. "Bilingual Minds, Bilingual Bodies." *Psychology Today.* Last modified October 7, 2015. https://www.psychologytoday.com/blog/life-bilingual/201510/bilingual-minds-bilingual-bodies.

Page on a Web Site, No Author Identified, No Date

"Bilingual Minds, Bilingual Bodies." *Psychology Today.* Accessed October 29, 2015. https://www.psychologytoday.com/blog/life-bilingual/201510/bilingual-minds-bilingual-bodies.

Chicago/Turabian (NB): Footnotes and Endnotes

In Chicago/Turabian Notes and Bibliography style, use footnotes or endnotes for citing sources in text.

Learning Objectives

Arrange footnotes in Chicago/Turabian NB style

Key Takeaways

Key Points

- A footnote is when you follow a quotation, a paraphrased idea, or a piece of information that otherwise needed to be cited with a superscript number.
- An endnote is exactly like a footnote, except the note on what source was used is at the end of the paper rather than the bottom of the page.
- There are two steps to creating a footnote. First, you need to place a number in the text to tell the reader what note to look for; then, you need to create the note itself.

Key Terms

- **endnote**: A note at the end of a paper, corresponding to a number in a text, which gives the reader citation information.
- **footnote**: A note at the bottom of the page, corresponding to a number in a text, which gives the reader citation information.

Footnotes and Endnotes

In your paper, when you quote directly from a source in their words, or when you paraphrase someone else's idea, you need to tell the reader what that source is so the author gets credit for their words and ideas. One method for doing this is creating a footnote.

A footnote is when you follow a quotation, a paraphrased idea, or a piece of information that otherwise needed to be cited with a superscript number (like this.)[1] Then, at the bottom of the page, you give a brief indication of where you retrieved that information. Fuller information about that source is then contained in the paper's bibliography. Think of the footnote as telling the reader where to go in your bibliography to find the source, and the bibliography entry as telling the reader where to go in the real world to find the source.

An endnote is exactly like a footnote, except that endnotes appear all together at the end of the paper, while each footnote appears on the bottom of the same page as its superscripted number.

Creating a Footnote

There are two steps to creating a footnote. First, you need to place a number in the text to tell the reader what note to look for; then, you need to create the note itself. As an example, let's say we are writing a paper about meerkat populations and we write the following sentences:

As of 2009, the meerkat population has increased by 20% in Eastern Botswana. "It's thrilling," says renowned biologist Elizabeth Khama, "The animals are truly making a comeback."

We need to create footnotes to cite our sources.

Numbering

The first step to creating a footnote is place a number next to the statement that needs to be sourced. To do this, place the number at the end of the sentence it refers to, after all punctuation.

As of 2009, the meerkat population has increased by 20% in Eastern Botswana.[1] "It's thrilling," says renowned biologist Elizabeth Khama, "The animals are truly making a comeback."[2]

Your first footnote of the paper should be numbered 1, your second should be 2, and so on until the end of the paper. If you are writing an exceptionally long paper, such as a doctoral thesis, numbers should restart at the beginning of every chapter.

Creating the Notes

Next, you need to create the note that the number refers to. Every number needs a note. In the note, you will have the author's name, the title of the work, the publication information, and the page number:

1. Andrew Byrd, "The Resurgence of the Meerkat," *Southern African Ecology* 32, no. 2 (2009): 221.

You only need to create a note that contains all of this information once per paper. If you cite this source again later in the paper (say, in your sixth note), you would simply write the author, title, and page number, separated by commas:

6. Byrd, "The Resurgence of the Meerkat," 256.

Using "Ibid."

However, if you cite the exact same source more than once in a row, without citing any other sources in between, there is a special shorthand you can use. Chicago NB style has very specific rules for what to do in this situation. If you cite the same source multiple times in a row, simply write "Ibid." in each note after the first—this means "this source is the same as the source in the previous note":

1. Andrew Byrd, "The Resurgence of the Meerkat," *Southern African Ecology* 32, no. 2 (2009): 221.

2. Ibid.

If you're citing a different page of the same source, add a comma and the new page number after "Ibid.":

1. Andrew Byrd, "The Resurgence of the Meerkat," *Southern African Ecology* 32, no. 2 (2009): 221.

2. Ibid., 225.

Once you cite a different source, your use of "Ibid." has to start over—you should not use it again until you have multiple notes in a row that cite the same source.

How to Reference Different Types of Sources in Footnotes

Different source types require different citation information when being cited in footnotes.

Learning Objectives

List the ways to cite different source types in Chicago/Turabian footnotes

Key Takeaways

Key Points

- Footnotes are like "mini- citations " at the bottom of the page, which direct your reader to a bibliography entry.
- Different types of source require different citation information.

Key Terms

- **Notes and Bibliography**: A subset of the Chicago/Turabian citation style, which uses footnotes to cite sources in the text.

Footnotes are the preferred citation method for the Chicago/Turabian Notes and Bibliography citation style. When using footnotes, you create what is essentially a "mini-citation" at the bottom of the page. These footnotes guide the reader to the corresponding entry in your bibliography.

Different types of source require different citation information, but they always follow the form of: author, title, publication information, and then either page number or website URL (all separated by commas). And remember, this information will also be contained, in a slightly different form, in your bibliography.

Book by a Single Author

1. Steven Pinker, *How the Mind Works* (New York: Norton, 1997), 223.

Book by Two to Four Authors

2. Stephen Dubner and Steven Levitt, *Freakonomics* (New York: William Morrow, 2005), 101.

Book by Five or More Authors

3. Theodore Brown et al., *Chemistry: The Central Science* (Upper Saddle River: Prentice Hall, 2005), 642.

Journal Article

4. Andrew Byrd, "The Resurgence of the Meerkat," *Southern African Ecology* 32, no. 1 (2009): 221.

Electronic Journal Article

5. Andrew Byrd, "The Meerkats Have All Gone Away," *African Ecology Online* 18, no. 2 (2006): 169, accessed October 31, 2015, http://www.afrecoonline.org/byrd1.htm.

Website with Author and Publication Date

6. Cara Nelson, "The Top Three Movies of All Time," *Best Movies*, last modified June 26, 1993, http://www.bestmovies.com/nelsoncara1.htm.

Website with Unknown Author and Publication Date

7. "Some Cool Movies," *Best Movies*, accessed October 14, 2015, http://www.bestmovies.com/anony-mous.htm.

Chicago/Turabian: Citations and References AuthorDate (AD) System

Chicago/Turabian (Author–Date): The References Section

In Chicago Author–Date style, the sources you cite in your paper are listed at the end in the References section.

Learning Objectives

Arrange the References section in a Chicago/Turabian Author–Date paper

---

Key Takeaways

Key Points

- In Chicago/Turabian style, there are two ways of formatting your citations: the Author–Date system or the Notes and Bibliography system (NB). If you are using the Author–Date system, you will need a References section.

- All the sources you cite throughout the text of your paper are listed together in the References section at the end of your paper.

- The References section has its own special formatting rules, including hanging indentation.

- In each citation style, formatting differs slightly based on source type; for example, you

> would format a citation differently if your source was an online book vs. a physical textbook.
> - There are different citation styles for types of sources, including books, online resources, journals, and many others.

In Chicago/Turabian papers using the Author–Date citation system, all the sources you cite throughout the text of your paper are listed together in full in the References section, which comes after the main text of your paper. (If you are using NB, this will be called the bibliography.)

Formatting the References Section

The top of the page, as the rest of your paper, should still include the page number in the right header. On the first line, the title of the page—"References"—should appear centered and not italicized or bolded. After the page title, leave two blank lines before your first citation.

Unlike the rest of your paper, this page should not be double-spaced: leave a blank line between each citation, but the citations themselves should not be double-spaced. Your citations should be in alphabetical order by the first word in each citation (usually the author's last name).

Each reference should be formatted with what is called a hanging indent. This means the first line of each reference should be flush with the left margin (i.e., not indented), but the rest of that reference should be indented one inch from the left margin. Any word-processing program will let you format this automatically so you don't have to do it by hand. (In Microsoft Word, for example, you simply highlight your citations, click on the small arrow right next to the word "Paragraph" on the home tab, and in the popup box choose "hanging indent" under the "Special" section. Click OK, and you're done.)

19

References

Broodbank, Cyprian. "The Spirit is Willing". Review of *The Cycladic Spirit* by C. Renfrew. *Antiquity*. Volume 66. Oxford: Thames & Hudson, 1992.

Cherry, John F. "Beazley in the Bronze Age? Reflections on Attribution Studies in Aegean Prehistory." In *Aegeum* Volume 8. *Aegean Bronze Age Iconography: Shaping a Methodology*. Liege: University of Liege, 1992.

Getz-Gentle, Pat. *Personal Styles in Early Cycladic Sculpture*. Madison: University of Wisconsin Press, 2001.

Getz-Preziosi, Pat. *Sculptors of the Cyclades*. Ann Arbor: University of Michigan Press, 1987.

Gill, David. Review of *Personal Styles in Early Cycladic Sculpture*, by P. Getz-Gentle. Bryn Mawr Classical Review. Accessed October 31, 2015. http://bmcr.brynmawr.edu/2014/2014-07-12.html.

Renfrew, Colin. *The Cycladic Spirit: Masterpieces from the Nicholas P. Goulandris collection*. New York: H. N. Abrams, 1991.

References page: This is a correctly formatted References page in Chicago/Turabian Author–Date style.

Constructing a Citation

The first step in building each individual citation is to determine the type of resource you are citing, since in each citation style formatting differs slightly based on source type. Some common types are a book, a chapter from a book, a journal article, an online book or article, an online video, a blog post, and personal communication such as an email or an interview you conducted. (You'll notice that "website" is not a category by itself. If the information you found is online, you want to determine if you're looking at an online book, an online article, or some other type of document.)

As an example, let's look in detail at the process of citing three particular sources in Chicago style: Joseph Conrad's *Heart of Darkness* (i.e., a book by one author), Project Gutenberg's online text of the same book (i.e., an online book), and an online journal article about the book.

Print Sources

Author Name

You always want to start with the author information. You should present the author information in the following order and format: the author's last name, a comma, the author's first name, the author's middle initial (if given), and then a period:

- Conrad, Joseph.

Title of Source

Next, you should include the title of the source in title case. For a book, the title is italicized.

- *Heart of Darkness.*

City of Publication

Next, you want to provide the location of the publisher's office. The location is generally a city, such as "London" or "New York, NY."

- London:

Publisher Name

Next, provide the publisher's name, followed by a comma:

- Everyman's Library,

Date of Publication

Now provide the year in which the source was published, followed by a period.

- 1993.

All together, then, the citation looks like this:

- Conrad, Joseph. *Heart of Darkness.* London: Everyman's Library, 1993.

Online Sources

Now let's take a look at the citation for the online version of the same book, available online through the publisher Project Gutenberg (gutenberg.org). Treat the online version of a print book exactly the same as a print book, but with an indication of where you found it online.

- Conrad, Joseph. *Heart of Darkness*. *Project Gutenberg*, 2006. https://www.gutenberg.org/files/ 219/219-h/219-h.htm.

Journal Articles and Multiple Authors

- NooriBerzenji, Latef S., and Marwan Abdi. "The Image of the Africans in *Heart of Darkness* and *Things Fall Apart*." *Interdisciplinary Journal of Contemporary Research in Business* 5, no. 4 (2013): 710–726.

Much of this citation will look familiar to you now that you know the basics. Again, we start with the author information. If the source has multiple authors, the citation rules are a little different. The first author will be listed with their surname first (Conrad, Joseph) but subsequent authors will be listed with their first names first (Joseph Conrad). Use the word "and" (not an ampersand, &) before the last author. Here we have only two authors, but if we had five, the "and" would come before the fifth author's last name, after the comma following the fourth author's name.

The date of publication and title are formatted the same. Note that even though APA style says that the article title should not be italicized, the book titles "Heart of Darkness" and "Things Fall Apart" within the article title are still italicized.

The new information here begins with citing the journal this article is from. Include the title of the journal in italicized title case (all major words capitalized, as in the title of a book):

- *Interdisciplinary Journal of Contemporary Research in Business*

Then include the journal volume:

- 5

If an issue number is provided in addition to the volume number, as it is here, add a comma after the volume number, the abbreviation "no.", and the issue number:

- 5, no. 4

Next, list the year of the article's publication in parentheses, followed by a colon:

- (2013):

Finally, list the page numbers of the article, followed by a period [note that the dash between the first and second numbers is an en-dash (–), NOT a hyphen (-) or em-dash (—)]:

- 710–726.

Multiple Publications by the Same Author

If you are referencing multiple publications by (or group of authors) that were published in the same year, there is a special rule for denoting this. You should first order those articles alphabetically by source title in the References section. But then, replace the author's name in all entries except the first one with an em-dash (—).

- Achenbach, Thomas. "Bibliography of Published Studies Using the ASEBA." *Achenbach System of Empirically Based Assessment*, 2012. http://www.aseba.org/asebabib.html.

- —. "School-Age (Ages 6–18) Assessments." *Achenbach System of Empirically Based Assessment*, 2012. http://www.aseba.org/schoolage.html.

Chicago/Turabian (Author–Date): How to Reference Different Types of Sources

In Chicago/Turabian style, there are different formats for citing sources at the end of your paper depending on the type of source.

Learning Objectives
List the ways to cite different source types in Chicago/Turabian Author–Date style

Key Takeaways
Key Points • If you are using the Author –Date method of Chicago/Turabian style, you will need a References section at the end of your paper. • In your References section, you will have to create a citation for every source you used in your paper; these citations will be formatted differently depending on the source type. • There are different citation styles for books, depending on how many authors they have. • There are different citation styles for articles, depending on where you found them. • There are ways to format sources that are not books or articles. **Key Terms** • **Author–Date**: A subset of the Chicago/Turabian citation style that uses in-text citations and a References page at the end.

Now that you know the different components of a book citation in Chicago/Turabian Author–Date style and how they should be formatted, you will be able to understand the citation formats for other source types. Here are some example citations for the most common types of resources you will use. These are how your citations will be formatted on your References page at the end of your Author–Date style paper.

Book by One Author

Doyle, Arthur. *The Memoirs of Sherlock Holmes.* Mineola: Dover Publications, Inc., 2010.

Book by Multiple Authors

Two or More Authors

(Write out all author names.)

Dubner, Stephen, and Steven Levitt. *Freakonomics: A Rogue Economist Explores the Hidden Side of Everything.* New York: Harper Perennial, 2005.

Brown, Theodore, H. Eugene Lemay, Bruce Bursten, Catherine Murphy, Patrick Woodward, and Matthew Stoltzfus. *Chemistry: The Central Science.* London: Prentice Hall, 2015.

Book with Author and Editor

Lovecraft, Howard Phillips. *Tales.* Edited by Peter Straub. New York: Library of America, 2005.

Article in a Journal with Continuous Pagination

Rottweiler, Frank, and Jacques Beauchemin. "Detroit and Sarnia: Two Foes on the Brink of Destruction." *Canadian/American Studies Journal* 54 (2012): 66–146.

Article in a Journal Paginated Separately

Rottweiler, Frank, and Jacques Beauchemin. "Detroit and Sarnia: Two Foes on the Brink of Destruction." *Canadian/American Studies Journal* 54, no. 2 (2012): 66–146.

Article in an Internet-Only Journal

Marlowe, Philip, and Sarah Spade. "Detective Work and the Benefits of Colour Versus Black and White." *Journal of Pointless Research* 11, no. 2 (2001): 123–124. Accessed October 31, 2015. http://www.jpr.com/stable/detectiveworkcolour.htm.

Page on a Web Site

Pavlenko, Aneta. "Bilingual Minds, Bilingual Bodies." *Psychology Today.* Last modified October 7, 2015. https://www.psychologytoday.com/blog/life-bilingual/201510/bilingual-minds-bilingual-bodies.

Page on a Web Site, No Author Identified, No Date

"Bilingual Minds, Bilingual Bodies." *Psychology Today.* Accessed October 29, 2015. https://www.psychologytoday.com/blog/life-bilingual/201510/bilingual-minds-bilingual-bodies.

Chicago/Turabian (Author–Date): In-Text References and Parentheticals

In Chicago/Turabian Author–Date style, in-text citations follow strict formatting rules.

Learning Objectives

Arrange in-text citations in Chicago/Turabian Author–Date style

---

Key Takeaways

Key Points

- In-text citations are where you tell the reader, within the text of your paper, the author's name and the date the source was published.

- The correct formatting for an in-text citation varies depending on how many authors created the source being cited.

- Formatting also varies depending on whether you cite the same source more than once, or whether you cite multiple works by the same author.

Key Terms

- **parenthetical**: A word or phrase within parentheses.

In your paper, when you quote directly from a source in the author's words, or when you paraphrase someone else's idea, you need to tell the reader where the words and ideas comes from so the original author gets credit. When you do this within the text the reader the author's name and the date the source was published in the text of your paper, this is called an in-text citation.

The Chicago/Turabian citation style uses in-text citations only in its Author–Date method, which is generally used for social science papers and is explained below. If your professor asks you to cite sources with footnotes and bibliography rather than in-text citations, make sure you use the Notes and Bibliography (NB) method rather than the Author–Date method described here.

Source by a Single Author

To cite this type of reference in the text, you should use what is known as a parenthetical —citation information enclosed in parentheses—at the end of the relevant sentence. The parenthetical should include the author's last name (with no first or middle initial) followed by the year the source was published. If you're citing a direct quotation, you also need to include the page number after a comma. For example:

- Social representations theory posits that reified scientific knowledge that exists at the boundaries of a given society will be interpreted in meaningful and often simplified forms by the majority (Pauling 2005).

- Social representations theory "proposes a new hypothesis…" (Pauling 2005, 113).

If you choose, you can integrate the author's name into the sentence itself—this is known as a " signal phrase "—and provide just the year in parentheses:

- Pauling (2005) posits that…

Source by Two or Three Authors

Authors should be presented in the order in which they are listed on the published article. If you include the authors' names in the parenthetical, use the word "and" between the two names. For example:

- Social representations theory posits that reified scientific knowledge that exists at the boundaries of a given society will be interpreted in meaningful and often simplified forms by the majority (Pauling and Liu 2005).

You may still choose to use a signal phrase instead, but make sure you keep both authors in it:

- Pauling and Liu (2005) posit that…

Source by Four or More Authors

For an article with more than four authors, the first time you cite the article in the text of your paper, you should use only the first author's name followed by "et al." and the year of publication. ("Et al." is short for "et alia," which means "and other people" in Latin—much like "etc." is short for "et cetera," which means "and other things" in Latin.)

- Social representations theory posits that reified scientific knowledge that exists at the boundaries of a given society will be interpreted in meaningful and often simplified forms by the majority (Pauling et al. 2005).

Using a signal phrase:

- Pauling et al. (2005) posit…

Citing Multiple Publications by Different Authors

If you need to cite multiple publications by different authors in the same sentence, you should list the multiple sources in alphabetical order by author and use a semicolon to separate them.

- … majority (Alford 1995; Pauling 2004; Sirkis 2003).

If within this citation you also have multiple sources by the same author, after that author's name, separate the multiple dates of publication with a comma, and order them chronologically (earliest to latest).

- … majority (Alford 1995; Pauling 2004, 2005; Sirkis 2003).

Citing Multiple Publications by the Same Author

If you need to cite multiple publications by the same author within a sentence, you use a comma to separate the years of publication in chronological order (oldest to most recent).

- … majority (Pauling 2004, 2005).

Using a signal phrase:

- Pauling (2004, 2005) suggests that…

Attributions

*Sample Chicago-Style Excerpt
(Notes and Bibliography)*

LIBERATION THROUGH LANGUAGE:
HOW THE EVOLUTION OF LINCOLN'S RHETORIC LED THE NATION
THROUGH CRISIS

Erin Herbst
History 302
December 12, 2017

1

On April 11, 1865, Abraham Lincoln spoke about the importance of Reconstruction in the state of Louisiana, and commended the people who voted in support of Union policies, namely emancipation. To help these people, he argued, was the right thing to do: "These twelve thousand persons are thus fully committed to the Union, and to perpetual freedom in the state—committed to the very things, and nearly all the things the nation wants—and they ask the nations [*sic*] recognition, and it's [*sic*] assistance to make good their committal."[1] Here, freedom meant for all, both blacks and whites. Lincoln concluded this speech with a strong message: "In the present '*situation*' as the phrase goes, it may be my duty to make some new announcement to the people of the South. I am considering, and shall not fail to act, when satisfied that action will be proper."[2] This sentiment, and the promise of Reconstruction, was seen as threatening to some staunch Southerners, including a young actor in the audience, John Wilkes Booth. This speech incited anger in Booth that could not be quelled without bloodshed. He decided this would be Lincoln's last public address. Just days later, John Wilkes Booth fatally shot President Abraham Lincoln, ending the life not just of one man, but of a political icon in American history. Booth's extreme actions gave credence to the significance of Lincoln's words; his speech full of hope for Reconstruction was enough to finally cause Booth, who had been plotting to kidnap Lincoln for months, to kill him. Lincoln's speeches had long inspired some while enraging others, but this speech proved to be too much; this paper will explore how these words gained the significance that changed the nation from Lincoln's early political speeches to his last days.

To understand Abraham Lincoln as a President is to understand Abraham Lincoln as a writer. As a man celebrated for his ability to guide the Union through crisis, it is essential to

---

[1] Abraham Lincoln, "Last Public Address," April 11, 1865, in *Collected Works of Abraham Lincoln* (University of Michigan, 2001), cited hereafter as CW.
[2] Ibid.

2

remember that his facility of language helped him to lead effectively. Without his cautious diction, extended metaphors, and keen awareness of his audience, his speeches, letters, and proclamations would not evoke the historical elevation that they reach today. It is often argued that Lincoln was the best communicator to ever occupy the position of President of the United States. His historical success is heavily intertwined with his literary prowess; he is an accredited politician, but a responsible study of his life and accomplishments must recognize him as a serious writer as well.

Lincoln's impeccable ability to use words in a concise, yet meaningful way has been the study of many historians. This is because there is a degree of shock when really examining Lincoln's written words due to his lack of official schooling. Our American idealization of the individual ability to elevate oneself, both in status and in elegance, is confirmed in the sixteenth President. Lincoln's rise from log cabins to the White House has been a center of fascination for many. In scholarship, this connection between Lincoln as writer and Lincoln as politician has been investigated; both career historians and literary critics have attempted to understand Lincoln's policies in connection to his written and oral language. Douglas L. Wilson states, "By almost any means of gauging his presidential activity, it becomes apparent that writing—both the activity and its products—was indispensible to Lincoln's way of performing his office."[3] This paper will show how, as Lincoln's words changed, he was able to promote change in national politics. These "products" of Lincoln's writings impacted American history in unprecedented ways and veered the country towards a path of liberty, truly for all.

---

[3] Douglas L Wilson, *Lincoln's Sword: The Presidency and the Power of Words* (New York: Vintage Books, 2006), 6.

. . .

19

other American, not excepting Washington."[47] Douglass' speech itself may have used Lincoln's

own texts as a model; he relies on sophisticated rhetoric and it is a piece of well-written prose,

including heavy repetition of "Dying as he did die."[48] Douglass revisited Lincoln's legacy in an

1876 speech entitled "Oration in Memory of Abraham Lincoln," given on the anniversary of

Lincoln's death. In this speech, Douglass tells his audience that Lincoln "saved for you a

country, he delivered us from a bondage, according to Jefferson, one hour of which was worse

than ages of the oppression your fathers rose in rebellion to oppose."[49] Douglass praises Lincoln

and focuses the speech using the words that Lincoln sought to define, stating, "under his wise

and beneficent rule we saw ourselves gradually lifted from the depths of slavery to the heights of

liberty and manhood."[50] Lincoln's words themselves were important to American history, but his

legacy was in part shaped by those who came after him and immortalized his language.

Throughout his tenure as a politician, the concepts of "liberty" and "equality" took on more

structured meanings in his texts, therefore showing both a progression of Lincoln as a man and

how his influence propelled a change in how the nation interacted with and defined these

concepts.

---

[47] Frederick Douglass, "Abraham Lincoln, A Speech,"
[48] Ibid.
[49] Frederick Douglass, "Oration in Memory of Abraham Lincoln," April 14, 1876
[50] Ibid.

20

Bibliography

Basler, Roy P. *The Collected Works of Abraham Lincoln.* New Brunswick, NJ: Rutgers University Press, 1953-1955. https://quod.lib.mich.edu/1/lincoln

Carpenter, Francis Bicknell. *Six Months at the White House with Abraham Lincoln.* New York: Hurd and Houghton, 1866.

Dodge, Daniel Kilham. *Abraham Lincoln: The Evolution of his Literary Style.* Urbana: University of Illinois Press, 2000.

Douglass, Frederick. *"Abraham Lincoln, a Speech".* Manuscript/Mixed Material. Retrieved from the Library of Congress, https://www.loc.gov/item/mfd.22015/.(Accessed November 20, 2017.)

Fehrenbacher, Don E. *Lincoln: Speeches, Letters, Miscellaneous Writings, The Lincoln-Douglas Debates.* New York: The Library of America, 1989.

Fehrenbacher, Don E. *Lincoln: Speeches, Letters, Miscellaneous Writings, Presidential Messages and Proclamations.* New York: The Library of America, 1989.

Gates Jr., Henry Louis and Yacovone, Donald. *Lincoln on Race & Slavery.* Princeton: Princeton University Press, 2009.

Guelzo, Allen C. *Lincoln: A Very Short Introduction.* New York: Oxford University Press, 2009.

New York Times, April 21, 1865 http://www.nytimes.com/1865/04/21/news/murderer-mr-lincoln-extraordinary-letter-john-wilkes-booth-proof-that-he.html?pagewanted=all

McPherson, James M. *How Lincoln Won the War with Metaphors.* (lecture, Pike Room, Fort Wayne, Indiana, May 9, 1985).

Oakes, James. "Disunion is Abolition" in *Freedom National: The Destruction of Slavery in the United States, 1861-1865,* New York: W.W. Norton, 2013.

Skillings, Jeffrey. "Abraham Lincoln: A World of Words." *New England Journal of History* 72, no. 2 (Spring 2016): 18-32. *America: History & Life,* EBSCO*host* (accessed October 17, 2017).

Willis, Garry. *Lincoln at Gettysburg: The Words That Remade America.* New York: Touchstone, 1992.

Wilson, Douglas L. *Lincoln's Sword: The Presidency and the Power of Words.* New York: Alfred A. Knopf, 2006.

Attributions

CC licensed content, Original

CPSIA information can be obtained
at www.ICGtesting.com
Printed in the USA
LVHW05s2050230818
587903LV00005B/355/P

9 781641 760287